P9-APH-235

REGIONAL BLOCS

Also by A. S. Bhalla

BLENDING OF NEW AND TRADITIONAL TECHNOLOGIES (*co-editor*)

ECONOMIC TRANSITION IN HUNAN AND SOUTHERN CHINA

ENVIRONMENT, EMPLOYMENT AND DEVELOPMENT (*editor*)

FACING THE TECHNOLOGICAL CHALLENGE

NEW TECHNOLOGIES AND DEVELOPMENT (*co-editor*)

SMALL AND MEDIUM ENTERPRISES: Technology Policies and Options (*editor*)

TECHNOLOGICAL TRANSFORMATION OF RURAL INDIA (*co-editor*)

TECHNOLOGY AND EMPLOYMENT IN INDUSTRY (*editor*)

TOWARDS GLOBAL ACTION FOR APPROPRIATE TECHNOLOGY (*editor*)

UNEVEN DEVELOPMENT IN THE THIRD WORLD

Regional Blocs

Building Blocks or Stumbling Blocks?

A. S. Bhalla

and

P. Bhalla

First published in Great Britain 1997 by
MACMILLAN PRESS LTD
Houndmills, Basingstoke, Hampshire RG21 6XS and London
Companies and representatives throughout the world

A catalogue record for this book is available from the British Library.

ISBN 0–333–64696–7

First published in the United States of America 1997 by
ST. MARTIN'S PRESS, INC.,
Scholarly and Reference Division,
175 Fifth Avenue, New York, N.Y. 10010

ISBN 0–312–17528–0

Library of Congress Cataloging-in-Publication Data
Bhalla, A. S.
Regional blocs : building blocks or stumbling blocks / A.S.
Bhalla, P. Bhalla.
p. cm.
Includes bibliographical references and index.
ISBN 0–312–17528–0 (cloth)
1. Trade blocs. 2. Regionalism. 3. International economic
integration. I. Bhalla, P. (Praveen), 1947– . II. Title.
HF1418.7.B47 1997
382'.91—dc21 97–9155
CIP

This book is printed on paper suitable for recycling and made from fully managed and sustained forest sources.

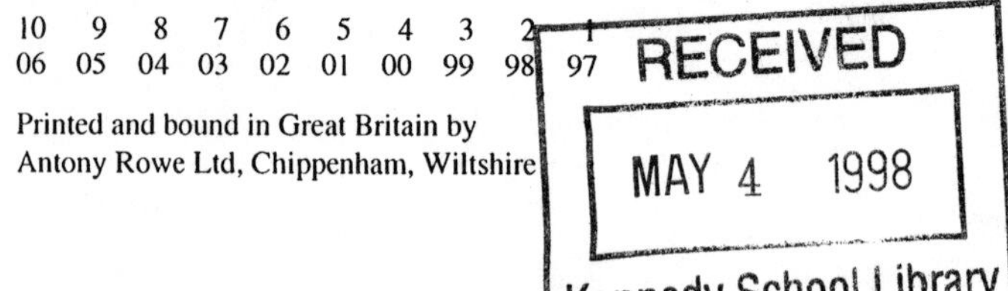
10 9 8 7 6 5 4 3 2 1
06 05 04 03 02 01 00 99 98 97

Printed and bound in Great Britain by
Antony Rowe Ltd, Chippenham, Wiltshire

Contents

List of Tables and Figures vii

Preface ix

Acknowledgements xii

List of Abbreviations xiii

1 Regional Cooperation in Historical Perspective **1**

Regional cooperation: a historical sketch 3
Lessons from past experience 11
Regional blocs or loose groupings? 14
Concluding remarks 15

2 The New Regionalism vs. Globalization? **17**

Different forms of the new regionalism 17
Globalization: concept and meaning 22
Regionalism or globalization? 24
Are regional blocs building blocks? 37
Concluding remarks 38

3 Regional Initiatives in Africa **40**

Southern African Development Community (SADC) and Southern African Development Coordination Conference (SADCC) 44
Southern African Customs Union (SACU) 58
Economic Community of West African States (ECOWAS) 63
Concluding remarks 67

4 Asia: ASEAN and SAARC **69**

Association of Southeast Asian Nations (ASEAN) 71
South Asian Association for Regional Cooperation (SAARC) 87
Concluding remarks 96

5 APEC: A Case of Open Regionalism **98**

Open regionalism in Asia Pacific Economic Cooperation forum (APEC) 101
Trade patterns in the Asia Pacific region 106
Regionalization/globalization of investments 109
A Pacific Free Trade Area (PAFTA)? 113
Challenges and prospects 116
APEC *vis-à-vis* the Uruguay Round 119

6 The Americas: NAFTA and MERCOSUR **121**

North American Free Trade Area (NAFTA) 121
Common market of the southern cone (MERCOSUR) 141
Prospects for Western Hemisphere integration 154
Concluding remarks 156

7 Regionalism in Europe **158**

The European Union (EU) 158
European Free Trade Area (EFTA) 178
Integration in Central and Eastern Europe? 180
Concluding remarks 190
Statistical Appendix 191

8 Future of Regional Blocs **196**

Trade and investment linkages 197
Blocs and big brothers 198
Building blocks or stumbling blocks? 199

Notes 208

Bibliography 215

Author/Name Index 229

Subject Index 232

List of Tables and Figures

Tables

1.1	Intensity Coefficients of Import Trade of ASA Countries	6
2.1	Characteristics of Old vs. New Regionalism	21
2.2	Indices of Trade Shares	27
2.3	Intraregional Trade of Major Groupings	28
2.4	Indices of Trade Intensity of Major Groupings/ Regions	30
2.5	Concentration of Inflows of Foreign Direct Investment (FDI)	34
2.6	GDP-Weighted Index of Inward and Outward Flows of FDI	35
3.1	African Economic Integration and Cooperation Groupings and their Membership	41
3.2	African Intra-Group Trade Performance	43
3.3	Basic Economic Indicators of SADC, SACU and ECOWAS Members	45
3.4	Intraregional Imports and Exports of SADC and ECOWAS Members	49
3.5	Ratios of Foreign Direct Investment to Gross Fixed Capital Formation and GDP for SADC, SACU and ECOWAS Members	56
4.1	Basic Economic Indicators of ASEAN and SAARC Members	70
4.2	Shares of ASEAN and SAARC Members in World Trade (%)	73
4.3	Indices of Intraregional Trade Intensity for ASEAN Countries	74
4.4	Shares of Foreign Direct Investment in GDP and Gross Fixed Capital Formation in ASEAN and SAARC Members	82
4.5	Indices of Intraregional Trade Intensity for SAARC Members	90
5.1	Basic Economic Indicators of APEC Members	99
5.2	Shares of APEC Members in World Trade (%)	106
6.1	Basic Economic Indicators of NAFTA and MERCOSUR Members	122

6.2 Indices of Intraregional Trade Intensity of NAFTA Members 129
6.3 Indices of Intraregional Trade Intensity of MERCOSUR Members 146
6.4 Estimates of Trade Diversion in MERCOSUR 148
7.1 Basic Economic Indicators of Members of the European Union 160
7.2 The Regional Structure of EC-12 Trade (as per cent of total EC-12 Trade) 164
7.3 FDI Intensity Ratios of Selected EU Countries By Host Region 177
7.4 Basic Economic Indicators of Central and Eastern European Economies 182
A7.1 Indices of Intraregional Trade Intensity of the EEC Members 191

Figures

6.1 FDI Inflows and Outflows: NAFTA Countries 134
6.2 United States: FDI Outflows to NAFTA and other Regions 134
6.3 Japan: FDI Outflows to NAFTA and other Regions 135
6.4 Mexico: FDI Inflows by Sector 136
6.5 United States: FDI Inflows by Sector 136
6.6 United States: FDI Outflows by Sector 137
6.7 FDI Inflows into MERCOSUR Countries 150
6.8 FDI Inflows into MERCOSUR from EC, US and Japan 150
7.1 Germany: FDI Flows to EC, NAFTA and Central and Eastern Europe 175
7.2 France: FDI Flows to EC, NAFTA and Central and Eastern Europe 175
7.3 United Kingdom: FDI Flows to EC, NAFTA and Central and Eastern Europe 176
7.4 Italy: FDI Flows to EC, NAFTA and Central and Eastern Europe 176
7.5 FDI Inflows into Central and Eastern Europe 187

Preface

A resurgence of regional economic and trade blocs throughout the world has raised new questions about their importance and role in trade, development and economic cooperation. The globalization of production and trade is another emerging phenomenon. It is characterized by trade liberalization with the breaking down of trade barriers and freer flows of capital, technology and goods and services across national boundaries. The objectives and performance of existing and emerging regional blocs needs to be examined in this global context, particularly with regard to their roles as promoters and deterrants to globalization. Are they promoting regionalism at the expense of globalization? Or would regionalization eventually give a boost to globalization?

Regional economic integration is high on the agenda particularly in North America, Europe and Asia. North America has witnessed the emergence of a rich–poor grouping – North American Free Trade Area (NAFTA) – consisting of Canada, Mexico and the United States. Although within Asia regional integration has not advanced as much as in Europe, the Association of Southeast Asian Nations (ASEAN) and the wider but looser grouping of Asia Pacific Economic Cooperation (APEC) has agreed to the eventual formation of a free trade area by 2010–20, and to a gradual reduction of tariff barriers within the region. In Latin America, Argentina, Brazil, Paraguay and Uruguay have negotiated to form a Southern Cone Common market – MERCOSUR.

There are already signs of increasing intraregional trade and growth of direct foreign investments within the blocs. In this monograph we argue that foreign direct investment plays a dynamic role in inducing growth and trade expansion. One of the premises on which the new blocs are being created among the developing countries is that they may not be able to expand their exports to the developed-country markets in North America and Europe in view of the growing protectionist tendencies as a result of the prolonged recession and high unemployment rates in the West. Promotion of trade with each other within a region is seen as an imperative alternative.

There is a growing concern that regional blocs may discriminate against goods and services of non-member countries and thus hinder the emergence of a global free-trade system as enshrined in the Uruguay Round agreement signed in Marrakesh in Morocco on 15 April

1994. Regional blocs are seen as stumbling blocks to the globalization process. Another more positive view is that regional blocs are a first step towards globalization including multilateralization of trade. It is argued that a fewer number of countries can more easily agree on harmonizing their national economic policies and on opening up their markets than a much larger number of countries. Thus regional blocs are seen as a gradual process towards multilateral trade and global competition.

The purpose of this monograph is to review a selected number of regional blocs in Asia, Africa, Latin America, North America and Europe to test the above hypotheses.

We owe a debt of gratitude for the completion of the monograph to a number of people. First and foremost, thanks are due to the International Development Research Centre (IDRC), particularly to its Board of Governors who offered the distinguished Pearson Fellowship to A.S. Bhalla. Secondly, many colleagues, friends and academics were most helpful in discussing issues, providing material and reviewing draft chapters of the manuscript. Notable among them are Rohinton Medhora and Réal Lavergne of IDRC; Maureen Molot, Director, Norman Paterson School of International Affairs, Carleton University, Ottawa; Gustavo Indart of the Centre for International Studies, University of Toronto; Professor Colin McCarthy of the University of Stellenbosch, South Africa; Robert Davies, Member of Parliament, Cape Town, South Africa; Rosalind Thomas of the Development Bank of South Africa; Joseph Tan of the Institute of Southeast Asian Studies (ISEAS), Singapore; Massoud Karshenas of the School of Oriental and African Studies of the University of London; Diana Tussie of *Facultad Latinoamericana de Ciencias Sociales* (FLACSO), Buenos Aires; Michael Mortimore of the Economic Commission for Latin America and the Caribbean, Santiago; and Messrs V.R. Panchamukhi and V.L. Rao of the Research and Information System for Non-Aligned and Other Developing Countries (RIS), New Delhi. None of them is however responsible for any errors or omissions. A. Bhalla gave seminars on Globalization and Regionalism at the Institute of Southeast Asian Studies (ISEAS), Singapore, and the Institute of Asian Research at the University of British Columbia, Vancouver. He is grateful to the Seminar sponsors and to the participants at these seminars whose comments and suggestions helped in the writing of the various chapters, particularly Chapters 2, 4 and 5.

At the policy level, A. Bhalla was privileged to meet, during a trip to South America in March 1996, senior negotiators of MERCOSUR in Argentina, Brazil, Chile and Uruguay. They were most helpful and gave freely their precious time to discuss the current status of MERCOSUR, its position *vis-à-vis* NAFTA and the future of Western

Hemisphere integration. Particular gratitude is due to Mr Pedro da Motta Veiga, Director, Operations Department, National Bank of Social and Economic Development (BNDES), Rio de Janeiro, Brazil; Mr Haroldo de Macedo Ribeiro, MERCOSUR Department, Ministry of Foreign Affairs of Brazil, Brasilia; Mr Alejandro Jara, Director, Multilateral Economic Affairs, Ministry of Foreign Affairs' General Directorate for International Economic Relations, Santiago; Mr Christian Larrain Pizzaro, Coordinator, International Finances, Ministry of Finance of Chile, Santiago; Alfred Raul Morelli, Minister, MERCOSUR Directorate, Ministry of Foreign Affairs of Argentina, Buenos Aires; and Mr Garcia Peluffo, Special Adviser to the Minister of Finance, Government of Uruguay and President of Uruguay Delegation to MERCOSUR.

A.S. Bhalla also benefited from discussions on NAFTA and MERCOSUR with a number of Latin American Scholars in Brazil, Chile, Argentina and Uruguay. Notable among them are: Patricio Meller, Director, Institute of Public Policy, University of Chile; Professor Manuel Agosin, Director, Graduate School of Economics and Management, University of Chile; Alberto van Klaveren, Director, Institute of International Studies, University of Chile; Jorge Katz and Osvaldo Rosales of the United Nations Economic Commission for Latin America and the Caribbean (UNECLAC), Santiago; Daniel Chudnovsky, Director, *Centro de Investigaciones para la Transformacion* (CENIT), Buenos Aires; Professors Reinaldo Goncalves and Eduardo Guimaraes, Institute of Economics, Federal University of Rio de Janeiro; Daniel Vaz, Manager, Research Department, Central Bank of Uruguay, Montevideo; Jose Manuel Quijano, Economic Adviser, Chamber of Industry of Uruguay, Montevideo; and Luis Macadar, former Director of the Centre for Economic Research (CINVE), Montevideo.

The APEC Secretariat in Singapore and the Asia-Pacific Economic Forum of Canada in Vancouver generously supplied useful material on Pacific economic and trade cooperation.

Finally, Jill Tansley and Eshete Hailu of IDRC and Haile Taye of the University of Ottawa provided very able research assistance. Haile Taye and Eshete Hailu also endured the unenviable task of tedious calculations and data processing. Ms Kafui Dansu of IDRC helped with translations of documents from Spanish into English while the word processing skills of Lucie Chatelain, Lauraine Clement and Carmen duBois assured the completion of the manuscript. We are deeply indebted to all of them.

A.S. BHALLA
P. BHALLA

Acknowledgements

The authors owe the sub-title of the book to Bhagwati (1991).

The authors and publishers gratefully acknowledge the following for permission to reproduce copyright material: United Nations Conference on Trade and Development (UNCTAD) for using Table 3.1 (Chapter 3) from *UNCTAD Review*, vol. 1, no. 2, 1989; United Nations Economic Commission for Latin America and the Caribbean (UNECLAC), for Table 6.4 (Chapter 6) taken from *CEPAL Review*, no. 51, December 1993; United Nations, New York and UNCTAD, Geneva, for Tables 2.3 (Chapter 2) and 3.2 (Chapter 3) taken from UNCTAD, *Handbook of International Trade and Development Statistics*; Tables 3.5 (Chapter 3) and 4.4 (Chapter 4) compiled from UNCTAD, *World Investment Report 1996*, and Table 7.3 (Chapter 7) taken from UNCTAD, *World Investment Report 1993*.

List of Abbreviations

ACP	Asia, Caribbean and Pacific developing countries signatories with the EU to the Lomé Convention
ADB	Asian Development Bank
AfDB	African Development Bank
AFTA	ASEAN Free Trade Area
AIC	ASEAN Industrial Complementation
AIJV	ASEAN Industrial Joint Venture
AIP	ASEAN Industrial Projects
ANZCERTA	Australia-New Zealand Closer Economic Relationship Trade Agreement (also CER)
APEC	Asia Pacific Economic Cooperation
ASA	Association of Southeast Asia
ASEAN	Association of Southeast Asian Nations
BLNS	Botswana, Lesotho, Namibia and Swaziland
CACM	Central American Common Market
CAP	Common Agricultural Policy of the EU
CARICOM	Caribbean Common Market
CARIFTA	Caribbean Free Trade Association
CBI	Cross-Border Initiative
CEAO	West African Economic Union
CEEAC	Economic Community of Central African States
CEEC	Central and Eastern European Countries
CEPGL	Economic Community of the Great Lakes Countries
CEPT	Common Effective Preferential Tariff (ASEAN)
CER	Closer Economic Relations trade agreement of 1983 (between Australia and New Zealand) – also known as ANZCERTA
CET	Common External Tariff
CFA	French Colonies of Africa
CGE	Computable General Equilibrium
CIS	Commonwealth of Independent States (of the former Soviet Union)
CMA	Common Monetary Area
COMECON	Common Market of the Centrally Planned Economies (also known as CMEA – Council for Mutual Economic Assistance)

COMESA	Common Market of Eastern and Southern Africa
CUSFTA	Canada-US Free Trade Agreement
EAC	East African Community
EAEC	East Asian Economic Caucus
EAI	Enterprise for the Americas Initiative
ECOWAS	Economic Community of West African States
EC	European Community
ECE	Economic Commission for Europe (United Nations)
ECM	European Common Market
EEA	European Economic Area
EEC	European Economic Community
EFTA	European Free Trade Association
EMS	European Monetary System
EPZ	Export Processing Zone
EU	European Union
EUROSTAT	Statistical Office of the European Communities
FDI	Foreign Direct Investment
FTA	Free Trade Area
GATT	General Agreement on Tariffs and Trade
GCC	Gulf Cooperation Council
GSP	Generalized System of Trade Preferences for developing countries
HTS	Harmonized Tariff System/Schedule
IDC	Industrial Development Corporation
IMF	International Monetary Fund
IT	Information Technology
IPA	Integrated Programme of Action
IRS	Increasing Returns to Scale
JETRO	Japan External Trade Organization
LAFTA	Latin American Free Trade Area
LAIA	Latin American Integration Association
MERCOSUR	Common market of the southern cone
MFA	Multi-Fibre Arrangement
MFN	Most Favoured Nation
MNE	Multinational Enterprise
MRU	Mano River Union
NAFTA	North American Free Trade Agreement
NIEs	Newly Industrializing Economies (of East Asia)
NTBs	Non-Tariff Barriers
OECD	Organization for Economic Cooperation and Development

PAFTA	Pacific Free Trade Area
PAFTAD	Pacific Trade and Development Conference
PBEC	Pacific Basin Economic Council
PECC	Pacific Economic Cooperation Conference
PTA	(ASEAN) Preferential Trading Agreement
PTA	Eastern and Southern African Preferential Trading Area
RIA	Regional Integration Agreements
ROW	Rest of the World
RSA	Republic of South Africa
SAARC	South Asian Association for Regional Cooperation
SACU	Southern African Customs Union
SADC	Southern African Development Community
SADCC	Southern African Development Coordination Conference
SAFTA	South American Free Trade Area
SAPTA	South Asian Preferential Trade Agreement
SAR	Southern African Region
SEM	Single European Market
SEZ	Special Export Zone
SIJORI	Singapore, Johor and Riau (growth triangle)
SREZ	Sub-regional Economic Zone
TRIMS	Trade-Related Investment Measures (GATT/WTO)
TRIPS	Trade-Related Intellectual Property Rights (GATT/WTO)
UDEAC	Central African Customs and Economic Union
UDI	Unilateral Declaration of Independence
UEMOA	West African Monetary Union
UMA	Arab Maghreb Union
UNCTAD	United Nations Conference on Trade and Development
UNCTC	United Nations Centre for Transnational Corporations
UNECE	United Nations Economic Commission for Europe
UNECLAC	United Nations Economic Commission for Latin America and the Caribbean
US	United States
VER	Voluntary Export Restraint
WACH	West African Clearing House
WHFTA	Western Hemisphere Free Trade Area
WTO	World Trade Organization

1 Regional Cooperation in Historical Perspective

Regional cooperation is not a new concept. During the sixties regional groupings were formed in almost all developing regions of the world in the wake of the creation of the European Common Market. However, in recent years interest in regionalism has been revived partly in response to increasing globalization. The new regionalism of the eighties and nineties envisages greater integration among members of both developed and developing countries through the establishment of closer economic and trade linkages. The creation of NAFTA, MERCOSUR and the Central European Free Trade Area, and a renewed interest on the part of ASEAN, SAARC and SADC to create free trade areas (see de Melo and Panagariya, 1993) are all testimony to this new trend. The context of earlier regionalism (that is, import-substituting industrialization) is very different from that of new regionalism (multilateralism and globalization). It is for this reason among others, that the issue of compatibility or conflict between regionalism and multilateralism has come to the forefront of the current debate about the global economy.

The formation of regional blocs or loose groupings in the sixties was based on a number of assumptions. First, that it would raise the demand for raw materials and foodstuffs, and with time, exports of manufactured goods among developing countries would reduce their economic and technological dependence on the industrialized countries. Second, that it could raise the bargaining power of the member countries *vis-à-vis* the developed countries. Meade (1955) argued that the larger the trading area as a single bloc the more likely it was to obtain 'better commercial policy treatment' in its negotiations with other (particularly developed) countries. The bargaining strength of countries forming an economic union lies in their position as potential importers or suppliers of essential products to the outside world. Thirdly, it was believed that regional groupings would enable economies of scale resulting from enlarged markets and thus lower the costs of production and raise economic efficiency. Fourthly, most developing countries are exporters of primary products the prices of which are subject to cyclical fluctuations. Adverse terms of trade can have a shattering effect on their economies which depend, by and large, on the exports of a single commodity or a few primary commodities. They are particularly vulnerable to fluctuations in world demand and commodity prices. Regional cooperation was seen as a means of reducing their vulnerability to external shocks.

Furthermore, with multilateral trade and investment flows biased in favour of the North (see Chapter 2), collective self-reliance through greater South–South cooperation was considered an important means of reducing the dependence of developing countries on the global economic and political regime, dominated as it was by the industrialized countries. It was, therefore, not surprising to see continuing experimentation by developing-country governments with a number of regional arrangements formed between the sixties and the eighties, viz. the Association of Southeast Asia (ASA) (1961), the Association of Southeast Asian Nations (ASEAN) (1967), the Southern African Development Coordination Conference (SADCC) (1979), the East African Community (1967), the Preferential Trade Area Treaty for Eastern and Southern Africa (1981), the Gulf Cooperation Council (1981), the Central American Common Market (1960), the Latin American Free Trade Association (LAFTA) (1960), the Andean Pact (1969) and the Caribbean Common Market (CARICOM) (1973).

The nineties have witnessed a revival of interest in regional integration by both developing and developed countries, possibly as an alternative, if not a stepping stone, to globalization. Among the developing countries, in particular, regionalism is a response to growing protectionist tendencies by the European Union, NAFTA and the major markets of Japan and the United States. It is also a bid to survive increasing global competition in trade and investments.

In this Chapter we examine lessons from the earlier experience of regional economic integration and cooperation in Latin America, Asia and Africa. The motivation of these earlier attempts at integration, in contrast to those which emerged in the late eighties and early nineties is considered in a historical perspective to determine what led to their failure. Does this experience provide any pointers for making the new regionalism of the nineties more successful? Some of the more recent regional arrangements represent rich-poor groupings and thus offer bigger market size and greater complementarity than the earlier poor-poor groupings (see Chapters 5 and 6).

REGIONAL COOPERATION: A HISTORICAL SKETCH

Most regions have witnessed the formation of one regional grouping or another during the past three or four decades. Below, we briefly describe these initiatives in different regions of the world.

Africa

The African region is unique in respect of the large number of groupings which have attempted economic integration. One of the earliest customs unions among developing countries was the East African Community of Kenya, Tanzania and Uganda. The East African Community had common external tariffs, free trade within the area, common customs and income tax administrations, a common currency and common communications services. It broke up in 1977. The origins of the economic community can be traced back to 1917 when free trade between Uganda and Kenya was established (see Okigbo, 1967). Tanganyika, the third member of the Community joined gradually between 1922 and 1927. Although there were some quantitative restrictions there were no tariffs among the three members. A common tariff against the outside world was imposed. Intraregional trade within the East African Community is known to have been quite large. Unlike ASA discussed below, transport and communications were well developed with railways and airways owned by the Community.

Why then did the Community break up? It had unequal partners with Kenya being far more developed than Tanganyika (Tanzania) and Uganda. Economic and political nationalism and growing ideological differences between Kenya with a capitalistic outlook and Tanzania with a socialist bias were contributory factors. Another major factor seems to have concerned the unequal distribution of gains. It is reported that most of the benefits from the Community accrued to Kenya to the detriment of the two poorer partners.

Some efforts were made by the African Community to compensate the poorer partners, for example, through a transfer tax and loans from the East African Development Bank. However, the transfer tax, which was intended to protect Ugandan and Tanzanian industries against Kenyan competition, ended up leading to a duplication of industries in the three countries. The exploitation of economies of scale required fewer industrial plants serving the whole common market, but the Community partners could not agree on the location of these plants. The East African Development Bank was meant to invest disproportionately more in Tanzania and Uganda but its resources were too limited to be effective. A coup in Uganda finally sounded the death knell for the Community. Hazlewood (1979) concludes that the African Community 'faded and died from a lack of interest in keeping it alive . . . the political will was lacking in the Partner States to keep the Community in being'.

Similar attempts at regional blocs were also made by the former French colonies in West Africa. For example, by a Treaty signed in December 1964, the countries of the former French Equatorial Africa, namely, Congo (Brazzaville), the Central African Republic, Chad, Cameroon and Gabon agreed to form a Customs Union with effect from January 1966. According to Okigbo (1967, p. 152) 'this customs union is more strictly defined and more far reaching than any other union in Africa'. The partner countries were characterized by a vast area sparsely populated and poorly served by transport and communications. Commercial production concentrated mainly on the export of primary products. As former French colonies they had special trading relationships with France and, to a lesser extent, the EEC countries. These countries continued to enjoy preferential treatment even after they introduced a common external tariff against third parties. The Treaty leading to the creation of a customs union allowed for the free movement of capital and goods but not labour (Robson, 1967). It also provided for fiscal, financial and industrial harmonization.

Another African grouping worthy of note is the West African Economic Union (CEAO). Founded in 1973 by the Treaty of Abidjan, it consists of the following countries of the former French Western Africa: Burkina Faso, Côte d'Ivoire, Mali, Mauritania, Niger and Senegal (Benin became a member in 1984). CEAO maintains the arrangements for monetary and economic union that prevailed during the French colonial period in West Africa. The monetary union was maintained through the Common Franc Zone linked to France which has continued to maintain its influence in its former colonies even after they gained independence, partly to counter the growing power of Nigeria in West Africa.

As we note in Chapter 3, Africa has, perhaps, the largest number of regional groupings. However, none of these groupings has worked well. At any rate, they have had little positive influence on the expansion of intraregional trade, which was one of their main goals.

Asia

Early attempts by the Asian countries aimed at promoting economic, political and cultural *cooperation* rather than economic *integration*.

Interest in economic cooperation grew partly as a reaction to the emergence of common markets in Europe and Latin America. In July 1961, Malaysia, Thailand and the Philippines established the Association of Southeast Asia (ASA). It was the first Asian regional economic bloc to promote cooperation in international commodity trade, in technical, economic and educational information, and in research and training. In 1966, the participating countries agreed on a number of programmes of economic coordination, viz. multilateral trade and navigation agreements, expansion of intraregional trade and the establishment of an ASA fund to finance regional projects.(For details, see Bhalla, 1964). Meanwhile, the creation of a Malaysian Common Market (Malaya, Singapore, Sabah and Sarawak) in 1963 amounted to a miniature economic union within the proposed bigger common market of ASA partners. However, the absence of any preferential treatment for the goods from Thailand and the Philippines made the Malaysian Common Market incompatible with the goal of an ASA free trade area.

Progress towards the achievement of the declared goals of ASA remained very slow due largely to strained political relations between the ASA partners especially between Malaysia and the Philippines. The political tensions between these two countries over Sabah finally led to the collapse of ASA in 1964.

Apart from the political factors, the economic rationale for the creation of an ASA customs union or a free trade area can be questioned. Attempts at trade liberalization among members had little effect on intra-ASA trade which remained quite small. Trade with the rest of the world continued to be limited to a few commodities and manufactured goods (see Table 1.1).

The ASA was followed by ASEAN formed by Singapore, Thailand, Indonesia, Malaysia and the Philippines (Brunei joined in 1984 and Vietnam in 1995). Several factors brought these countries together: the need to bring stability to a region rocked by internecine regional disputes and ethnic problems, the external communist threat, mainland China's links with its overseas Chinese, many of whom lived in the ASEAN countries, the war in Vietnam, growing instability in the Indo-China zone, and so on. So far progress in the field of economic cooperation within the ASEAN has been rather slow, although recent initiatives suggest a renewed interest in the formation of a free trade area through a progressive reduction of tariff barriers (see Chapter 4).

South Asia presents a striking contrast in terms of the motivation, or rather the lack of it, for forming the regional grouping of SAARC on 8 December 1985 among India, Pakistan, Bangladesh, Sri Lanka,

Table 1.1 Intensity coefficients of import trade of ASA countries

	1958	*1960*	*1964*	*1965*
1. Malaysia				
United States	0.87	0.90	1.08	1.14
United Kingdom	1.92	1.34	1.08	0.70
Philippines	0.26	0.24	0.17	1.80
Thailand	4.14	2.47	7.21	1.90
2. Thailand				
United States	1.48	1.23	1.08	0.53
United Kingdom	0.54	0.46	0.48	0.46
Philippines	3.90	0.23	4.19	4.61
Malaysia	26.93	26.84	22.10	14.29
3. Philippines				
United States	4.55	4.34	4.05	3.69
United Kingdom	0.13	0.22	0.14	0.12
Thailand	0.06	0.11	0.13	0.06
Malaysia	0.08	0.07	0.26	1.03

Source: Our estimates. The coefficients are based on data from IMF, *Direction of Trade Statistics Yearbook* – calculated using the Anderson–Norheim formula (equation 2.1)

Nepal and Bhutan. Here geopolitical factors have played a divisive role rather than providing an incentive to regional cooperation. The main motivation for the creation of SAARC would appear to be the common fear by the region's smaller countries of domination by India and the expectation that collective pressure by members within the framework of a regional grouping might serve to contain Indian ambitions to regional hegemony.

Political and ethnic tensions among the South Asian neighbours, the asymmetrical structure of South Asia from the standpoint of size and resources, and the extreme contrasts in the levels of industrialization as well as a lack of complementarity in resources and production are formidable constraints to regional cooperation. Such constraints are exacerbated in turn by India's view of South Asia as a single security unit which it alone is responsible for policing to the exclusion of outside interference – an attitude which has encouraged other SAARC members in the past to seek to offset Indian domination by establishing closer ties with China and the United States. Recent attempts to redefine regional cooperation in SAARC and ASEAN are discussed in Chapter 4.

Latin America and the Caribbean

The motivation for regional economic groupings arose from a recognition that the national import-substitution policies followed by most countries of the region shielded by protectionist barriers did not help them overcome their foreign exchange constraints. Integration efforts gave a regional dimension to the inward-looking nationalist policies (Nogues and Quintanilla, 1993). Economic interdependence within the Latin American region and independence from the advanced countries were the major objectives of regional integration in the early sixties. The integration programmes were intended to promote intraregional trade even if this involved trade diversion away from traditional trading partners outside the region (for example, the United States) (Baumann, 1993). Regional economic integration in Latin and Central America dates back to 1960 when both the Latin American Free Trade Association (LAFTA) and the Central American Common Market (CACM) were established. These were some of the earliest attempts at forming a customs union and a common market. The Andean Pact, which followed in 1969, consisted of Bolivia, Chile, Colombia, Ecuador, Peru and Venezuela (Chile left the Pact in 1976). The Caribbean Common Market (CARICOM) established in 1973 consisted initially of Jamaica, Trinidad and Tobago, Barbados and Guyana. They were subsequently joined by Antigua and Barbuda, the Bahamas, Belize, Dominica, Grenada, Monserrat, St Christopher-Nieves, St Lucia, and St Vincent. CARICOM grew out of the earlier Caribbean Free Trade Association (CARIFTA) which was established in 1968.

The Latin American Free Trade Association (LAFTA) consisted of Argentina, Brazil, Chile, Mexico, Paraguay, Peru and Uruguay. The original treaty provided for the creation of a free trade area to expand intraregional trade and the promotion of industrial integration. In 1980, after 20 years of existence, LAFTA was replaced by the Latin American Integration Association (LAIA) founded by the Treaty of Montevideo. The reduction of trade barriers within LAFTA did not significantly raise intraregional trade. The LAFTA/LAIA trade ratios (total trade as a percentage of combined GDP of the region) rose from 2 per cent in the sixties to only 2.6 per cent in the eighties (see Nogues and Quintanilla, 1993, Table 2). On the other hand, in the case of the Central American Common Market (CACM) consisting of El Salvador, Guatemala, Honduras and Nicaragua, the lowering of tariff barriers contributed to a substantial growth in intraregional trade. Unlike LAFTA, the trade ratios increased from 1.8 per cent in 1960 to nearly 7 per cent during the 1980–90 period.

Following the example of Latin American countries, the Caribbean countries formed a common market (CARICOM), and also aimed at regional cooperation in health, education as well as transport, and co-ordination of foreign policies of the member states. Despite the last objective, political integration was not envisaged. Payne (1994) states that CARICOM represents 'neither nationalism nor regionalism but a hybrid creature consisting of elements of both'.

CARICOM member countries are at varying levels of development which made negotiations often difficult. CARICOM owed its creation largely to the more developed member countries like Jamaica. To placate the smaller less-developed island members and to promote their economic development, a Caribbean Investment Corporation was established. However, ever since the creation of CARICOM, such members as Guyana and Jamaica have suffered from international economic crises. While Trinidad and Tobago benefited from the oil boom of the early seventies, Jamaica experienced recession. The structural adjustment and balance of payments problems led Guyana and Jamaica to impose restrictions on the import of goods from within the region. This measure was clearly inconsistent with the formulation of a common market which required the elimination of tariff and non-tariff barriers.

Bilateral agreements between Caribbean countries like Jamaica and Latin American countries such as Venezuela also stood in the way of regional economic cooperation within the Caribbean.[1]

In 1989, an attempt was made to revitalize the integration process within CARICOM. This led to an agreement among the members for the creation of a new scheme of CARICOM industrial programming, the establishment of a common external tariff by January 1991, regional air and sea transport systems by the middle of 1992, and the introduction of an intraregional capital movement scheme by 1993. These plans do not seem to have materialized. With the emergence of NAFTA and an invitation by the United States for all Latin American countries to join the Enterprise for the Americas Initiative (see Chapter 6), the future of CARICOM has become uncertain.

The Andean Pact was somewhat different from other efforts at trade cooperation. It envisaged the establishment within 10 years of coordinated development plans harmonizing economic and social policies, joint industrial development programmes and science and technology policies and a common régime regulating direct foreign investments. To achieve some of these goals, sectoral industrial programmes to set up key industries were adopted with a view to attaining regional import substitution. The Pact has been regarded as the 'most sophisticated integration scheme to foster import-substitution at the regional level with the most complex of regulations to implement the agreement' (Nogues and Quintanilla, 1993).

Middle East

The Arab Common Market and the Arab Maghreb Union established in the sixties are two examples of regional cooperation which were not implemented. A more encouraging example of economic integration in the region is the Gulf Cooperation Council (GCC) which was formed in 1981 by Bahrain, Kuwait, Oman, Qatar, Saudi Arabia and the United Arab Emirates. The Council aimed at the free movement of goods and services and capital and labour. Trade within the Council countries was liberalized by a gradual reduction and harmonization of tariffs. However, local content was specified at 40 per cent of value added to be provided within the GCC region. Similarly, 51 per cent of the capital of trading firms was expected to be owned by the GCC citizens (Harmsen and Leidy, 1994).

Arab regional integration efforts failed to make much headway partly due to the political conflicts between Iran and Iraq, between Iraq and the countries of the Gulf coalition, and between Israel and the Arab States. Despite efforts at the formation of the Arab Common Market, intraregional trade in the Middle East has remained small at only 6 per cent in 1983 (Fischer, 1993). Taking individual countries, Bahrain, Jordan, Syria and Yemen recorded much greater intraregional trade than other countries in the region. In the foreseeable future, a regional grouping of the type of NAFTA or the European Union for the whole of the Middle East is unlikely for both economic and political reasons.

Industrialized Countries

So far we have considered regional integration among developing countries. In the industrialized countries, early examples of regional groupings include: European Common Market (ECM), Common Market of the Centrally Planned Economies (COMECON) and European Free Trade Association (EFTA). Perhaps the oldest and most effectively functioning case of regional integration is that of the European Community which was established in 1958 by the Treaty of Rome to achieve both political and economic objectives. Its precursors were the Benelux (Belgium, Netherlands and Luxembourg) customs union (1944) and the European Coal and Steel Community (1953–4). The Treaty aimed at phasing out tariffs and quantitative restrictions to free trade among the participating countries (Belgium, France, Germany, Italy, Luxembourg and the Netherlands) over the period of twelve years ending in January 1970. National tariffs against non-members were to be harmonized gradually so as to arrive at a common external tariff throughout the Community area. By the middle of 1962, the six members of the Community had already lowered their tariffs *vis-à-vis* other members by 50 per cent on industrial products (Dell, 1963, p. 89). The 1986 Single European Act aimed at the creation of a single European market, and common community policies in the fields of social and regional development, science and technology and monetary union.

The Maastricht Treaty adopted in 1992 took the European Common Market a step further by providing for the establishment of a monetary union and a common European currency by 1997. In January 1993, a Single European Market Programme was introduced, leading to free movement of capital, goods and people.

Unlike the European Union, the European Free Trade Association (EFTA) was formed in November 1959 purely as an economic entity. It did not provide for any common external tariff which limited its efforts towards economic integration. Free trade was restricted only to industrial goods although some arrangements were also envisaged for trade in agricultural commodities and fish. Dell (1963, p. 94) notes the 'character of EFTA as a low tariff club designed to exert pressure on the EEC rather than as a serious exercise in economic integration'.

Parallel to economic integration in Western Europe, the former central and eastern European countries and the former Soviet Union established their own regional grouping, COMECON (CMEA – Council for Mutual Economic Assistance) in January 1949. This regional economic grouping of the then communist countries differed from those of Western Europe in the sense that trade liberalization and economic cooperation were centrally planned and markets did not play a role in the allocation of goods and resources. Quantitative regulations and restrictions, rather than tariffs, regulated trade among the member countries. COMECON collapsed with the disintegration of the former Soviet Union and the end of communism in Central and Eastern Europe. More recent attempts at integration among some countries in this region include the Central European Free Trade Area between the Czech Republic, Hungary, Poland and Slovakia established in March 1993, and the Baltic Free Trade Agreement signed in April 1994 between Estonia, Latvia and Lithuania.

Within North America, the formation of a free trade area between

Canada and the United States in 1988 and the North American Free Trade Area (NAFTA) among Canada, Mexico and the United States in 1993, are the most recent attempts at economic integration (see Chapter 6). NAFTA differs fundamentally from the European Union which is aiming at Union-wide policies on several issues. Unlike the EU, these North American attempts do not involve any harmonization of national economic and monetary policies which entail a certain loss of national sovereignty to supranational regional bodies. While NAFTA is an example largely of a market-led process of integration, that of the EU is a policy and institution-led approach to integration. The other regional arrangements discussed above can similarly be classified into these two main models of integration. While APEC is largely market-led, other groupings such as MERCOSUR, ASEAN, ECOWAS, SADCC, SACU, and so on were essentially government or policy induced.

Regional integration in industrialized countries was motivated much more by static gains from trade creation than by the objective of economic development. In the developing countries on the other hand, it was seen in more dynamic terms with a developmental goal of changing production structures, promoting industrialization and enhancing productive capacity through import substitution (see McCarthy, 1994).

LESSONS FROM PAST EXPERIENCE

What lessons, if any, can be learnt from these past experiments with regionalism?

Among the developing countries most of the regional groupings consisted of poor countries with very limited size of national, regional and sub-regional markets. Even when the combined populations of the regional groups were large, the low per capita income and purchasing power kept the market size relatively small. Most of the regional groups were formed among low-income countries which did not allow much market expansion through regionalization. The lesson that follows is that poor–poor country groupings are likely to be unsuccessful because of market limitations. At least one of the member countries in the group should have a reasonably big market to enable the reaping of economies of scale at a regional level (see Chapter 8 for elaboration of this point).

It was believed that integration would raise industrial efficiency by promoting competition within an integrated market. Once the (sub) regional producers could successfully face competition from each other within a bloc they would gain the confidence to compete successfully with developed-country producers in the global markets. In many cases in practice, the adoption of national import-substitution policies obstructed the regional groupings' efforts aimed at import-substitution at the sub-regional or regional level. This explains their failure to introduce regional industrial joint ventures. As we noted above, amongst poor countries even the combined size of the market may be too small to make regional import-substitution economically viable. This seems to have been the case with many African groupings (see Chapter 3).

Furthermore, even when minimum size of markets is assured, a number of preconditions for regional trade expansion and growth need to be fulfilled. These may, *inter alia*, consist of harmonization of foreign investment legislation, linkages between governments, industrialists and enterprises across national boundaries, mechanisms for financing trade such as long-term credit facilities, multilateral clearing and payments arrangements and convertibility of national currencies, and so on. The experience of SACU discussed in Chapter 3 shows how monetary coordination is essential for the functioning of a customs union. The poor performance of ECOWAS is in part attributed to the lack of convertible currencies and the absence of other preconditions cited above.

In Latin America, the balance of payments problems and debt crises have inhibited efforts at economic cooperation. Persistent macroeconomic imbalances often led to overvalued exchange rates which made trade liberalization difficult and generated pressures to increase protection within the region.

The experiences of the various South–South groupings were also closely linked to the international economic climate. During the seventies when the international economy was growing, economic cooperation also developed rapidly, particularly in the case of ASEAN and CACM. In the eighties however, these blocs suffered setbacks especially in intraregional trade and in the operation of clearing and payments arrangements. Rather than reacting collectively *en bloc* to external economic crises, member states responded individually and placed their national concerns ahead of their commitment to the integration process.

A related aspect concerning external factors is that South-South regional integration can be promoted through assistance from a third country or another regional grouping. In the case of ASEAN, Japanese aid has played a major role in assisting regional industrial projects such as automobile assembly and parts production. In the case of CACM, the European Union is assisting the process of subregional economic integration.

A major lesson from the past experience of regional blocs is that political harmony and cohesion is an important precondition for successful cooperation. Serious political disagreements and disputes over territory often led to the failure or break-up of many well-functioning groupings. This was, for example, the case of the East African Community, the Andean Pact and the Association of Southeast Asia.

In many of the developing countries, the ruling élites have derived their power and support from relatively small groups of vested interests whose economic and political clout has been created and sustained by traditional North–South linkages. The leadership, therefore, has been wary of the political costs in seeking to reorient such linkages which regional integration requires. Furthermore, such reorientation of linkages calls for structural adjustment measures which most developing countries were reluctant to undertake, perhaps at the time, but are now undergoing in response to pressures from the Bretton Woods institutions (the International Monetary Fund (IMF) and the World Bank).

In the absence of any mechanisms to ensure compensation for any loss of production or tariff revenues, regional cooperation among unequal partners is likely to lead to unequal or uneven distribution of perceived or actual gains from trade and economic liberalization. Generally, benefits from integration tend to gravitate towards the advanced members. This is to be expected on economic logic; industry tends to be located where skills and infrastructure are available and economies of large-scale production can be exploited. As we noted above, in the former East African Community, Kenya benefited disproportionately at the expense of Uganda and Tanzania. Despite a compensation mechanism, the Community failed to satisfy the poorer members that they were getting a fair share of the gains. For integration schemes among countries to be lasting and successful, it is necessary for all members, both poor and rich, to benefit adequately from them. Appropriate regional policies (as in the case of the European Union, see Chapter 7) and other compensatory arrangements (such as fiscal transfers, foreign investment codes, joint industrial planning and programmes) are an essential precondition for integration schemes among unequal partners to function well.

In the past, regional blocs failed to expand intraregional trade even through trade diversion. Net trade creation did not occur owing both to limited market size, noted above, and to slow economic growth in member countries. Rapid economic growth in East Asia on the other hand, has led to trade expansion without any explicit institution-based regional integration.

Most past groupings consisted of countries with similar production structures resulting in lack of complementarity among partners. Diversified production structures are a precondition to expansion of intraregional trade as well as to trade with the rest of the world. Therefore, cooperation in production is as important as cooperation in trade. Strengthening of production linkages will *inter alia*, depend on adequate flows of foreign investments, and adequate and well-developed transportation and communications infrastructure and distribution and marketing networks. In ECOWAS and SAARC weak industrial production and infrastructure linkages (for example, transport and telecommunications, information sharing and so on) among member countries have limited the prospects of enhanced economic and trade cooperation. Regional integration schemes need to be dynamic and growth-inducing which, as we note in the following chapters, calls for reinforcement of linkages between trade and foreign direct investment.

Finally, in the case of South–South groupings the process of regional integration is likely to require a longer time frame than for the North–South or North–North groupings, owing to the need to overcome greater socioeconomic problems, achieve industrial growth and develop greater regional complementarities.

REGIONAL BLOCS OR LOOSE GROUPINGS?

Different meanings have been attached to regional cooperation, integration and blocs. Despite the plethora of new literature on regional blocs and open regionalism the conventional categories of free trade areas, customs unions and common markets are still valid for depicting different types and degrees of regional economic integration.

Free trade areas (FTAs) are defined in terms of free trade within the area (absence of tariff barriers) and discrimination against third countries in terms of external tariffs determined by the individual members of the FTAs. Customs unions are an advanced form of free trade areas in which, besides regional free trade, the members agree to introduce common external tariffs against third countries. Common markets are characterized by free flows of all factors of production as well as of goods and services. Economic unions are the most advanced form of integration in which fiscal, monetary and other economic policies are harmonized at a supranational level. Many other regional arrangements take the form of associations or consultative bodies engaged in weaker economic cooperation on a sectoral or case-by-case basis.

The term, regional blocs, in this book is defined to cover all the above forms of integration as they are all capable of making an impact on the globalization of trade and investments. The specific blocs discussed in Chapters 3 to 7 can be classified as follows according to the categories noted above.

1. Regional economic cooperation association: SADC, ASEAN, SAARC and APEC;
2. Free Trade Area for example, NAFTA, MERCOSUR, APEC and AFTA;
3. Customs Union MERCOSUR, SACU;
4. Common Market (the European Union); and
5. Economic Union (the European Union).

As noted above, some blocs belong to more than one category. This is because they aim to move from a lower category of integration to a higher level of integration. For example, ASEAN which was slow to introduce economic cooperation now aims at the formation of a free trade area (AFTA) by the year 2003 (see Chapter 4). The European Union, currently a common market, is preparing for supranational bodies (for example, a European Central Bank) and a common currency.

CONCLUDING REMARKS

It is clear from the above discussion that most geographical regions of the world have in the past witnessed several attempts at economic cooperation and/or integration. The European Union is the most experienced and advanced form of integration among developed countries. NAFTA is the single example of a free trade area representing a grouping of two developed and one developing country. APEC, a weaker form of economic cooperation also includes both developed and developing countries of Asia and the Pacific region. The ASEAN involves economies at varying levels of development but owing to their proximity to the rapidly growing economies of East Asia, are able to benefit more from extraregional than intraregional linkages.

Besides NAFTA and APEC, other new regional economic initiatives include the Central European Free Trade Area (Czech Republic, Hungary, Poland and Slovakia) in place of the now defunct COMECON, and MERCOSUR.

What explains the renewed interest in regional groupings in the eighties and nineties? How are these more recent attempts at free trade and regional integration different from the earlier ones? These are some of the questions discussed in the following Chapter which also outlines the approach and methodology of the subsequent chapters. Chapters 3 to 7 deal with pairs of specific regional groupings relating respectively to Africa, Asia and the Pacific, the Americas and Europe. A separate chapter is devoted to APEC. The last chapter speculates on the future of regional blocs. We argue that regional blocs need not be stumbling blocks to freer multilateral trade and the emerging global economy. However, much will depend on how these blocs are implemented and on the attitudes and policies of some key players: the European Union, the United States and a possible Japan-dominated East Asia. Static gains from trade need to be combined with dynamic gains from foreign investment, and regionalism needs to be non-discriminatory towards third countries. Thus, in principle, non-discriminatory regional arrangements are likely to be more compatible with a freer multilateral trading system and globalization. On the other hand, customs unions and common markets could hinder globalization of trade by discriminating against third parties.[2]

2 The New Regionalism vs. Globalization?

The past decade has witnessed the emergence of new regional economic groupings and the revitalizing of existing ones. This development raises questions about whether such groupings are 'building blocks or stumbling blocks' towards efforts to create a global multilateral trading system and a unified global economy. One view is that by gradually introducing free trade or trade liberalization at a regional level, they could be considered the initial steps towards global liberalization of trade. Such liberalization may initially be easier when a small number of countries is involved.

Another view is that regionalism might pose a threat to a global trading system especially if the regional blocs create tariff walls around them. Growing protectionism (for example, anti-dumping practices, local content requirements in manufacturing) especially by European countries and North America against imports from developing countries has prompted the latter to create their own retaliatory protectionist blocs. Regionalism in this context is regarded as a defensive reaction to the new economic and political trends. It is also often regarded as a possible alternative to multilateralism.

This Chapter examines different forms of the new regionalism in the context of the process of globalization and puts forward conditions under which regional blocs will act as building blocks. It attempts to consider the extent to which regionalization of trade, investment and production is taking place.

DIFFERENT FORMS OF THE NEW REGIONALISM

Regionalism in the eighties and nineties differs substantially from the old regionalism discussed in Chapter 1. This is largely due to a vastly different economic and political context in which the new regionalism is taking shape. From the fifties to the seventies, the newly independent developing countries were anti-colonial and thus sought independence from the North through South–South cooperation. Regional groupings were considered a means of promoting such cooperation. However, the earlier regional groupings were created when their member countries were at early stages of development. Owing to the small size of their markets, it was believed that regionalism would provide economies of scale, which, in conjunction with import-substitution strategies, would promote rapid industrialization. The regional groupings were inevitably formulated within the framework of economic planning and government regulation.[1]

The new groupings, on the other hand, have emerged under the paradigm of economic liberalization and market deregulation. The world economy has become increasingly interdependent following the end of the Cold War, as a result of rapid technological diffusion and economic and trade liberalization by most countries. Many developing countries are liberalizing trade unilaterally as a component of reforms in macroeconomic, trade and industrial policies. Such reforms are being introduced with the aim of raising productive efficiency and coping with increasing international competition. Thus, the new regional groupings are being established within an open multilateral trading framework (Oman, 1994).

While the earlier groupings were inward-looking and viewed protective tariffs as a means to promoting growth, the new groupings are generally outward-looking and view intraregional and interregional trade as an engine of growth. In some ways, the new regional arrangements are a response to the increasing competition under a global economy, and for many, they represent a first step towards enabling economies to benefit from the process of globalization.

The new wave of regional integration is being viewed less in terms of gains from trade creation/diversion and more in terms of scale economies, product differentiation, efficiency gains, and policy coordination (see Robson, 1993). There is also an increasing emphasis on the role of foreign investment in regional integration and globalization and a genuine drive towards trade liberalization with the ultimate aim of creating free trade areas (FTAs). Such FTAs are viewed as a means of attracting foreign direct investment and achieving global competitiveness in trade. In the past, most regional integration schemes did not go beyond limited preferential arrangements.

Unlike most old groupings (with the exception of the African ones), the new ones are characterized by overlapping membership by countries in a number of different groupings (for example, membership of the US, Canada and Mexico in NAFTA and APEC). It would appear that the primary motivation for this multiple membership is to secure access to different regional markets, particularly where regional blocs demonstrate protectionist tendencies against non-members. Individual countries' fears of losing shares of the European market (in the wake of a possible 'fortress Europe') have led them to seek access to rapidly growing markets elsewhere especially in the Asia Pacific. Given the increasing number of regional agreements, there is a growing compulsion for those left out to either form their own agreements or join into existing ones for fear of being marginalized.

Besides market access, members of regional groupings may also be interested in diversifying their trade and investment linkages so as to reduce their dependence on major trading partners such as the US. Multiple membership by the major industrialized countries may also be indicative of the desire to bring regionalism in line with multilateralism. Such a desire is likely to be stronger for a large country with global markets than for smaller countries. However, US trade policy in recent years, with its linking of social and environmental conditions to trade, has raised questions about its commitment to the multilateral process (see Chapter 8 for more details).

The dominant position of the United States in world markets in the fifties and sixties has been weakened by its trade and budget deficits and by increasing competition from the European Union and Japan. Once the champion of multilateral free trade, the US is now turning increasingly towards regional and bilateral arrangements where it has more control over the rules of the game.[2] These circumstances may have led to the US acceptance of regionalism in North America but not necessarily elsewhere. In fact, it has consistently opposed an Asian trade bloc dominated by Japan. It is, perhaps, for this reason that the US subscribed to APEC where it could counterbalance Japanese influence by becoming a major participant in the forum.

For the first time regional integration is taking place between the North and the South. APEC (1989), 'the Enterprise for the Americas Initiative' (EAI) (1990) proposed by former President George Bush, and NAFTA (1992), are three concrete examples of varying forms of North–South bilateral/multilateral trading arrangements. A common element in all three initiatives is the participation of the US. The tendency to shift from import-substitution to export-oriented trade and industrial policies in Latin American countries (and deregulation measures by many of their governments) has made agreement with the US easier. The geographical and physical proximity and restoration of democracies in some countries of the region have also played a significant role in facilitating negotiations for guaranteed access to the US market. Foreign direct investment has been a major incentive for participation in the agreements. Although the above agreements were bilateral, they encouraged the creation of sub-regional groupings in Latin America (for example, MERCOSUR) as a means of strengthening the position of participating countries for negotiating trade liberalization agreements with the US (Oman, 1994).

This increasing trend towards bilateral trade arrangements aims to counter protectionist forms of regionalism and to supplement regional arrangements. But it is also creating 'hub and spoke' arrangements most evident in the Western Hemisphere where the United States with its large market could be viewed as a 'hub' and the smaller countries as 'spokes'. The greatest advantages from such an arrangement accrue to the US as it can negotiate agreements on its own terms without the need to accommodate regional partners. The hub benefits from trade liberalization agreements signed with the spokes but the spokes do not benefit from other spokes. There is also a tendency to combine membership of regional arrangements with bilateral agreements with countries outside the regional bloc. For example, Mexico's membership of NAFTA has not precluded its entering into free-trade agreements with Chile and Venezuela. Currently, Mexico is negotiating an agreement with MERCOSUR similar to that negotiated by Chile (see Chapter 6).

Conversely, some developing countries that are not in a position to undertake the structural adjustments necessary to subscribe to a regional free trade agreement, may prefer bilateral agreements so as to liberalize at their own pace.

Table 2.1 summarizes the characteristic features of the old and new regionalism.

There seems to be a growing consensus that the new regionalism can only be consistent with globalization if it is outward-oriented or 'open'. This is discussed below.

'Open' Regionalism

'Open' regionalism is generally associated with the outward-looking export-oriented economies of East Asia and the Pacific, which, unlike NAFTA and the European Union, are not formally grouped into any regional bloc. Yet, over the past decade or so, this region has been the fastest growing with exports as a proportion of GNP expanding faster than for any other region. Intraregional trade expansion has been accompanied by growth in interregional trade. As we shall discuss in Chapter 5, open regionalism à la APEC is characterized by trade

Table 2.1 Characteristics of old vs. new regionalism

Old Regionalism	*New Regionalism*
Institutions/Government driven	Market driven
Import-substitution as basis of industrialization	Export promotion and trade liberalization
Discrimination against the rest of the world	No discrimination against the rest of the world
Regional or sub-regional competition	Global competition
Emphasis on intraregional trade and security	Emphasis on open trade, investment and growth
South–South or North–North membership	North–South membership (e.g. NAFTA, APEC)
Generally membership of one group (with the exception of Africa)	Overlapping membership of a country in a number of groups

liberalization and expansion independent of the sort of governmental or institutional interventions which were responsible for the formation of blocs in other regions.

Garnaut (1994, p. 273) notes that 'open regionalism involves regional economic integration without discrimination against economies outside the region'. He defines it in terms of three analytical elements, namely: (i) 'open' policies in relation to official barriers to trade (protection); (ii) the role of regional cooperation in reducing non-official trade barriers such as transport and communications barriers, risk and uncertainty resulting from imperfect information and social, psychological and institutional factors; and (iii) regional integration through market processes, independent of government. There is however no clearcut theory of open regionalism. Neither is it clear whether in practice 'open' regionalism is fundamentally different from 'discriminatory' integration. Any regional arrangements for trading purposes are bound to give preferences to members as against non-members. In the absence of such discrimination the rationale of groupings would be reduced only to some perception of increased bargaining power *vis-à-vis* non-members.

A distinction is sometimes made between *market* integration and *policy-led* or *institutional* integration (see Cooper, 1974; Drysdale and Garnaut, 1989, 1993; UNCTAD, 1994; UNCTC, 1992). Market integration relies on market forces instead of any institutional mechanisms or public policy, whereas institutional integration (as in the case of the European Union) involves supranational bodies and harmonized policies in favour of members often at the expense of the rest of the world.

The latter generally tends to be discriminatory. However this distinction can be misleading since the integration process may be governed by both market forces and government policies (Molot, 1995). This is shown by the experience of the Asia Pacific region. Market forces are important in this region; yet governments there have also played an important role in promoting a favourable economic environment for private investors, in overcoming possible national resistance to international specialization and in providing such 'public goods' as infrastructure and telecommunications. Although governments play a role, there are no supranational institutions to regulate and monitor trade expansion and foreign direct investment (FDI) inflows.

GLOBALIZATION: CONCEPT AND MEANING

The term, globalization, which is used to describe the state of multilateral economic relations in the world today, has become fashionable but its meaning and implications, particularly for developing countries, are far from clear. Globalization is generally understood in terms of multilateral trade and reduction of barriers to trade and the flow of goods and services, capital and finance across nations. Apart from multilateral free trade, internationalization of production, increased flows of foreign direct investment, and financial integration are also noted as important features of globalization. The corporate strategies of multinational corporations regarding trade, technology and foreign direct investment are an important driving force propelling the process of globalization. The rapid pace of technological change and the widespread use of information and telecommunications technologies also play an important role in this process.

Barriers to trade have been progressively lifted and the Uruguay Round has been ratified by a large number of countries. During the past five decades the average OECD levels of tariffs are known to have been reduced from 40 per cent to 5 per cent (see Oman, 1994, p. 31). Most developing countries have also liberalized their trade, investment and economic policies. World trade is growing faster than output and the structure of world trade has changed significantly. The share of manufacturing exports in total world exports has increased. Barriers to international capital movements have been considerably reduced (see below).

Globalization has been described as the 'increasing internationalization[3] of the production, distribution and marketing of goods and services'

(Harris, 1993). This trend is largely the result of the globalization of financial and capital markets, increased flows of foreign direct investment (FDI), the rapid diffusion of new communications technologies and the adoption by multinational enterprises of new organizational forms of production. Information technology has contributed to the fragmentation of production on a global basis in a number of ways: by providing cheap data over long distances, it has contributed to the globalization and integration of financial markets; by providing information to buyers and sellers worldwide, it has contributed to the globalization and homogenization of demand, and as a consequence, it has led to the globalization of competition among suppliers of goods and services (Doz, 1987; Oman, 1994).

FDI flows have increased in response to expanding markets and resulting growth prospects. Under the old import-substitution policies adopted by most developing countries, FDI acted as a substitute for trade. Increased restrictions on commodity trade tended to eliminate trade but led to factor movements of capital for example. The exporting countries, faced with high tariff barriers, invested in countries to produce for the domestic sheltered markets (Mundell, 1957). Import-substitution has now been abandoned by most developing countries. This strategy has been replaced by that of export promotion. FDI has become complementary to both intraregional and global trade through technology upgrading, market expansion, and export competitiveness (For a discussion of substitution and complementarity between trade and FDI, see Kojima (1975) and Purvis (1972)). Bhagwati (1978) argued that a country adopting an export-promotion strategy would attract more growth-inducing FDI inflows catering for larger regional or international markets. Using cross-section data from 46 developing countries, Balasubramanyam, Salisu and Sapsford (1996) have provided some empirical support to the Bhagwati hypothesis. Larger market size and resulting growth prospects also played an important role in US firms' decisions to invest in the European Community (Balasubramanyam and Greenaway, 1993, Chapter 7).

At a microeconomic level, globalization is defined in terms of corporate strategies of the multinational enterprises, 'strategic alliances' between firms as well as inter-firm competition, and the evolution of global firms and industries (Porter, 1986). An increasing number of mergers and acquisitions have been occurring in the early nineties to create global competitive advantage, reap greater economies of scale in new technology research and development and reduce risk and uncertainty about market shares. The product development costs have risen, which induces firms to cater for the world market in order to spread R & D costs over larger output. It is reported that cross-border mergers and alliances of MNEs largely explain the growth of FDI and globalization in the second half of the eighties (Bailey *et al.*, 1993).

Multinationals also contribute to the process of globalization through their strategies concerning foreign direct investment, technology transfer and international subcontracting. But these strategies are also a response to the process of globalization: global competition resulting from market liberalization, deregulation of trade and investments, and freer capital flows.

REGIONALISM OR GLOBALIZATION?

Having examined the nature of regionalism and globalization, it is now appropriate to ask whether globalization is indeed taking place or whether regionalism instead is the order of the day. There is no agreement yet on whether regionalism and globalization are complementary or competitive. There are those who believe that regional blocs are stepping stones towards a global trading system (Anderson and Blackhurst, 1993; de Melo, Panagariya and Rodrik, 1993a; Lawrence, 1991; Schott, 1991; Summers, 1991). Others (notably Bhagwati, 1993) believe that multilateral trade would have grown faster in the absence of various regional integration agreements.

Critics of the new regionalism fear that a tripolar fragmentation of world trade will undermine the goal of globalization and that trade diversion will occur as a result of the creation of free trade areas or customs unions. For example, the fear of 'fortress' Europe following the creation of the Single European Market is a subject of serious debate. Although tariff barriers within Europe have decreased, non-tariff barriers against developing countries have increased (Chapter 7). The creation of NAFTA in North America (Chapter 6) and the increasingly inward-looking position of the US is also interpreted as a form of regionalism which may be harmful to the multilateral trading system. A third major trading bloc may emerge in the Asia Pacific region where Japan's dominant role is considered worrying. It is assumed that Japan's extensive investments in Southeast Asian countries give it control of those markets and effectively protect them (like the Japanese market) against foreign goods and services (see Lawrence, 1991). The formation of APEC (Chapter 5), with the participation of the US, Australia and Japan, may help to check such protectionist tendencies. Furthermore, in theory the threat of trade wars between the US and Japan and increasing protection by NAFTA and the Single European Market, may force East Asia and the Pacific to create a defensive bloc. While the US and Japan have opposed Prime Minister Mahathir of Malaysia's proposal for an East Asian Economic Group (comprising the four 'tigers' (Korea, Hong Kong, Singapore and Taiwan), China, Japan and the ASEAN-4), it has appeal for many countries in the region. This would effectively split the global trading system into three competing trade blocs (Krugman, 1991; Oppenheim, 1992; Kitson and Michie, 1995).

We noted above that apart from open trade liberalization, globalization is being promoted at a microeconomic level through the activities of multinational corporations. The critics of regionalism argue that these corporations would change their strategies from global to regional markets if protectionist tendencies were to grow (see Han, 1992). By serving different regions through local production facilities, the corporations may begin to accept trade barriers and weaken the forces of global trade liberalization (Lawrence, 1991) (see below).

In trade theory it is generally assumed that expansion of markets and economies of scale resulting from trade blocs create an environment for trade expansion which is welfare enhancing for all the member countries. However, trade diversion *per se* does not necessarily mean that regionalism will conflict with multilateralism. In the old Vinerian sense, trade creation and trade diversion can occur at the same time and the former may more than compensate to create a *net* positive effective on growth of global trade. However, as Lal (1993) notes, trade diversion may lead to the creation of new interest groups who would tend to oppose a move towards an open trading system.

Thus, regionalism and the growth of regional trade agreements may or may not conflict with the goals of globalization and multilateral trade. The Uruguay Round accord is supposed to insure against the growth of inward-looking tendencies by regional blocs, though experience shows that in practice this is hard to enforce (see Chapter 8 for discussion relating to Article XXIV of GATT and the new WTO). Past experience with trade expansion shows that it can occur when countries join a bloc or equally without any such regional integration. The case of East Asia is often cited in defence of the second possibility. Here, the rapid growth of trade among the countries of this region has occurred without government-induced membership of any regional bloc.

One way to determine whether globalization is taking place or not is to examine whether world trade, production and foreign direct investment (FDI) are becoming regionalized or globalized. Below we turn to this issue.

Regionalization of World Trade?

The substantial changes in the pattern of world trade can be summarized as follows. First, the share of OECD countries in world trade (as a proportion of exports) has increased significantly. Secondly, trade in services is expanding much faster than merchandise trade. Thirdly, with the exception of Asia the share of developing countries in world exports has also declined (Khan, 1994). Fourthly, intraregional trade shares of developing countries have increased in some regions more than in others (see Table 2.3). Fifthly, the share of developing countries' trade with OECD countries has declined, due *inter alia*, to economic recession, slow growth and a decline in demand. The decline in value of trade could also be explained by a decline in commodity prices as well as synthetic substitutes for the mainly primary commodities exported by developing countries.

The decline in developing-country exports to OECD countries can also be explained by the growing protectionism adopted by these countries. It is estimated that 21 out of 24 OECD countries were on balance, more protectionist at the end of the eighties than a decade earlier (see World Bank, 1991, p. 9 and Chapter 7 for more details).

But East and Southeast Asia have been successful in managing export expansion despite protectionism and worldwide economic recession, suggesting their effective competitiveness. In the last two decades, East Asia's trade has been estimated to grow at 16 per cent per annum in current US dollars. This rate of growth is much faster than in any other region (Young, 1993). China's rate of growth in trade is even faster.

The bulk of increase in world trade is among the industrialized countries of the OECD. The share of intraregional trade for Western Europe rose consistently between 1960 and 1994 (see Table 2.2). Earlier estimates by Anderson and Norheim (1993) for 1928 to 1958 showed rather stable shares.

This suggests that Western Europe's intraregional trade was boosted by the formation of the European Community in 1958 and the European Free Trade Area (EFTA) in 1960 and its trade with the rest of the world has declined since then. The situation in North America is somewhat different. While the share of GDP traded with the rest of the

Table 2.2 Indices of trade shares (1960–1994)

	1960	*1970*	*1980*	*1990*	*1994*
1. Intraregional trade share (%)					
Western Europe	57	62	63	71	71
Eastern Europe	18	59	53		
TOTAL, Europe	**65**	**76**	**70**	**75**	**78**
North America	27	35	27	31	39
Latin America	17	17	21	18	20
TOTAL, America	**47**	**49**	**45**	**45**	**59**
Australasia*	26	40	45	52	56
Japan*	40	30	49	35	42
Developing Asia	37	31	47	55	66
TOTAL, Asia	**36**	**41**	**52**	**52**	**59**
Africa	7	7	4	7	10
Middle East	5	10	6	10	7
TOTAL WORLD	**52**	**49**	**46**	**52**	**61**
2. Share (%) of world trade					
Western Europe	42	46	44	46	39
Eastern Europe	10	9	7	4	4
TOTAL, Europe	**52**	**55**	**51**	**50**	**43**
North America	15	16	15	17	20
Latin America	8	6	6	4	3
TOTAL, America	**23**	**22**	**21**	**21**	**23**
Australasia	2	2	1	1	1
Japan	3	5	6	6	6
Developing Asia	10	8	12	14	18
TOTAL, Asia	**15**	**15**	**19**	**21**	**25**
Africa	5	4	4	2	2
Middle East	5	3	6	3	3
3. Share (%) of GDP traded					
Western Europe	24	35	49	47	46
Eastern Europe	13	14	32		
TOTAL, Europe	**21**	**29**	**45**	**45**	**45**
North America	11	11	20	19	18
Latin America	29	23	27	22	19
TOTAL, America	**13**	**12**	**22**	**19**	**18**
Australasia	43	40	46	29	29
Developing Asia	11	13	32	24	24
Japan	7	8	16	18	19
TOTAL, Asia	**9**	**10**	**25**	**21**	**22**
Africa	43	28	53	58	62
Middle East	15	16	61	53	58
TOTAL WORLD	**20**	**20**	**35**	**33**	**32**

Source: Our estimates based on UNCTAD: *Handbook of International Trade and Development Statistics* and *Direction of Trade Statistics Yearbook* (various years).

Note: * Calculated as a share of the Asian region.

Table 2.3 Intraregional trade of major groupings

Groupings	*Share of intraregional trade in total trade of the groups (per cent)*				*Share of intraregional trade in world trade (per cent)*	
	(1970)	*(1980)*	*(1990)*	*(1993)*	*(1980)*	*(1993)*
I. North America						
NAFTA	36.0	33.6	41.4	45.4	5.0	8.0
II. Europe						
EU (12)	53.2	55.7	60.6	56.0	19.0	19.7
EU (15)	59.5	61.0	66.0	61.2	22.7	23.8
EFTA	18.1	14.7	13.5	11.4	0.8	0.6
III. Asia and the Pacific						
ASEAN	21.1	16.9	18.7	20.0	0.6	1.1
SAARC	4.6	5.0	3.0	3.5	0.03	0.3
APEC	57.1	57.5	69.0	67.2	16.9	29.0
IV. Africa						
ECOWAS	3.0	10.2	7.9	8.6	0.03	0.4
SADC	5.2	5.1	5.2	5.1	0.005	0.009
UDEAC	4.9	1.8	2.3	2.3	0.004	0.003
PTA	9.6	12.1	7.6	7.0	0.03	0.02
V. Latin America and the Caribbean						
ANDEAN	1.8	3.8	4.1	9.2	0.06	0.08
MERCOSUR	9.4	11.6	8.9	17.5	0.17	0.25
CARICOM	4.6	4.3	7.8	8.5	0.02	0.01
CACM	26.0	24.4	15.4	14.2	0.06	0.02
LAIA	9.9	13.7	10.8	15.9	0.5	0.6

Source: UNCTAD, *Handbook of International Trade and Development Statistics*.

Note: Based on exports.

world rose from 11 per cent in 1960 to 18 per cent in 1994, its intraregional trade share was the same in 1960 and 1980 although it has increased since then. This seems to suggest that in the case of North America, global trade is as important as regional trade.

With the exception of the EEC, NAFTA and APEC, intraregional trade in other regional groupings is quite small. Countries in these groupings tend to trade more with non-members than with members. This seems particularly the case with developing-country groupings in Africa, Asia and the Middle East, the regions whose shares of GDP traded increased substantially between 1960 and 1994 (see Table 2.2).

Estimates of intraregional trade as a share of total trade in Tables 2.2 and 2.3 can, however, be misleading since they do not adequately measure the effects of preferential policy-induced bias in regional trade (Anderson and Norheim, 1993). Besides government policies, historical and geographical reasons also influence patterns of international trade. Intraregional trade shares can be distorted also by the differences in the number and size of countries in different regions. For example, the European Union has 15 countries, ASEAN seven and NAFTA only three. To overcome some of these problems indexes of trade intensity, which make adjustments for these factors, have been proposed. In other words, they show the relative importance of a country's bilateral trade on intraregional trade relative to its shares in world trade. An index of trade intensity is defined as a ratio of a country's (or region's) exports to a partner country (or region) relative to the partner country's (or region's) share in world total imports. Trade intensity estimates in Table 2.4 and those in subsequent chapters, are based on the following estimating equation taken from Anderson and Blackhurst (1993):

$$\begin{aligned}\mathbf{I}_{ij} &= \mathbf{X}_{ij} \,/\, \mathbf{M}_j \\ &= \mathbf{X}_{ij} \,/\, (\mathbf{q}_j \cdot \mathbf{r}_j)\end{aligned}$$

where

X_{ij} = country i's share of exports going to country j,
M_j = country j's share in world imports (less country i's imports),
q_j = country j's share in world GDP (less country i's GDP) and
r_j = country j's imports-to-GDP ratio divided by total world imports-to-GDP (less country i's) ratio.

The advantage of the above formula is that it captures the extent to which regional trade preferences exist. In the absence of trade preferences or bias, the index will have the value of unity, that is, the share of country i's exports going to country j is proportional to the share of country j's imports from the rest of the world. A value of the index above unity, indicates that the country (or region) has larger trade than would be expected on the basis of the country's (or region's) share in world trade. Despite its appealing features in adjusting for size and number of countries in a region, however, the intensity index does not account for other determinants of trade flows. For instance, the Anderson–Blackhurst formula

Table 2.4 Indices of trade intensity of major groupings/regions

	East Asia	*Australasia*	*North America*	*South America*	*EEC*	*Africa*	*Middle East*	*EFTA*
East Asia								
1970	3.19	1.70	1.93	0.20	0.49	0.96	2.39	0.49
1980	2.80	2.01	1.42	0.38	0.42	0.61	0.93	0.28
1990	2.21	1.30	1.56	0.44	0.33	0.55	0.74	0.32
1994	1.42	1.05	1.10	0.35	0.27	0.40	0.56	0.21
Australasia								
1970	0.77	3.83	1.63	0.22	0.77	0.47	1.45	0.10
1980	3.17	5.76	1.31	0.27	0.46	0.25	1.45	0.12
1990	2.47	6.36	1.05	0.45	0.36	0.37	1.36	0.35
1994	2.10	7.14	0.64	0.18	0.30	0.45	0.85	0.24
North America								
1970	1.20	1.24	2.78	1.94	0.67	0.47	1.78	0.42
1980	1.05	1.47	2.15	2.42	0.63	0.59	0.88	0.47
1990	1.29	2.14	3.44	4.52	0.67	0.74	1.14	0.50
1994	0.90	1.62	3.01	3.52	0.63	0.55	1.07	0.40
South America								
1970	0.17	0.12	3.17	2.88	0.86	0.25	1.89	0.04
1980	0.22	0.13	3.00	3.76	0.61	0.41	0.37	0.04
1990	0.34	0.26	2.98	5.66	0.53	0.50	0.65	0.24
1994	0.29	0.25	3.20	4.16	0.49	0.44	0.40	0.19
EEC								
1970	0.33	0.62	0.58	0.43	1.48	0.90	1.82	0.34
1980	0.24	0.41	0.34	0.35	1.32	0.93	0.76	0.31
1990	0.18	0.37	0.32	0.32	1.80	0.73	0.54	0.15
1994	0.18	0.31	0.30	0.29	1.91	0.60	0.55	0.27

EFTA								
1970	0.61	0.56	0.72	0.62	1.94	1.31	1.20	2.52
1980	0.83	0.60	0.48	0.51	1.83	0.87	0.89	2.24
1990	0.48	0.69	0.57	0.52	1.44	0.59	0.69	1.95
1994	0.32	0.56	0.45	0.36	1.55	0.51	0.66	1.96
Africa								
1970	0.47	0.27	0.87	0.29	1.46	2.95	0.49	0.81
1980	0.21	0.17	2.11	1.02	1.06	1.04	0.15	0.38
1990	0.29	0.17	1.26	0.40	0.94	2.93	0.45	0.16
1994	0.31	0.24	0.96	0.47	1.04	3.76	0.57	0.26
Middle East								
1970	1.07	1.13	0.71	0.11	2.77	1.42	1.70	1.95
1980	1.23	0.90	1.06	0.90	2.52	0.33	0.80	0.61
1990	1.14	0.62	1.09	0.98	2.09	0.95	2.71	0.29
1994	0.98	0.80	0.70	0.41	2.19	0.79	1.75	0.38

Source: Our estimates based on data from IMF, *Direction of Trade Statistics Yearbook.*

Note: East Asia includes China, Hong Kong, Indonesia, Korea, Malaysia, the Philippines, Singapore, Taiwan and Thailand does not account for trade flows due to relative differences in transaction costs between countries, and due to trade complementarities.[4] As Drysdale and Garnaut (1982) pointed out, the degree of complementarity in the commodity composition of trade determines the opportunities for bilateral trade. It is for this reason that Drysdale (1967) had refined trade-intensity indices by separating the commodity composition factor from other factors influencing trade. However, Drysdale's decomposition of the trade intensity index also suffers from limitations in so far as it assumes that the commodity composition of a country's foreign trade is independent of factors determining bilateral trade. In fact, changes in structures of tariffs and transport costs may affect both complementarity and country bias in trade.

Table 2.4 gives the indices of trade[5] intensity by different regions. In most cases, the trade intensity index value exceeds unity but in some cases it does not. This may be partly because trade between some partners is already high (so-called natural partners) which shows low intensities, whereas high values of intensity may be due to low initial intraregional trade (for example, in the case of Africa). While Africa's intensity index seems to be high, it is not as high as that of some developing regions (for example, South America) or regional economic groupings such as SAARC or MERCOSUR (see Chapters 4 and 6). An increase in the value of the index for Africa for the early nineties may be due to the inclusion of South Africa.

South Africa's share in Africa's intraregional trade increased from 3.3 per cent in 1990 to 5.6 per cent in 1993 and 7.2 per cent in 1994 (IMF, *Direction of Trade Statistics Yearbook*, 1995). The increase in the index for 1993 and 1994 coincided with the lifting of the trade embargo. Furthermore, despite Africa's dependence on other regions for import of manufactured goods and intermediate inputs, the share of such trade in total trade is very small. Therefore, border trade and trade in other basic goods is likely to dominate the overall trade flows. Consequently, trade intensity might be high (due to the flow of basic goods across the borders) despite the absence of trade in manufactured goods among African countries.

Since 1970, the index values for East Asia's trade with North America and that of North America with East Asia have declined, suggesting the growing importance of the openness of these regions' trade with the rest of the world. East Asia's trade links are mainly with North America and Australasia; South America also has important trade links with North America whereas its trade links with the European Union are rather limited, and those with EFTA almost insignificant.

In examining post-war trade flows, Anderson and Norheim (1993) and Srinivasan, Whalley and Wooton (1993) found that the evolution of these flows outside Western Europe showed little evidence of a 'regionalization' of world trade. Most studies of the modelling of the global economy suggest that net trade creation has occurred in Western Europe. Whether such trade creation has also occurred in other regions is much less clear. It is also difficult to attribute whatever trade creation might have occurred to the creation of regional blocs. While there has been some tendency for an increase in intraregional trade, the more important feature of the past several decades has been faster growth of world trade than world output. Anderson and Norheim (1993) argue that this rapid growth in world trade cannot necessarily be attributed to the proliferation of regional blocs at least not in East Asia.

Regionalization of FDI?

We now turn to trends in investment flows to determine whether these flows are concentrated in a few regions or are being globalized. Table 2.5 gives investment trends by regions and shows that foreign direct investment is heavily concentrated in Europe and North America bypassing most other regions, particularly Africa. In fact, it is often argued that Africa is becoming increasingly marginalized as reflected in the decline in trade and foreign investment in the region. In contrast, in the case of the East Asian region a virtuous circle of trade and foreign investment has propelled growth of the region and strengthened links with the world economy. Between 1986 and 1992, flows of FDI to developing East Asian economies increased six times, rising from US$3 billion to US$19 billion. Their share of total FDI to developing countries increased from about 24 per cent in 1986 to about 38 per cent in 1992 (World Bank, 1994, pp. 41–2). The share of Western Europe is about 33 per cent and of the US, 22 per cent (see Table 2.5). A recent empirical study also confirms that both foreign direct investment (FDI) and trade are regionally concentrated, but the former is less concentrated (Petri, 1994).

Table 2.5 Concentration of inflows of foreign direct investment (FDI)

	Average (US$ billions)				*Share in Total (percentage)*			
	1984–89 (Annual average)	*1991*	*1993*	*1995*[a]	*1984–89 (Annual average)*	*1991*	*1993*	*1995*[a]
All countries	115.37	157.77	207.94	314.93	100	100	100	100
Developed countries	93.12	114.00	129.30	203.17	80.71	72.26	62.18	64.51
Developing countries of which:	22.19	41.32	73.13	99.67	19.24	26.19	35.17	31.65
China	2.28	4.37	27.51	37.50	1.98	2.77	13.23	11.91
Western Europe	39.76	80.57	77.48	115.63	34.46	51.06	37.26	36.71
North America	48.66	24.76	46.12	71.42	42.17	15.69	22.18	22.68
of which: USA	43.94	22.02	41.13	60.24	38.09	13.96	19.78	19.13
Other developed countries[b]	4.71	8.67	5.70	16.12	4.08	5.50	2.74	5.12
of which: Japan	0.08	1.73	0.23	0.04	0.07	1.10	0.11	0.01
Central and Eastern Europe	0.06	2.45	5.50	12.09	0.05	1.55	2.65	3.84
Africa	2.73	2.81	3.30	4.66	2.36	1.78	1.59	1.48
Asia	11.54	22.69	49.98	68.05	10.00	14.38	24.0	21.61
of which:								
East, South and Southeast Asia	9.85	20.77	46.48	65.03	8.54	13.16	22.35	20.65
West Asia	1.69	1.92	3.30	2.47	1.46	1.22	1.59	0.78
Latin America and the Caribbean	7.74	15.36	19.45	26.56	6.71	9.74	9.36	8.43

Source: UNCTAD (1996).

Note: a = estimates.
b = includes Australia, Israel, Japan, New Zealand, South Africa.

Table 2.6 GDP-weighted* index of inward and outward flows of FDI

	Inward FDI flows			*Outward FDI flows*		
	1986	*1990*	*1994*	*1986*	*1990*	*1994*
Regions						
Western Europe	1.17	1.66	1.00	–	1.95	1.62
North America	1.42	1.01	0.88	–	0.49	0.77
Australasia	3.07	2.87	2.13	–	0.73	2.26
Africa	0.96	6.73	1.82	–	–	–
South, East & Southeast Asia**	1.37	1.55	2.99	–	0.50	1.73
Latin America & the Caribbean	1.05	2.00	1.80	–	1.00	0.33
Groupings						
EEC (12)	1.08	1.71	0.90	–	1.75	1.43
NAFTA	1.44	1.03	0.94	–	0.47	0.73
APEC	1.16	0.94	1.00	–	0.79	0.86
MERCOSUR	0.60	0.61	0.59	–	0.13	0.15
ASEAN	2.77	4.21	3.00	–	0.79	0.95
SAARC	0.17	0.14	0.33	–	0.0	0.01

Source: Our estimates. Investment data are from the UNCTC/UNCTAD, *World Investment Report*; GDP data are from World Bank, *World Development Report*.

* calculated as a ratio of investment share relative to each region's/country's share in GDP.
** excluding Taiwan — = not available.

We attempted an estimate of the index of GDP-weighted inward and outward flow of FDI (see Table 2.6) on the basis of the following formula:

$$\frac{\left(\frac{FDI_i}{FDI_w}\right)}{\left(\frac{GDP_i}{GDP_w}\right)}$$

where *i* refers to region and *w* to world.

An FDI index value of 1 implies that the investment flow as a proportion of world FDI is proportional to the region's or country's GDP share in world GDP; when the index exceeds unity, it shows the country's or region's relative attractiveness in the case of FDI inflow. Table 2.6 shows the attractiveness of Asia, Australasia, and to a lesser extent,

Latin America and the Caribbean for FDI inflows in 1994. Among the regional groupings, NAFTA and APEC are more attractive as is to be expected. However, the investment data are incomplete and not strictly comparable and the results may not be reliable in all cases.

The emergence of regional blocs may not only increase intraregional trade but also intraregional investments especially as countries continue to remove barriers to FDI inflows and trade.

Regionalization of Production?

There is no consensus that globalization of production has taken place. Some authors argue that regionalization rather than globalization of production is increasingly noticeable (Oman, 1994; Wells, 1993). In defense of his argument, Oman (1994) presents two new features of the production process today. First, the share of low-skilled labour in the total costs of production has considerably declined thereby reducing the importance of relocating production to low-wage areas. Secondly, flexibility of production and specialization has also raised the importance of physical proximity between producers and customers (so-called 'global localization') and between producers and suppliers of spare parts and components. This latter tendency implies regionalization of production most evident in the dynamic East Asian economies where producers have an incentive to serve their fast-growing markets rather than the global markets. Lowering or eliminating of tariff barriers within regional blocs has given further impetus to the regionalization of production.

Wells (1993) argues that US multinationals organise manufacturing production on a regional basis because the gains from global manufacturing are not significant, that regional economies of scale are just as important, and that world-integrated manufacturing systems are more difficult to manage than regional ones. Similarly, in the context of the American MNEs Morrison and Roth (1992) show that a global strategy may be inappropriate for US companies with extensive network of international subsidiaries. On the basis of a research project covering 150 parent MNEs and 125 subsidiaries in the United States, Canada, France, Germany, Japan and the United Kingdom, the authors argue that the US companies have not adopted the Japanese model of trade-based (instead of FDI-based) globalization. They have relied much more on FDI to capture shares of the international market. The US companies are known to have failed to adopt global strategies which call for tight central control and coordination of activities worldwide and a high degree of standardization of products for all markets. The international subsidiaries have resisted tight control by parent companies and have preferred a regional strategy on the grounds that local product features and technical differences (for example, in the case of the television industry) continue to prevail, and that a regional strategy permits faster delivery and smaller inventories. The growing emergence of regional trading blocs may reinforce regional strategies of MNEs as opposed to global strategies. Inadequate language skills and low level of awareness of world conditions may also encourage US companies to adopt regional strategies (Morrison and Roth, 1992).

The extent of globalization of production may also depend, *inter alia*, on the nature of the industry. Production of some goods, such as automobiles, is more global than others (for example, textiles, garments and food). The latter tend to be more subject to local consumer tastes which make product standardization difficult. Industries linked to information technology lend themselves more easily to globalization than other industries. Service industries or functions such as accounting, banking, insurance, and so on are easier to relocate to low-wage economies without incurring high transaction and transportation costs. Global industries sell their products worldwide and integrate their activities across national markets. The nature, characteristics and strategies of these industries are likely to vary according to the nature and structure of their markets.

ARE REGIONAL BLOCS BUILDING BLOCKS?

We noted above that economists are divided on whether regional blocs are stumbling blocks or building blocks to multilateral trade and globalization. Positions naturally vary depending on the assumptions made. A pragmatic approach is to define conditions and circumstances under which regional blocks can be 'building blocks'. The following are *necessary* though not *sufficient* conditions for such complementarity:

(i) the regional blocs should lead to *net* trade creation rather than trade diversion. Even when some trade diversion occurs away from third countries, trade creation should be greater than trade diversion in order to promote welfare-enhancing effects on both members and non-members. Thus, any new regional blocs will not reduce welfare in third countries so long as the *volume* of their trade with the bloc members does not fall. In other words, if both intraregional and interregional trade expand (which would be the situation under the 'open' regionalism of the APEC kind), the existence of regional blocs will not act as stumbling blocks to growth of global trade. A condition for both intraregional and extraregional trade to increase, is the lowering of trade barriers against non-members. Bhagwati (1993) has suggested that the lowest pre-union tariff on a particular item or product group should become the common external tariff for that item.[6]

(ii) Regional integration needs to be growth-inducing besides creating trade. To the extent that regional blocs contribute to growth, they will generate demand for extra-regional exports and imports from the rest of the world. Higher growth would in principle result from regional integration through increased income gains from trade, greater investor confidence and induced investment.[7]

(iii) The formation of regional blocs should make possible more effective negotiations for achieving the positive results of multilateral trade under the Uruguay Round. The historical experience of the European Union suggests that it is easier to make trade concessions along with other partners in a customs union or a free trade area than unilaterally. Negotiations under the Kennedy Round of trade are said to have been facilitated by the existence of the European Union (Hufbauer, 1990). Similarly, the NAFTA trade negotiations may have revived Uruguay Round negotiations while APEC also claims credit for giving an impetus to this multilateral agreement. Global trade liberalization is easier through a step-wise process whereby a small number of regional blocs can negotiate and relate to each other more effectively than a large number of individual countries.

The above conditions can be summarised into factors relating to (a) trade (b) growth and foreign investment, and (c) others.

CONCLUDING REMARKS

In this Chapter we have outlined the main contours of globalization as well as of regionalism in its old and new manifestations. We have shown that globalization is a much broader concept than trade liberalization *per se*. Its scope extends to trade and investment flows, spread of financial and capital markets and production beyond national boundaries and the activities of MNEs. In the growing climate of liberalization, multinational enterprises and their corporate strategies are playing an increasingly important role in determining the nature, shape and extent of regionalism and globalization.

We also noted that regionalism can be both consistent and in conflict with the goals of the multilateral trading system as defined in the Uruguay Round. In order that regional blocs act as building blocks towards globalization, certain conditions need to be met. Primarily these blocs should be both trade creating and growth-inducing.

We defined different forms of regionalism including 'open' regionalism which is compatible with globalization more than the earlier more protective forms of regionalism. Globalization would gain ground if all the different regions adopted open regionalism. However, protectionism practised by some regions acts as a stumbling block to this process.

In the following Chapters, we examine whether regional blocs act as stumbling blocks towards globalization through, for example, trade and investment diversion. We study specific cases of regional blocs in different parts of the world, comparing pairs in respect of intraregional trade, trade and investment linkages and MNE strategies.

3 Regional Initiatives in Africa

In Chapters 1 and 2 we examined regionalism in a historical perspective and in the context of globalization which distinguishes, *inter alia*, the new phase of regionalism from the old. Whereas the earlier forms of regionalism during the Cold War era were politically motivated, driven largely by a search for greater security and stability, the recent proliferation of regional groupings has been more of a response to the process of globalization in trade, investment and production.

The following chapters will attempt to analyze those specific regional blocs (defined rather loosely) which are significant enough to have an impact, or potential impact on the multilateral trade liberalization process, and to determine whether they are moving in the spirit of the Uruguay Round agreement. By promoting regional integration, are they serving as building blocks to GATT/WTO agreements for the globalization of trade or are they leading to a fragmentation of trade and economic linkages, thereby undermining the globalization process?

The African region is unique in respect of economic integration for two reasons. First, one of the earliest customs unions in developing countries was the East African Community of Kenya, Tanzania and Uganda. Second, a very large number of regional economic groupings have existed in Africa during the past three decades. It is noted that 'Africa accounts for about half the 30 or so sub-regional and regional cooperation and economic integration arrangements existing among developing countries' (Joshua, 1989).

A list of the regional groups along with their country membership is given in Table 3.1. These groups can be classified into the following geographical regions:

Western Africa: ECOWAS, CEAO.
Central Africa: UDEAC, CEEAC.
Eastern and Southern Africa: PTA, SADCC, EAC.

The groups vary in the degree of economic integration. Some groups, such as SADCC (see below), concentrated on particular sectors and specific projects; others, like the East African Community and the Equatorial Union, were more ambitious and aimed at creating a common

Table 3.1 African economic integration and cooperation groupings and their membership*

Groupings / *Countries*	*UDEACS*	*CEEAC*	*ECOWA*	*CEPGL*	*MRU*	*PTA***	*CEAO*	*SADCC*	*CPCM*	*EC*	*CILSS*	*LCBC*	*NBA*	*OKBA*	*OMVG*	*OMVS*	*ALGR*	*SACU*
Algeria									X									
Angola								X										
Benin			X				X			X			X					
Botswana								X										X
Burkina Faso			X				X			X	X		X				X	
Burundi		X		X		X								X				
Cameroon	X	X										X	X					
Cape Verde			X															
Central African Republic	X	X																
Chad	X	X									X	X	X					
Comoros						X												
Congo	X	X																
Côte d'Ivoire			X				X			X			X					
Djibouti						X												
Equatorial Guinea	X	X																
Ethiopia						X												
Gabon	X	X																
Gambia			X												X			
Ghana			X															
Guinea			X		X								X		X			
Guinea Bissau			X												X			
Kenya						X												
Lesotho						X		X										X
Liberia			X		X													
Mauritius						X												
Malawi						X		X										
Mali			X				X				X		X			X	X	
Mauritania			X				X		X		X					X		
Morocco									X									
Mozambique								X										
Niger			X				X			X	X	X	X				X	
Nigeria			X									X	X					
Rwanda		X		X		X								X				
Sao Tomé & Principe		X																
Senegal			X							X				X	X			
Sierra Leone			X		X													
Somalia						X												
South Africa																		X
Swaziland						X		X										X
Togo			X							X								
Tunisia									X									
Uganda						X								X				

Table 3.1 *continued*

United Republic of Tanzania			X	X			X
Zaire	X	X					
Zambia			X	X			
Zimbabwe			X	X			

Source: Joshua (1989).

Notes to Table 3.1

Frequency of membership:

Frequency	*Groupings*
7	Niger
6	Burkina Faso, Mali
5	Chad, Mauritania
4	Benin, Burundi, Cameroon, Côte d'Ivoire, Guinea, Rwanda, Senegal
3	Nigeria, United Republic of Tanzania

* As of December 1987

** The PTA Agreement is open for signature and ratification by Angola, Botswana, Madagascar, Mozambique, Seychelles.

Abbreviations (groupings and date of establishment)

UDEAC	Central African Customs and Economic Union founded in 1966 (revised in 1975)
CEEAC	Economic Community of Central African States founded in 1983
ECOWAS	Economic Community of West African States founded in 1975
CEPGL	Economic Community of the Great Lakes Countries founded in 1976
MRU	Mano River Union founded in 1973
PTA	Eastern and Southern Africa Preferential Trade Area founded in 1981
CEAO	West African Economic Community founded in 1973 (but dates to UDAO and UDEAO founded in 1959 and 1966 respectively)
SADCC	Southern African Development Co-ordination Conference founded in 1980
CPCM	Maghreb Permanent Consultation Committee founded in 1964
CE	Council of the Entente founded in 1959
CILSS	Permanent Inter-State Committee on Drought Control in the Sahel founded in 1973
LCBC	Lake Chad Basin Commission founded in 1964
NBA	Niger Basin Authority founded in 1980 (but dated back to 1963)
OKB	Organization for the Planning and Development of the Kagera River founded in 1977
OMVG	Organization for the Development of the River Gambia founded in 1978
OMVS	Organization for the Development of the Senegal River founded in 1972
ALGR	Authority for the Integrated Development of the Liptako-Gourma Region founded in 1970
SACU	Southern Africa Customs Union founded in 1969 (replacing preceding agreement which dated from 1910)

Table 3.2 African intra-group trade performance (1970–1993)

Country / Group	*1970*	*1980*	*1985*	*1990*	*1993*
A. Value of intra-group trade (in millions of dollars)					
CEPGL	3	2	9	7	14
CEEAC	29	98	118	168	169
ECOWAS	86	693	1026	1539	1699
MRU	1	7	4	3	1
PTA	306	693	407	837	746
SADC	100	107	198	356	338
UDEAC	22	84	85	139	129
UEMOA	54	476	431	625	578
UMA	60	109	274	958	823
B. Intra-group trade as a percentage of total exports of each group					
CEPGL	0.4	0.1	0.8	0.5	1.1
CEEAC	2.4	1.5	2.1	2.2	2.5
ECOWAS	3.0	10.2	5.3	7.9	8.6
MRU	0.2	0.8	0.4	0.1	0.0
PTA	9.6	12.1	5.5	7.6	7.0
SADC	5.2	5.1	4.7	5.2	5.1
UDEAC	4.9	1.8	1.9	2.3	2.3
UEMOA	6.4	9.9	8.7	12.0	10.4
UMA	1.4	0.3	1.0	2.8	3.2

Source: UNCTAD, *Handbook of International Trade and Development Statistics*.

market with free flows of factors of production and goods and services. As most African countries are at early stages of development, with inadequate infrastructure and industrial production, emphasis on the integration of productive sectors (as in SADCC) seems appropriate. Trade liberalization alone is unlikely to offer bloc members any meaningful benefits from economic integration.

In Chapter 1, we noted that small size of national markets was one of the rationales for regional integration which was meant to offer economies of scale through enlarged regional markets necessary for industrialization. In the case of Africa, by world standards, even combined regional markets remain small in view of the very low per capita incomes. This may have been an important factor explaining failures in industrial development, besides lack of skills and inadequate infrastructure.

Although intraregional trade within Africa has increased somewhat, it is still quite small compared to the Asian and Latin American regions (see Table 3.2 and Chapter 2). It is generally assumed that an increase in intraregional trade within Africa is conducive to economic growth and development, and that the current levels of such trade are below what might be expected among countries with similar economic characteristics and levels of development. Using a gravity model, Foroutan and Pritchett (1993) show that intra-Sub-Saharan African (SSA) trade is, however, not lower than what one would expect. For the 19 countries in their sample, the actual SSA share of imports and exports was a little over 8 per cent whereas the gravity model predicted a 7.5 per cent level.

In this Chapter we discuss three regional groupings, namely, SADC (formerly SADCC), SACU and ECOWAS. With the end of apartheid in South Africa and its subsequent membership of SADC, greater potential now exists for economic growth and diversification through integration in the Southern African region. ECOWAS is included as a point of comparison with the rest of Africa.

The basic economic indicators for member countries for these groupings are presented in Table 3.3. Most of the ECOWAS members have a GNP per capita lower than US $500. The level of development in SADC countries is somewhat higher, particularly in Botswana, Mauritius, South Africa and Zimbabwe. The share of GDP originating in industry is also generally higher in the SADC than in the ECOWAS member countries. The Forouton-Pritchett (1993) study, noted above, concludes that the low intra-SSA trade flows are accounted for by a low level of development reflected in low GDP rather than by inappropriate policies and inadequate infrastructure.

SOUTHERN AFRICAN DEVELOPMENT COMMUNITY (SADC) AND SOUTHERN AFRICAN DEVELOPMENT COORDINATION CONFERENCE (SADCC)

SADCC was established in 1980 as a nine-member grouping consisting of Angola, Botswana, Lesotho, Malawi, Mozambique, Swaziland, Tanzania, Zambia and Zimbabwe. South Africa joined SADC in August 1994. The two other new members are Namibia and Mauritius. As the *raison d'être* of SADCC, that is, to fight apartheid and reduce dependence on South Africa disappeared, its continued existence was questioned in the early nineties. In August 1992, under the Treaty of Windhoek SADCC was restructured as the South African Development Community (SADC) to concentrate on trade cooperation.

SADCC presents a model of a grouping which sets it apart from other groupings in several respects. First, in its original formulation, trade cooperation was meant to play a minor role whereas most other

Table 3.3 Basic economic indicators of SADC, SACU and ECOWAS members

Grouping/ Country	*GNP per capita (US$) (1994)*	*GNP per capita Average annual growth (%) (1985–94)*	*Population (millions) (mid-1994)*	*Share of industry in GDP (%) (1994)*	*Export to GDP ratio (%) (1995)*	*Import to GDP ratio (%) (1995)*	*Share in world exports (%) (1995)*	*Share in world imports (%) (1995)*
I. SADC (including SACU)								
Angola	410	–4.0	10.4	–	–	–	–	–
Botswana	2800	6.6	1.4	49	51.8[1]	51.6[1]	0.05[1]	0.04[1]
Lesotho	720	0.6	1.9	46	21.4[1]	113.9[1]	0.003	0.02
Malawi	170	–0.7	9.5	21	29.9	35.5	0.007[1]	0.01
Mauritius	3150	5.8	1.1	33	58.4	61.5	0.02	0.04
Mozambique	90	3.8	15.5	12	24.3	63.6	0.003	0.01
Namibia	1970	3.3	1.5	29	53.6	62.2	0.03	0.03
South Africa	3040	–1.3	40.5	31	24.3	24.7	0.5	0.6
Swaziland	1190[2]	2.3[2]	0.88[2]	49	101.9[1]	111.6	0.01	0.02
Tanzania	140	0.8	28.8	17	26.4[1]	54.3[1]	0.01	0.04
Zambia	350	–1.4	9.2	35	40.2[2]	41.4[2]	0.02[1]	0.02[5]
Zimbabwe	500	–0.5	10.8	36	32.1[3]	31.4[3]	0.05[1]	0.04[1]

(*Continued on page 46*)

Table 3.3 continued

Grouping/ Country	*GNP per capita (US$) (1994)*	*GNP per capita Average annual growth (%) (1985–94)*	*Population (millions) (mid-1994)*	*Share of industry in GDP (%) (1994)*	*Export to GDP ratio (%) (1995)*	*Import to GDP ratio (%) (1995)*	*Share in world exports (%) (1995)*	*Share in world imports (%) (1995)*
II. ECOWAS								
Benin	370	–0.8	5.3	12	27.6	35.8	0.003[1]	0.01[1]
Burkina Faso	300	–0.1	10.1	27	12.2[1]	19.6[1]	0.01	0.01
Cape Verde	930	2.0	0.37	–	–	–	–	–
Côte d Ivoire	610	–4.6	13.8	26	29.9[2]	27.5[2]	0.2[5]	0.1[5]
Gambia	330	0.5	1.1	15	11.7[1]	59.4[1]	0.0007[1]	0.004[1]
Ghana	410	1.4	16.6	16	19.7[2]	35.8[2]	–	–
Guinea	520	1.3	6.4	31	15.2[1]	20.2[1]	0.01	0.01
Guinea-Bissau	240	2.2	1.0	18	12.4[2]	39.1[2]	0.0004[2]	0.001[2]
Liberia	–	–	2.7	–	44.1[4]	23.3[4]	–	–
Mali	250	1.0	9.5	15	21.8[1]	46.9[1]	0.007[1]	0.009[1]
Mauritania	480	0.2	2.2	30	38.8[1]	34.3[1]	0.009[1]	0.008[1]
Niger	230	–2.1	8.7	18	13.1[2]	18.8[2]	0.005[1]	0.006[1]
Nigeria	280	1.2	108.0	32	23.7[1]	18.6[1]	0.23[1]	0.2[1]
Senegal	600	–0.7	8.3	20	35.0[1]	40.2[1]	0.03[1]	0.04[1]
Sierra Leone	160	–0.4	4.4	18	28.6	18.8	0.003	0.004
Togo	320	–2.7	4.0	21	31.8	36.4	0.007	0.008

Sources: *World Development Report 1996* for GNP, population and share of industry; IMF, *International Financial Statistics*, Nov. 1996, for shares of export and import to GDP and shares in world exports and imports.

1 = 1994; 2 = 1993; 3 = 1990; 4 = 1989; 5 = 1988. – 1992 not available.

African groupings are concerned mainly with preferential trade agreements and customs unions. Preferential arrangements tend to lead to trade diversion which SADCC avoided. Its members continued to trade freely with the rest of the world. Secondly, SADCC's primary goal was to reduce dependence on apartheid Africa. Thirdly, SADCC concentrated on less ambitious but more realistic and attainable programmes and projects (for example, development of infrastructure, water and electricity and transport and communications) and thematic cooperation in respect of food security or cross-border investments (McCarthy, 1995a). One can argue that this incremental approach is a surer path to longer-term market integration which the other African groupings have been trying to achieve without much success. Fourthly, SADCC started off as a pledging aid coordination conference which meant that its evolution and performance depended largely on the willingness of aid donors and international organizations to support particular programmes and projects. Finally, the old SADCC structure also differed from that of other African groupings. Although SADCC's central secretariat is located in Gaborone (Botswana), responsibility for particular sectoral portfolios rests with individual members; for example, Mozambique for transport; Tanzania for industrial development, South Africa for finance and investment, and Zimbabwe for food security. These sectoral functions are coordinated by a Ministerial Council.

SADCC functioned on the basis of consensus between the members rather than on the will of individual governments. In the past, projects aimed at attaining independence from South Africa and orienting individual economies towards development of their own resources. With the end of apartheid in South Africa, this situation has now changed and the Southern African economies are becoming more and more interdependent. Step-by-step cooperation, rather than any established model of integration, however, continues to be the main approach followed by the present SADC. While most other African groupings, for example, PTA and ECOWAS (see below) believed that trade expansion was a precondition to development, SADCC assumed that coordinated production and economic development of the region was a precondition to expansion of intraregional and interregional trade. SADCC saw trade merely as a means to economic development. Strategies and approaches followed by the old SADCC and new SADC can also be distinguished by a shift from an import-substitution model to an export-oriented one for achieving economic cooperation and development.

There is a greater potential for the development of Southern Africa now that both Mauritius and South Africa, two dynamic economies, have joined SADC. Although the South African economy has been growing very slowly, if at all, in the past few years, it is still in a much stronger economic position (with well-established infrastructure and communication systems, financial services and private sector) than most of the neighbouring economies with the possible exception of Zimbabwe. Furthermore, South Africa is much more industrialized and diversified than its neighbours. By participating in joint ventures with SADC members, in principle, the South African private sector and financial services industry can help stimulate the development of the entire region (as discussed below).

Intra-SADCC Trade

Intraregional trade within SADCC is extremely low, less than one-tenth of the total foreign trade of every member of SADCC. The share of such trade was 5–6 per cent between 1981 and 1988. This pattern is similar for Africa as a whole for which intraregional trade has not only been very low compared with other regions (see Chapters 1 and 2) but has also 'experienced a consistent decline . . ., from 10 per cent in 1928, to 6 per cent in 1979 and 1990'. (McCarthy, 1995). This decline may be explained, in part, by two historical events. First, following the Unilateral Declaration of Independence (UDI) by Southern Rhodesia (today's Zimbabwe) its borders with Malawi, Mozambique and Zambia were closed during the seventies. Secondly, substantial trade between Angola and Mozambique ceased once the two countries became independent (Blumenfeld, 1991). The civil war in these two countries may further explain low trade. In normal circumstances, intra-SADCC trade would, perhaps, have been higher.

Since the joining of Mauritius and South Africa, the share of intraregional trade may have increased but it remains quite small compared to other regions outside Africa. Each SADC country trades more with South Africa than with any other SADC member. The African Development Bank (AfDB, 1993, p. 37), notes that SADC-South Africa trade flows 'exceed intra-SADC trade flows by a factor of more than three-to-one'. Many SADC member governments have entered into bilateral trade agreements with post-apartheid South Africa which may explain this situation.

As we noted earlier, trade was not a priority subject area within SADCC until its restructuring into the Southern African Development Community (SADC). Table 3.4 gives trends of intraregional imports and exports for SADCC (including SACU) and ECOWAS between 1975

Table 3.4 Intraregional imports and exports of SADC and ECOWAS members

Country	*Exports to Africa as % of total exports*					*Imports from Africa as % of total imports*				
	1975	1980	1985	1990	1994	1975	1980	1985	1990	1994
I. SADC (including SACU)										
Angola	3.2	3.2	0.1	0.4	0.3	13.9	12	1.6	2.3	9.8
Botswana	–	–	–	–	–	–	–	–	–	–
Lesotho	–	–	–	–	–	–	–	–	–	–
Malawi	17.8	15.5	20.9	18.5	24.2	39.7	43.6	48.1	41.8	56.5
Mauritius	3.2	3.6	2.9	4.1	4.5	13.1	18.1	11	12.8	11
Mozambique	14.3	9.9	–	2.7	16.5	24.5	2.1	–	12.4	49.6
Namibia	–	–	–	–	–	–	–	–	–	–
South Africa	6	5.5	4.4	5.8	9.5	4.5	2	2	2.5	2.8
Swaziland	–	–	–	–	–	–	–	–	–	–
Tanzania	15.8	17.3	5.7	4.9	12.6	7.5	2.6	6.4	4.5	14.9
Zambia	3	3.7	5.5	7.8	12.1	9.5	18.6	9.5	31.5	49.8
Zimbabwe	–	9.2	26.4	31.8	34.4	–	16.6	24.7	32.9	43.5
Average	9.0	8.5	9.4	9.5	14.3	16.1	14.5	14.8	17.6	29.7

(*Continued on page 50*)

Table 3.4 continued

Country	*Exports to Africa as % of total exports*					*Imports from Africa as % of total imports*				
II. ECOWAS										
Benin	18.5	14.48	3.9	4.0	8.6	5.9	7.14	6.2	27.7	5.3
Burkina Faso	54.7	43.15	10.3	22.6	21.7	23.4	23.34	33.2	28	36.4
Cape Verde	26.7	18.42	16.7	2.9	12.3	12.5	8.93	2.9	4	6.8
Côte d'Ivoire	15.3	15.39	14.1	31.9	29.8	5.2	6.23	20.61	29.7	37.3
Gambia	3.1	29.04	88.05	6.8	24.2	5.3	8.51	7.11	9.6	21.9
Ghana	1.3	0.4	0.7	2.5	17.3	2.4	23.1	15.7	23.1	21.5
Guinea	3.6	4.6	6.6	8.4	6.2	10.9	4	4.2	14.4	23.5
Guinea-Bissau	15.3	15.1	2.3	4.4	4.2	3	6.6	10.1	12.8	8.8
Liberia	1.2	1.9	1.1	0.2	0.2	1.2	1.9	1.4	0.7	1.7
Mali	47.5	9.9	14.3	14.4	4.9	24.7	36.7	27.1	44.8	43.5
Mauritania	1.7	1.7	2.1	5.6	14.5	13.8	13.5	7.5	6.7	7.9
Niger	7	12.5	15.1	–	0.1	20.7	17.9	23.2	0.8	2.4
Nigeria	2	2.1	2.8	6.5	8.5	0.9	1.4	0.82	0.7	3.3
Senegal	16.9	30.9	22.9	19	27.6	6.6	14.5	23.5	21.1	18.3
Sierra Leone	1.8	1.1	1.1	0.8	2	2.9	1.6	19.1	24.4	18.8
Togo	4.9	26.3	5.3	18.3	25.7	4.5	19.6	3.7	20.3	33.9
Average	13.8	14.2	13.0	12.3	13.0	9.0	12.2	12.9	16.8	18.2

Source: Our estimates based on IMF, *Direction of Trade Statistics Yearbook.*

and 1994. The average share of intraregional exports for SADCC as a whole remained rather stagnant between 1975 and 1990, but increased substantially between 1990 and 1994. The recent increase was accounted for by an increase in intraregional exports of Malawi, Mozambique, South Africa, Tanzania, Zambia and Zimbabwe. The average share of SADCC intraregional imports increased between 1975 and 1994, the increase being most significant for Malawi, Mozambique, Swaziland, Tanzania, Zambia and Zimbabwe.

Efforts are now being made to encourage freer trade among SADC members. At a meeting in Maseru (Lesotho) in August 1996, SADC members (including South Africa) signed protocols to create a regional free trade zone by eliminating all tariffs within eight years. South Africa promised to set the ball rolling by lowering tariffs and allowing imports from other SADC member countries whose economic development is also in its own interests. A failure of these economies to develop could lead to mass influx of their citizens into South Africa.

Apart from official or recorded trade, account needs also to be taken of the substantial amount of cross-border illegal trade that takes place among SADCC countries on the basis of the market rate of exchange which is above the officially controlled rate. Such unrecorded trade is estimated to be in the range of 15–50 per cent of the officially recorded cross-border trade within SADCC and PTA (AfDB, 1993, p. 21). Controlled exchange rates tend to encourage smuggling and undeclared trade across borders. As one scholar has stated, 'these unofficial transactions which take place entirely outside state control . . . represent a dynamic, popularly based means to overcome monetary and economic barriers to intra-African trade' (Barad, 1990, p. 102). Although these activities are illegal and represent an underground economy, economic decline has led many officials and workers in the formal sector to participate in these activities.

Lack of complementarity of national economies and foreign exchange constraints are the two main obstacles to the expansion of intraregional trade. With the exception of South Africa, most SADC members have a limited production base and few goods and services to trade. The foreign exchange constraints are further aggravated by the inconvertibility of national currencies into either other regional currencies or hard currencies. Other reasons for low trade in the region include lack of transport and other infrastructure, limited credit facilities, lack of information about trade possibilities and low level of development in general. Nevertheless, an early SADCC study identified more than 60 products for which there was spare production capacity within the region.

Yet these products were being imported from outside SADCC, often from the Republic of South Africa.

The AfDB (1993, p. 38) concludes that 'there is still considerable potential for expanding intraregional trade in the intermediate term by (a) further substitution of RSA's (Republic of South Africa) imports of primary agricultural commodities from the rest of the world (ROW) by shifting sourcing to efficient producers in the SAR (Southern African region) and (b) further substitution of the region's imports from ROW by shifting sourcing of imported manufactures to RSA and Zimbabwe as well as Kenya and Mauritius'.

The current shares of each member of SADC (including South Africa) in world imports and exports are insignificant (see Table 3.3). The shares of exports and imports in GDP are, however, quite large for many SADC members. This suggests that while these economies are quite open and depend on trade, their weight in the world economy is very small. This is not surprising considering that most of the economies still rely heavily on the exports of a limited number of primary commodities. Those countries which do trade in manufactured goods are also characterised by a low level of industrial development.

The low level of industrial development in most SADC countries (with the exception of South Africa, Mauritius and Zimbabwe) means that these countries do not have the capacity to produce manufactured goods for exports. But lack of productive capacity is only part of the problem. In some cases, factories produce below capacity owing to small local demand, or more often, because the country cannot afford to import the raw materials. In some countries (for example, Zimbabwe) the scope for exporting to South Africa is limited by high tariff barriers imposed by the latter.[1] However, these barriers are now being reduced, perhaps in the spirit of the Uruguay Round agreement. In Zimbabwe industrial capacity exists at least in such sectors as clothing, textiles and footwear. South Africa could certainly import more from within the SADC-region provided its tariffs and non-tariff barriers to trade were reduced and even eliminated (McCarthy, 1995a).

SADCC aimed at changing existing trade patterns to reduce dependence on South Africa. Notwithstanding its efforts however, each SADCC member had more trade with South Africa than with all its SADCC partners combined. (All countries with the exception of Tanzania continued to trade with apartheid South Africa). For many SADCC countries, the cost of disengagement from South Africa was too high. They were, therefore, reluctant to sever trade relations with South Africa. About two-thirds of SADCC trade with South Africa was accounted for by Botswana, Lesotho, Namibia and Swaziland (countries that form part of the South African Customs Union) (see below).

The above objective of SADCC has been overtaken by events. South Africa has become a SADC member and apartheid has come to an end. But the problem of trade imbalances remains. South Africa exports far more to SADC than it imports, leading to an enormous trade surplus *vis-à-vis* SADC members. This problem of trade imbalances also remains intractable within SACU. But potential exists for South Africa to import from within the region such inputs as energy, water and food. An open trading and investment pattern in the region may also encourage investment flows from South Africa to other lower labour-cost countries in the region to establish enterprises catering for the regional market. The lack of South Africa's competitiveness due to a relatively high cost of labour and low labour productivity may further encourage this possibility. It is reported that hourly wages have risen much faster than in the US, Japan or Germany while rates of labour productivity growth have been much lower. Labour costs in South Africa are noted to be about three times those in some newly industrializing economies of East Asia (AfDB, 1993, p. 63).

SADC and PTA (COMESA)

All SADC members except Botswana are members of the Preferential Trade Area (PTA). This aims to expand trade in a larger region than SADC, by lowering tariff and non-tariff barriers. In spirit, this conflicts with SADC's preference for counter trade and its stress on new bilateral trade agreements. Its scepticism about free trade areas inevitably led to some conflicts with the PTA. However, since 1992, SADC's new mandate for regional integration through trade liberalization has converged with the PTA. PTA was established in December 1981 with a membership of 19 African countries making it the biggest African regional grouping. It envisages a regional common market by the year 2014 and an African Economic Community (economic and monetary union) by the year 2034. In January 1993, the PTA approved the creation of a Common Market of Eastern and Southern Africa (COMESA) by the year 2000. In December 1994, the PTA was transformed into COMESA.

Removal of all trade barriers is the major goal of COMESA. With this aim, products have been selected on which tariff barriers are reduced gradually and progressively to be totally eliminated by the end of 1996. Despite this however, non-tariff barriers such as licensing and exchange controls remain in force. This may partly explain why the level of intra-COMESA trade has not increased and may actually be declining. Much of intra-COMESA trade is dominated by trade flows between Kenya and Zimbabwe, the two relatively more diversified economies. Lack of convertible currencies and monetary collaboration (which prevails in SACU as we discuss below) may also explain limited intraregional trade. COMESA members prefer to trade with non-members in order to earn much-needed foreign exchange.

SADC will simply duplicate COMESA if it concentrates only on trade liberalization. It would, therefore, be desirable for SADC to maintain its original approach of concentrating on the coordination of production and economic development at the same time as it emphasizes trade liberalization and promotion of intraregional trade.

Foreign Direct Investment (FDI)

The past experience of SADCC suggests that member countries followed divergent national policies towards foreign direct investment (FDI). Regulation and control of foreign investment varied significantly. In general, foreign capital inflows were assumed to increase dependence on the West which SADCC was supposed to overcome. Since the transformation of SADCC into SADC, this hostile attitude towards foreign capital and the private sector has been abandoned.

Although all the SADC members encourage private foreign investment there is no uniform investment code. In general, preference is given to joint ventures and to involvement of parastatals. More foreign control is permitted if advanced technology is involved. Since 1987, SADCC has also emphasised the role of the private sector. Generally, preference is given to foreign firms that use local resources and are engaged in exporting. The state generally controls allocation of foreign exchange, and remittance of profits, dividends and fees.

In an effort to promote private business and investments, SADC member countries are engaged in establishing business councils and organizations. A number of such organizations already exist in Zimbabwe. In 1988, the SADCC Council of Ministers pleaded for its members to join the World Bank's Multilateral Investment Guarantee Agency. Many members are already known to have joined the Agency (see Hanlon, 1989). The structural adjustment programmes and economic reforms in most SADCC member countries have led to a liberalization not only of trade but also of foreign investment which is an essential precondition for encouraging FDI inflows.

However, private foreign investment is unlikely to be encouraged until a favourable business environment is created and the high risk of investing in Southern Africa is reduced. High risk factors may include frequent and unpredictable policy shifts due partly to political instability. To some extent, these policy changes are imposed through donor conditionality, for example, in the case of the structural adjustment programmes. Concentration on a few primary commodities for export also contributes to uncertainty and instability especially in conditions of declining terms of trade for these commodities. Institutional preconditions for foreign investment in the form of investment codes, property right laws and formal insurance systems, and well-developed capital and equity markets are also missing in many SADC countries (exceptions are South Africa and Zimbabwe).

Rules of origin are a constraint to foreign investment in SADC and COMESA countries. In order to qualify for preferential treatment, products must be produced by local firms or by foreign firms in which 51 per cent of the equity is owned by nationals. This rule is likely to discourage multinational firms from investing in these countries. Waivers to these conditions of localization would be necessary to encourage FDI inflows and promote intra-SADC and COMESA trade in manufactures.

Most SADC members (apart from Angola and Botswana) are dependent, in varying degrees, on capital inflows from abroad. SADCC leaders' pragmatism led them to accept that Western governments (particularly the UK under Mrs Thatcher) were not willing to support total sanctions and disinvestment in apartheid South Africa. Therefore, they changed their strategy and requested these governments to (i) make new investments in SADCC states and not in South Africa and (ii) make industrial and commercial investments directly rather than through the back door of South Africa. Most investments in SADCC states have originated from states with little or no investments in apartheid South Africa (viz. Scandinavian countries, France, Italy and India), and less from the three states with most investments in apartheid South Africa (viz. Germany, the UK and the US).

It is difficult to assess the magnitude or trends of FDI inflows into SADC due to the paucity of data and its non-comparability. Bearing this in mind, we present the ratios of FDI to GDP and gross fixed investment. These are very low with the exception of Angola, Botswana, Namibia, Swaziland and Zambia (see Table 3.5). These economies have traditionally relied on multinational corporations and FDI for exploitation of their rich mineral resources. For example, in Angola, FDI inflows went into petroleum exploration and mining. Another reason for

Table 3.5 Ratios of foreign direct investment to gross fixed capital formation and GDP for SADC, SACU and ECOWAS members

Country	*Gross fixed capital formation*[1]*(%)*			*Gross domestic product*[2] *(%)*		
	1984–89 (Annual average)	*1991*	*1994*	*1985*	*1990*	*1994*
I. SADC (Including SACU)						
Angola	31.3	107.5	55.8	11.1	12.4	30.2
Botswana	13.4	–0.6	–3.4	45.3	26.6	13.8
Lesotho	4.6	1.7	3.3	6.2	11.0	14.5
Malawi	7.7	4.9	0.7	12.2	11.6	18.3
Mauritius	4.3	2.4	1.9	3.5	6.3	6.7
Mozambique	0.4	2.6	3.3	0.7	2.9	10.6
Namibia	1.2	34.0	5.8	151.7	89.5	73.6
South Africa	–	–	–	–	–	–
Swaziland	31.1	49.5	27.8	55.0	49.0	69.5
Tanzania	–	–	–	–	–	–
Zambia	28.4	8.9	19.1	4.4	15.8	23.9
Zimbabwe	–0.9	0.2	2.7	66.6	36.6	42.2
II. ECOWAS						
Benin	0.1	5.1	2.0	3.1	2.0	4.5
Burkina Faso	0.5	0.1	0.2	2.4	1.1	1.1
Cape Verde	0.5	1.0	0.1	–	0.8	0.9
Côte d'Ivoire	4.5	1.8	1.9	7.9	10.1	8.9
Gambia	6.2	20.0	16.8	9.4	11.9	24.3
Ghana	1.1	2.3	22.6	4.9	6.0	12.8
Guinea	2.2	7.8	0.5*	0.1	2.3	4.2
Guinea-Bissau	1.4	3.3	–2.6*	0.8	3.3	6.0
Liberia	133.0	8.2	9.4	124.8	211.7	214.8
Mali	0.8	0.7	10.4	2.8	1.2	2.9
Mauritania	2.3	0.9	0.9	4.8	4.9	8.2
Niger	3.5	0.5	0.5	14.1	10.6	11.5
Nigeria	16.5	19.8	50.5	5.4	24.7	31.1
Senegal	0.9	3.0	1.1	7.7	5.5	5.9
Sierra Leone	–25.2	13.9	81.3	5.0	–0.5	3.3
Togo	1.5	0.6	0.2	28.7	15.2	20.3

Source: UNCTAD (1996). 1 – FDI inflows. 2 – Inward FDI stock.

* – for 1993.

the attraction of FDI inflows into SADC is services, notably finance and banking services, particularly in the case of Mauritius (which is attempting to become an offshore banking centre) but also post-apartheid South Africa. In the latter case however, FDI outflows also increased in 1992, with opportunities for investment growing in the neighbouring countries with which South Africa's political relations have become normal.

However, given the state of economic and political transition to a post-apartheid liberal regime, the existence of severe welfare gaps between the black and white population, and the need to mitigate poverty by providing housing and social and economic infrastructure in shanty towns, the economy's capacity to provide sizeable investments abroad may be limited, at least in the near future.

The capacity of other SADC members, such as Zimbabwe and Zambia, for intra-SADC investments may also be limited. However, a beginning has been made in this direction. Zimbabwe is investing in Botswana and Mozambique. But its investment is a drop in the ocean since the absence of a well-developed capital market and shortage of skills within the region discourages FDI inflows.

Lack of cross-border investments hinders the capacity of the region to export and import from within the region. But privatization that is now underway in the SADC region should attract some FDI. It is estimated that 'approximately $10 billion worth of public assets in Angola, Malawi, Mozambique and Zambia are scheduled for sale' (AfDB, 1993, p. 55). Both SADC and PTA (COMESA) have expressed interest in the promotion of cross-border investments and the PTA Charter on Multinational Industrial Enterprise (1990) is intended to offer incentives for intraregional joint venture investment. However, FDI is unlikely to be attracted without the support of bilateral and multilateral donors in sharing risk and bolstering investor confidence. Multilateral donors (for example, the World Bank, the European Union and the African Development Bank) have shown some interest by proposing the implementation of a cross-border initiative (CBI) under which 'balance of payments support is provided in exchange for bilateral liberalization of the capital account with respect to cross-border investment flows'. (AfDB, 1993, p. 56). This donor-dominated initiative may provide a first step towards the implementation of a more ambitious proposal, namely, the SADC Cross-Border Investment Facility.

There is evidence that some SADC members have been able to build export capabilities through FDI inflows by multinationals. This is particularly true in the case of Mauritius where FDI in textiles and garments is intended for exports of these goods to European and other markets. In other SADC members, especially those which are primarily agriculture-based, foreign affiliates are likely to be engaged mainly in primary commodity exports and processing of minerals.

SOUTHERN AFRICAN CUSTOMS UNION (SACU)

Originally established in 1910, SACU first consisted of the Union of South Africa (later the Republic of South Africa) and the three High Commission Territories of Bechuanaland, Basotholand, and Swaziland. These three Territories became independent in the course of the sixties as respectively, Botswana, the Kingdom of Lesotho and the Kingdom of Swaziland. In 1969, these three countries concluded the South African Customs Union agreement with South Africa. In 1990, on gaining independence, Namibia (formerly South West Africa) also joined SACU.

Thus SACU is a legacy of the colonial era. It is one of the oldest functioning customs unions in Africa. The origins of SACU can be traced to political as well as economic factors. Apartheid South Africa clearly reaped political mileage by entering into a customs union agreement with its three neighbouring independent states. This agreement also enabled South Africa to flout efforts at sanctions against it. McCarthy (1992) considers it as a 'marriage of convenience' and notes that by and large this marriage has been a success. The other three members of the Union benefited in terms of payments they received from South Africa as compensation for their loss of national tariff revenue, fiscal autonomy and trade diversion. In 1978, the revenue-sharing formula was stabilized at between 17 and 23 per cent of the import and excisable production revenue going to the BLNS (Botswana, Lesotho, Namibia and Swaziland) countries (McCarthy, 1994). Significant and regular contributions to state revenue of BLNS offered them financial security. In 1990–91, SACU revenue accounted for 14.5 per cent of total government revenue in Botswana, and nearly 60 per cent of the total government revenue in Lesotho (Thomas, 1995).

SACU consists of very unequal partners; South Africa, a sophisticated relatively rich and fairly industrialized country on the one hand, and BLNS, rather poor countries with limited skills and infrastructure, on the other. These two groups of countries are therefore bound to differ in their perceptions of costs and benefits from the Union. The BLNS argue that they do not receive enough compensation through the current revenue-sharing arrangements. They have to rely on more expensive South African imports instead of cheaper goods from the rest of the world.[2] Apart from the higher financial cost, this raises the costs of industrialization in these countries and prevents them from becoming competitive in the international market. South African exports to BLNS (an assured market) retard growth in domestic industrial production. This can be regarded as BLNS subsidizing South African industry for which they would like to receive compensation in addition to what they obtain under the revenue-sharing arrangement. Furthermore, there is a two-year delay in disbursements from the common revenue pool which amounts to the BLNS offering an interest-free loan to South Africa for which they receive no compensation. South Africa, on the other hand, believes that the revenue transfers to BLNS are too generous and are a fiscal burden. It would not like its obligations to SACU to stand in the way of its fiscal discretion and freedom to change its tax structure (AfDB, 1993, p. 229).

Unlike most other customs unions, particularly of developing countries, SACU's main objective was not the economic development of member countries. This is clear from the reluctance of South Africa to allow growth of industry in BLNS countries producing for the South African market. Walters (1989) has noted that the location of television assembly in Lesotho and Swaziland using components from outside the union was prevented in order to protect South African component producers. Lundahl and Petersson (1991) have reported restrictions and controls in certain industries by South Africa by requiring standardization of circuit design and components (for example, components industry) in order to prevent entry of certain industrial enterprises into the country. Davies (1994) has stated that 'price dumping' or 'aggressive retaliatory action' by South African producers blocked Swaziland's attempt to establish a fertiliser factory, and Botswana's and Lesotho's efforts to set up breweries. Thus competition to South African industry is effectively eliminated.

A number of non-tariff barriers also prevent access of BLNS goods in the South African market (cf. Articles 11 and 17 of the secret memorandum attached to the 1969 Treaty). Although Article 7 of the 1969 Treaty allows BLNS to specify industries of strategic importance (on which tariffs and duties could be lowered), it was extremely difficult to invoke this Article. The secret memorandum noted above 'requires that, before tariff protection can be considered, 60 per cent of the quantitative requirements of all countries in the union must be met and the quality of goods produced must be high. Also tariff relief for the goods will not be granted unless there are no suitable substitutes for the good in the customs union area'. (Mayer and Zarenda, 1994, p. 29).

The foregoing clearly indicates that South African industry is heavily protected against competition from BLNS and that the articles of the 1969 Treaty are inherently biased in favour of industrial growth in South Africa at the expense of the other member countries.

Intra-SACU Trade

The Protectionist policy of South Africa towards BLNS is clearly inimical to intra-SACU trade on a reciprocal basis. Trade within SACU is one-sided with South Africa exporting far more to BLNS than it imports from them. To some extent this is due to the much more diversified economy of South Africa. But as we noted above, it is also partly due to the efforts of South Africa to prevent BLNS from industrializing. Any trade diversion from the rest of the world to SACU resulting from a common external tariff, is likely to gravitate towards the more developed economy of South Africa. Since the South African economy is producing under protection, its products are not competitive. The BLNS countries suffer a loss of economic welfare due to inefficient high-cost production, as they have to import expensive goods from South Africa instead of cheaper ones from the rest of the world.

Thus, SACU is clearly an unusual kind of a customs union in which (against expectations) there is no sub-regional common market or a free flow of goods and services due to lack of reciprocity. While South African goods have free access to BLNS markets, the BLNS goods do not have free access to the South African market. Trade is therefore heavily biased in favour of South Africa. It enjoys growing trade surpluses with BLNS which are unsustainable for long periods. It is paradoxical that this one-way trade relationship is inimical to economic development in the region as the objective of an economic or customs union is to promote development through enlarged markets and more efficient production.

Recent extraregional bilateral trade agreements of South Africa with the United States, the European Union and Asia may also hurt the SACU members and the process of greater integration of the region (Cassim, 1995). At present, the poorer SACU members enjoy non-reciprocal duty-free access to the European Union under the Lomé Convention which South Africa does not enjoy. South Africa's bilateral free trade agreement with the European Union is likely to involve a reciprocal lowering of tariffs which might hurt the SACU members through trade diversion. If SACU members were to be included, it would harm their economies further by slowing their efforts towards industrialization. Thus, while bilateral agreements within SACU and SADC may be seen as a step towards greater regional integration, extraregional bilateral agreements may hinder such integration and make distribution of gains more unequal.

One reason for serious trade imbalances in favour of South Africa is its higher level of industrial development and diversified production structure. Also tariff and non-tariff barriers imposed by South Africa discourage imports from the BLNS. Trade imbalances could be reduced by widening trade liberalization to include non-manufactures such as agriculture and minerals. This should help BLNS to export more since they are primarily agricultural and mineral-producing countries. Secondly, intra-SACU trade can also be expanded by widening cooperation in tourism, and financial and commercial services. Thirdly, greater cooperation is needed in the exploitation of such (natural) resources as electricity and water. The ongoing Lesotho Highlands Water Project, for example, should be a good source of additional water supply to South Africa's industrial heartland. It will also generate hydro-electricity in Lesotho which will replace power currently imported from South Africa (McCarthy, 1995a; Davies, 1995).[3]

Can SACU be downgraded to a free trade area, or upgraded to a common market of the five member countries? While a free trade area may be in the interest of South Africa with its more developed and competitive industry, it is unlikely to be in the interest of the BLNS. The absence of all tariff and non-tariff barriers within SACU is likely to wipe out whatever incipient industries exist in the BLNS. It is therefore more appropriate to aim at a *preferential* trade agreement under which infant industries of the BLNS can be temporarily protected to promote industrialization. Elimination of trade barriers among the very low-income countries of SACU is unlikely to raise allocative and productive efficiency which, in theory, is the main purpose of trading blocs.

Can SACU be upgraded into a common market with free mobility of goods, capital and labour? This would certainly overcome problems associated with labour migration from the BLNS to South Africa. A number of scholars consider this possibility (Lundahl and Petersson, 1991; Davies, 1993; Maasdorp and Whiteside, 1993) since SACU, together with the Common Monetary Area (CMA) of which all SACU members, except Botswana participate, already resembles a common market.[4] CMA integrates the monetary policies of Lesotho, Namibia and Swaziland into that of South Africa. The currencies of these three countries are pegged to the South African *rand*. The *rand(R)* is legal tender in Lesotho and Namibia, and it circulates freely in Swaziland (Johnson, 1995). CMA enables SACU to operate within the framework of convertible currencies (even though Botswana is not a member of CMA, its currency, *pula,* is convertible) which does not exist either in ECOWAS or any other grouping in Africa. The existence of CMA and convertible currencies should, in principle, facilitate intra-SACU trade.[5]

SACU Trade with SADC

SACU trade with SADC is as unbalanced as South African trade with the other members of SACU. Since the reintegration of South Africa into Southern Africa, SACU trade with other SADC countries has steadily increased with the latter importing more and more from industrially developed South Africa. It is reported that between 1988 and 1994, 'SACU exports to the rest of SADC quadrupled in value . . . rising from R (rand) 1.8 billion to R 7.2 billion' (Industrial Development Corporation, 1995, p. 5). In 1994, Zimbabwe accounted for 34 per cent of SACU's exports to SADC and Mozambique, 24 per cent. Manufactured goods account for most of these exports. SACU's imports from SADC have also been expanding rapidly, rising from R 500 million to R 1.5 billion between 1988 and 1994. Again, Zimbabwe was the main trading partner.

Greater potential exists for increasing intraregional trade within SACU and SADC and between the two groupings. Rough estimates made by the South African Industrial Development Corporation (IDC) show that 'SACU as a whole could benefit to the extent of a 1.1 per cent increase in GDP, a 4.6 per cent increase in total exports and an 8 per cent increase in manufactured exports from the removal of all tariffs within the SADC area'. (Davies, 1995, p. 5). However, tariff removal would have adverse effects on the economies of the remaining members of SADC. According to the IDC estimates, South African exports into these economies would provide tough competition to their domestic manufacturing industries, leading to a net negative impact on their GDP.

Foreign Direct Investment (FDI)

We noted above that such members of SACU as Angola, Botswana and Swaziland have relatively greater FDI inflows than the other SADC members. This is explained partly by the exploitation of rich natural resources such as oil and diamonds. For example, investment by De Beer Corporation of South Africa in diamond mining accounted for over three-quarters of total exports of Botswana during the eighties (see UNCTAD, 1995a). That Botswana's economy has benefited from FDI is reflected in its rise from a low-income to a middle-income country. The SACU members may have also benefited from membership of the common monetary area with South Africa and from their special status as signatories of the Lomé Convention with the European Union. Added to this, their membership of the Preferential Trade Area gives them locational advantage as a base to export to the region as well as to Europe (UNCTAD, 1994).

Constraints to FDI flows into SACU will be very similar to those that are discussed above under SADC. However, SACU is organized as a customs union which may offer a bigger assured market to foreign investors. This factor is also likely to promote greater intra-SACU investment flows than intra-SADC flows.

Intra-SACU flows of direct investment from South Africa to other partners are likely to be greater than those from South Africa to other SADC members. The economies of SACU have traditionally been better integrated and mutually interdependent than the other SADC countries. As we noted above, higher labour costs in South Africa and slow productivity increase may encourage it to invest in lesser-developed SADC members where labour is cheaper.

Having discussed Southern African integration, below we discuss the experience of integration in West Africa.

ECONOMIC COMMUNITY OF WEST AFRICAN STATES (ECOWAS)

Established in 1975, ECOWAS is one of the largest economic communities with 16 members. The Treaty establishing ECOWAS aimed at the liberalization of trade through a gradual tariff reduction schedule, introduction of a common external tariff, industrial cooperation and harmonization of fiscal policies. However, the Treaty did not spell out how tariff reduction was to be implemented. But it envisaged rather unusually for 'trade liberalization to take place in advance of tariff harmonization' whereas 'in most other communities liberalization is made conditional on prior tariff harmonization in order to provide stimulus to the formation of a common external tariff and to avoid possible misallocation of resources. . . .' (Ezenwe, 1990, p. 29). Since customs duties form a sizeable proportion of total government revenue in Sub-Saharan Africa, there is a reluctance on the part of African countries (particularly the least developed ones) to incur revenue loss through tariff liberalization. This seems to be one of the reasons for extremely slow progress in meeting Treaty targets for tariff reduction in ECOWAS. As member countries are at different stages of development, the least developed countries genuinely fear that the more developed partners such as Côte d'Ivoire, Nigeria and Senegal will benefit more simply because they enjoy alternative sources of income (for example, through the export of manufactures to the lesser developed partners). Article 25 of the ECOWAS Treaty provides for fiscal compensation to partners who suffer loss of revenue, but it does not allow for compensation for any income losses resulting from trade creation and trade diversion. Thus the problem of unequal distribution of gains from regional integration persists.

In 1983, ECOWAS Heads of State decided to extend the mandate of the Community from a common market to a full monetary union which required harmonization of national monetary policies of the member states. It was felt that inconvertibility of national currencies of member states thwarted efforts towards trade liberalization within the Community. The proximity of the West African Monetary Union (UEMOA), which provided for international convertibility of currencies, may have further impelled the ECOWAS leaders to expand the mandate of the grouping. Frimpong-Ansah (1990, p. 55) suggests that this collective action for harmonization of monetary policies was motivated by a serious economic decline rather than a spontaneous commitment. In 1991, the original Treaty was revised to conform to the changing economic and political realities in the West African region as well as opening up of the world economy. In 1993, these revisions were approved by the Heads of State. The revised Treaty reiterates the need for regional integration, reaffirms the role of ECOWAS as the sole economic community of the Western African region, and spells out the relationship between ECOWAS and other intergovernmental bodies in the region. The Treaty reaffirms the goal of a common market and a monetary union. It also emphasizes the important role of the private sector in the process of regional integration (Bundu, 1997).

On paper, ECOWAS is a more advanced form of regional integration than either SACU or SADC. Apart from intraregional trade liberalization, it aims at the free flow of labour throughout the region. However, the ECOWAS Protocol on Labour Mobility signed in 1979 had not obtained the seven ratifications necessary by 1992. ECOWAS has promoted regional agricultural and industrial cooperation programmes, joint development of regional transport and communications networks and regional defence cooperation. It also aims at harmonization of the national monetary and fiscal policies of members. The West African Clearing House is being transformed into a West African Monetary Agency with a mandate to implement the ECOWAS monetary programme. This is intended to create a single monetary zone with a single West African currency (see Bundu, 1997).

In practice, ECOWAS has been much less effective than SACU and SADC. Since its creation in 1975, most of the agreements remain to be implemented. McCarthy (1995) cites ECOWAS (and UDEAC) as examples of non-implementation in intraregional trade liberalization. As we noted above, as far back as 1983 ECOWAS had planned to create a Single Monetary Zone by 1994. There is no progress on this front. In July 1992, this target date was pushed back to the year 2000 (Bach, 1997).

Nevertheless, some similarity exists between SACU and SADC on the one hand and ECOWAS on the other. While South Africa is a dominant economy in the former, Nigeria is dominant in the latter. Indeed, Nigeria was instrumental in the creation of ECOWAS in order to check French influence in the region. But the similarity seems to end there. With the participation of South Africa, both SADC and SACU represent a much bigger market than that of ECOWAS.

Intra-ECOWAS Trade

As in SADC, intra-ECOWAS trade is extremely limited and has remained so despite two decades of so-called integration efforts (see Tables 3.2 and 3.4). Foroutan and Pritchett (1993, p. 97) note that 'intra-ECOWAS and intra-UDEAC trade patterns . . . appear to be unrelated to the two groupings. . . .' Between 1980 and 1994, the share of intraregional trade in total trade was highest for Côte d'Ivoire, followed by Burkina Faso and Togo. In the case of the English-speaking members of ECOWAS, at below 5 per cent this share was particularly low for Nigeria, the dominant country in the grouping. The share was much higher for Ghana and Sierra Leone, ranging between 8 to 13 per cent. The francophone countries, with a common CFA currency and links with France, trade more within the region. This phenomenon may be explained by the convertibility of their currencies. The Western African Monetary Union, with a fully convertible common currency – the CFA franc, backed by France, has the effect of lowering transaction costs and thus contributes towards enhancing the scope for intraregional trade. The currencies of the English-speaking countries are non-convertible. The English-speaking members of ECOWAS are reluctant to accept the CFA franc as a common currency. Thus the idea of West African monetary integration, though debated, cannot be implemented for political reasons. While a West African Clearing House (WACH) exists within ECOWAS, to promote the use of domestic currencies to settle payments among member states, there is no central bank to supervise financial transactions. Instead, a Committee of governors of national central banks plays that role. However, all trade does not go through clearing houses; private banks are free to bypass WACH.

One solution to the problem of common currency, has been suggested by Johnson (1995), namely, that the non-CFA member countries of ECOWAS fix their national currency exchange rates *vis-à-vis* the CFA franc which already enjoys a fixed parity relationship with the French franc. These fixed exchange rates can be realigned if necessary, as has indeed been done in the European Union.

Lack of harmonization of national macroeconomic and industrial policies, apart from the monetary policies, also stands in the way of promoting intra-ECOWAS trade. A common external tariff, though a goal of ECOWAS, is not yet a reality. Due to differences in the degree of industrialization and the level of development of member states (Nigeria, Ghana, Senegal and Côte d'Ivoire are much more developed than Mali, Mauritania and Burkina Faso) different tariff schedules have been adopted with different implications for national comparative advantage.

Foreign Direct Investment (FDI)

Historically, ECOWAS members have been linked to the two main metropolitan countries, namely, France and the United Kingdom, in respect of both direction of trade and inflow of foreign capital required to exploit natural resources. In general, for Africa as a whole, FDI is insignificant as we noted in Chapter 2. It is particularly low for low-income ECOWAS countries without good infrastructure or sizeable markets. The major recipients of FDI included the Gambia, Ghana, Liberia and Nigeria (see Table 3.5). Recent policies of economic liberalization and privatization of state or parastatal organizations may encourage some inflow of foreign investments. However, the African situation is not encouraging. It is reported that sub-Saharan Africa's share in the total revenue for developing countries from privatization was only 0.4 per cent, accounted for by US$ 250 million from a sale of 80 enterprises: 8 in Benin, 37 in Ghana, 29 in Nigeria and six in Togo (Ndulu, 1994). Only 21 out of these cases involved foreign participation. This situation contrasts with MERCOSUR (see Chapter 6) where most FDI is linked to privatizations. It is estimated that during the 1988–93 period, the share of FDI inflows as a proportion of privatization transactions in sub-Saharan Africa was a little over 6 per cent compared to nearly 15 per cent for Latin America and the Caribbean (UNCTAD, 1995a).

Ratios of FDI to gross domestic product and fixed gross investment for ECOWAS countries are also very low (see Table 3.5). This reconfirms the findings in Chapter 2 that FDI flows are concentrated in a few developing countries and that Africa is not very attractive to foreign investors. The reasons for this situation are manifold: small markets, slow progress with economic reforms, slow growth of the private sector, and a high level of indebtedness which creates severe foreign exchange shortages which in turn makes it difficult to guarantee the transfer of FDI income.

Linkages of FDI and trade are also weak in ECOWAS. The role of manufacturing multinationals in exports of host countries is likely to be limited except perhaps in the cases of Nigeria and Côte d'Ivoire, countries with some manufacturing activity. However, mention should be made of trading multinationals which provide a useful supportive marketing function in a number of African countries. For example, such companies are known to act as buying agents on behalf of wood firms in Côte d'Ivoire (UNCTAD, 1995, p. 53).

CONCLUDING REMARKS

African integration is a story of mixed results. In the case of Southern Africa, the fruits of regional trade and economic cooperation are a little more visible than those in West Africa. This may be due to the existence of the more sophisticated economies of South Africa, Mauritius and Zimbabwe among the regional groupings. Western Africa is also fraught with divisions on linguistic and colonial lines with overlapping memberships between ECOWAS and CEAO and the CFA Franc Zone countries linked to France and the French Franc. For political reasons, ECOWAS is unlikely to adopt the CFA franc as its currency. The existence of two different monetary zones in West Africa may partly explain low intraregional trade in the region.

In Southern Africa, particularly SACU, South Africa is the most industrialized and developed economy where labour costs are much higher than in the other member countries. Over time, South Africa's situation may be somewhat similar to that of Japan in East Asia. It may be driven to invest in BLNS to produce labour-intensive goods in order to take advantage of lower labour costs. It may also be forced to leave labour-intensive production increasingly to other SACU members. The extent to which a similar situation may prevail in SADC is less certain since the South African economy is much less integrated with its non-SACU members.

Despite over three decades of regional integration, Africa's exports, as a share of GDP and as a share of total world trade, remain quite low. In fact, its shares of total trade and investment have both declined. Recent liberalization of economic policies and encouragement of the private sector seems to have been too half-hearted to have had any positive effect on investments. Political instability, risk and the lack of institutional requirements for foreign investments have kept their inflows very low.

Thus, Africa has become and remains marginalized in the world economy. As most regional groupings (including ECOWAS) have remained largely ineffective, they are unlikely in the future to be a hindrance to the emergence of a global trading system. However, the long-term goal of an African Economic Community by the year 2025 could, in principle, slow down the pace of multilateralism. But during these three decades multilateralism is likely to be so well entrenched that a more effective Pan-African regional integration can only be favourable especially through links with such other regional blocs as the European Union.

4 Asia: ASEAN and SAARC

Recent initiatives by regional and sub-regional groupings in the Asia Pacific testify to the growing belief in the need to liberalize in response to globalization trends. The oldest of the existing Asia Pacific regional groupings, the Association of Southeast Asian Nations (ASEAN), formed in 1967, has only recently begun to take economic cooperation seriously with its launching of the ASEAN Free Trade Agreement (AFTA) in January 1993. In South Asia, the South Asian Association for Regional Cooperation (SAARC) formed in 1985, though intended to 'promote and strengthen collective self-reliance through joint action' has been unable to move beyond modest efforts at economic cooperation. However at its eighth summit in 1995, it announced the implementation of the South Asian Preferential Trade Agreement (SAPTA) by November 1995. In 1990, the lukewarm reception given to the Malaysian Prime Minister's proposal for an East Asian Economic Group led, nevertheless to its modification resulting in an East Asian Economic Caucus (EAEC), a pressure group which, while not particularly active at present, has the potential to influence trends in the Pacific region.

The regional groupings in Asia which form the subject of analysis in this chapter are: ASEAN and SAARC. The Asia Pacific Economic Cooperation Forum (APEC), which is not a regional bloc as such but more of a consultative body, is discussed in Chapter 5.

As Table 4.1 shows, the ASEAN countries are at a much higher level of development than the SAARC countries. According to World Bank indicators, the latter figure among the world's low-income economies and thus differ in significant respects from the middle-income countries of the ASEAN. ASEAN countries switched from import-substitution to export-led growth in the eighties which has enabled them to form important trade and investment linkages outside the region and thereby to take advantage of the new liberal global trade regime. SAARC countries, on the other hand, are latecomers to market liberalization and are still struggling to open up their economies. Recent liberalization policies of SAARC countries, and attempts by

Table 4.1 Basic economic indicators of ASEAN and SAARC members

Grouping/ Country	GNP per capita (US$) (1994)	Average annual growth rate of per capita GNP (%) (1985–94)	Population (millions) (mid-1994)	Share of industry in GDP (%) (1994)	Export to GDP ratio (%) (1995)	Import to GDP ratio (%) (1995)	Share in world imports (%) (1995)	Share in world exports (%) (1995)
ASEAN								
Brunei	14,240	–	0.28	–	–	–	–	–
Indonesia	880	6.0	190.4	41	26.0	25.2	0.8	0.9
Malaysia	3,480	5.6	19.7	43	89.7[1]	91.3[1]	1.5	1.5
Philippines	950	1.7	67.0	33	36.2	44.0	0.5	0.3
Singapore	22,500	6.1	2.9	36	139.0	138.0	2.4	2.3
Thailand	2,410	8.6	58.0	39	41.4	48.4	1.4	1.1
SAARC								
Bangladesh	220	2.0	117.9	18	14.1	22.4	0.1	0.05
Bhutan	400	4.4	0.67	–	32.6[2]	45.5[2]	0.02[1]	0.0001[1]
India	320	2.9	913.6	28	11.1[3]	11.0[3]	0.7	0.6
Maldives	950	7.7	0.24	–	2.5	12.1	0.005	0.001
Nepal	200	2.3	20.9	21	24.2	35.6	0.02	0.007
Pakistan	430	1.3	126.3	25	16.4	19.4	0.21	0.16
Sri Lanka	640	2.9	17.9	25	36.0	45.5	0.1	0.08

Sources: World Bank, World Development Report, 1996 for GNP per capita, population and share of GDP in industry; IMF, *International Financial Statistics*, Nov. 1996 for import and export shares, and ratios of exports and imports to GDP.

[1] = 1994; [2] = 1991; [3] = 1993; – = not available

the group as a whole to open up, bodes well for any eventual ASEAN–SAARC collaborative arrangements. This would be attractive to ASEAN particularly for the purpose of tapping the large and growing Indian market. SAARC countries would benefit enormously from such cooperation. As the ASEAN economies grow and lose comparative advantage in certain labour-intensive sectors, SAARC countries could gain a competitive edge in these sectors, particularly if trade, investment and production linkages are established with the Asia Pacific region.

ASSOCIATION OF SOUTHEAST ASIAN NATIONS (ASEAN)

ASEAN encompasses the nations of Brunei, Malaysia, the Philippines, Singapore, Thailand, and Vietnam which joined the grouping in 1995. Observers believe it is only a question of time before Cambodia, Laos and Myanmar also join but this would be conditional on their ability to achieve the objectives of the free trade agreement signed by existing ASEAN members in 1992. The present grouping represents a combined population of over 300 million. It was created mainly out of a mutually-perceived need to stem the threat of spreading communism in the region and to establish stability in an area that was rife with internal and bilateral conflicts. Progress on economic cooperation was therefore very slow. Some authors (Wong, 1985) believe that any early attempts at railroading measures to promote trade and economic cooperation could well have threatened the continued existence of the group as the newly independent states (except Thailand) were still sensitive about their sovereign rights. In addition, the member countries were at different levels of development, and therefore had different perceptions of how far regional integration should go and how it could serve their national interests.

It took a decade before ASEAN countries agreed on a programme of economic cooperation through a cautiously drafted preferential trading arrangement (PTA). The instruments of PTA launched in 1977 included: the extension of tariff preferences, liberalization of non-tariff measures on a preferential basis, long-term commodity contracts, financing of procurement of ASEAN commodities at preferential interest rates, and preference in procurement by government institutions.

Along with the PTA, other schemes introduced to promote intraregional trade through industrial cooperation included the ASEAN Industrial Projects (AIPs), the ASEAN Industrial Complementation and the

ASEAN Industrial Joint Ventures (AIJV). The AIPs encompassed new large-scale government-sponsored industrial projects which, because they were intended to serve the region as a whole, rather than a limited domestic market, would have promoted a regional import-substitution strategy. The ASEAN Industrial Complementation scheme, on the other hand, sought to promote complementarity in existing medium and small-scale industries in the private sector. However, the performance of these schemes has been disappointing owing to bureaucratic delays, the failure of member states to agree on the various proposals for joint projects, and member countries' continued protection of competing infant industries in order to safeguard national interests.

Several factors account for low PTA trade: relatively small tariff cuts, a limited number of products included relative to the number of items traded by the ASEAN countries, inclusion of items in the preference list which were not traded at all by the ASEAN countries, and low price elasticities of relevant product groups (Yam, Heng and Low, 1992). The success of the scheme was also undermined by members drawing up long national exclusion lists of 'sensitive' items (items whose preferred entry into a country might damage domestic interests).

The PTA also had the effect of creating a bias in favour of the more advanced members of the grouping (Singapore and Malaysia), as they had the industrial capability to fulfil import demands by the other ASEAN members for the machinery and technology required for rapid industrial growth. Non-tariff barriers such as quantitative restrictions and cumbersome customs regulations and procedures, have further inhibited intra-ASEAN trade.

Intra-ASEAN Trade

The share of ASEAN in total world trade rose from 3.35 per cent in 1980 to almost 6.5 per cent in 1995 (see Table 4. 2). The share of intraregional trade of ASEAN is quite small. During the eighties and early nineties, intraregional trade has hovered at around 17–20 per cent of the region's total trade compared with the EU range of 56–66 per cent (see Table 2.3, Chapter 2).

A striking feature of the trade pattern is the pivotal role played by Singapore. If Singapore is excluded, intraregional trade accounts for less than 5 per cent of the group's total trade. Almost half of ASEAN's trade in 1990 was between Singapore and Malaysia and another 30 per cent involved Singapore and Indonesia and Singapore and Thailand. This implies that the only appreciable degree of complementarity within

Table 4.2 Shares of ASEAN and SAARC members in world trade (%)

	1980	*1985*	*1990*	*1995*
ASEAN				
Indonesia	0.85	0.78	0.70	0.85
Malaysia	0.61	0.75	0.87	1.50
Philippines	0.36	0.27	0.31	0.45
Singapore	1.12	1.32	1.68	2.40
Thailand	0.41	0.44	0.83	1.25
Total ASEAN	**3.35**	**3.56**	**4.39**	**6.45**
SAARC				
Bangladesh	0.09	0.10	0.08	0.10
India	0.61	0.68	0.61	0.64
Maldives	0.001	0.002	0.003	0.003
Nepal	0.01	0.02	0.01	0.016
Pakistan	0.21	0.23	0.19	0.19
Sri Lanka	0.08	0.08	0.07	0.09
Total SAARC	**1.00**	**1.11**	**0.96**	**1.03**

Source: Our estimates based on IMF, *International Financial Statistics Yearbook*, 1995 and *International Financial Statistics,* November 1996. See Chapter 2 for method of estimation.

the region is between Singapore and the other members. Its entrepôt trade in manufactures has grown rapidly since the eighties, while petroleum refining from crude imported from Indonesia and Malaysia remains an important component of trade. The Philippines economy, on the other hand, is particularly weakly integrated (Hill, 1994).

Table 4.3 presents trade intensity indices for the ASEAN countries. It shows some interesting features: Trade intensities for all ASEAN countries have shown a declining trend; Singapore has the highest trade intensity with all its partners while Indonesia's trade intensity with other ASEAN countries is among the lowest; Singapore's trade intensity with Malaysia has declined over time suggesting that Malaysia has begun to export directly rather than through Singapore. Also, it is not clear how much of Malaysia's exports to Singapore are re-exported to the rest of the world (Ariff and Chye, 1992).

Higher value-added manufactures are gradually becoming a growing component in ASEAN countries' exports, following a similar pattern to the East Asian Newly Industrializing Economies (NIEs) before them. By 1991 the share of manufacturing in ASEAN exports had risen – to 71 per cent in the Philippines, 67 per cent in Thailand, 61 per cent in Malaysia and 41 per cent in Indonesia. By 1993, when Singapore's

Table 4.3 Indices of intraregional trade intensity for ASEAN countries

	1970	*1975*	*1980*	*1985*	*1990*	*1994*
Indonesia						
Malaysia	6.60	2.07	0.49	0.63	1.15	1.54
Philippines	5.48	0.97	1.93	3.69	1.64	1.73
Singapore	17.93	9.02	9.16	6.27	4.15	–
Thailand	0.04	0.06	0.34	0.89	0.75	0.81
Total ASEAN	9.43	4.52	4.67	3.77	2.44	0.73
Malaysia						
Indonesia	1.88	1.16	0.47	0.78	1.81	1.70
Philippines	3.73	3.72	3.57	8.22	3.49	1.97
Singapore	25.96	20.15	15.47	13.87	12.83	8.62
Thailand	1.97	3.67	3.06	6.95	3.58	2.97
Total ASEAN	12.22	9.81	8.30	9.40	7.63	5.44
Philippines						
Indonesia	0.52	1.48	3.35	0.73	1.18	0.76
Malaysia	0.06	0.49	2.96	5.79	1.84	1.20
Singapore	0.85	1.40	1.59	3.90	1.67	2.22
Thailand	0.72	0.47	2.31	3.69	1.98	0.99
Total ASEAN	0.59	1.10	2.33	3.70	1.70	1.53
Singapore						
Indonesia	–	–	–	–	–	–
Malaysia	45.58	39.14	26.81	23.55	15.01	13.96
Philippines	0.66	2.32	3.27	3.27	3.29	3.06
Thailand	7.47	8.55	9.10	8.41	6.68	4.31
Total ASEAN	15.24	11.44	10.22	10.34	7.23	6.79
Thailand						
Indonesia	6.82	3.17	6.51	1.12	1.04	0.93
Malaysia	11.76	10.68	8.09	7.63	2.90	1.90
Philippines	0.28	3.45	0.84	2.57	1.89	0.96
Singapore	8.27	9.02	6.25	5.70	4.10	4.03
Total ASEAN	5.99	5.93	4.99	4.24	2.41	2.14

Source: Our estimates based on data from IMF, *Direction of Trade Statistics Yearbook.*

re-exports constituted nearly 37 per cent of its total exports, manufactures accounted for 80 per cent of its entrepôt exports (Chia, 1994). The dramatic rise in the share of manufactures in ASEAN trade is particularly noticeable in the case of Indonesia – this rose from only 7 per cent in 1980 to 47 per cent in 1990. Similarly, the share of manufactures in Thailand's trade with ASEAN rose from 31 per cent in 1980 to 64 per cent in 1990 (Naya and Imada, 1992).

Exports have shifted from primary products to textiles and clothing, chemicals, basic metals, machinery and electronics. The main markets for these goods have been in North America and Western Europe, but the sources of capital and intermediate goods are largely from within the East Asian region.

Intra-ASEAN trade continues to remain a low proportion of its overall trade as member countries produce similar resource-based and labour-intensive manufactures exported to the richer markets of Australia and the United States, and to a lesser extent, Japan. However, it is not clear whether ASEAN countries can sustain such market penetration in the future in the face of non-tariff barriers on food and textiles imposed on their exports by the US. Both Australia and the US have often resorted to anti-dumping duties, and quantitative restrictions have inhibited ASEAN exports of products such as canned tuna fish, shrimp, crab meat and pineapple.

The persistent US trade deficit is likely to exacerbate this situation. There may therefore be some scope for trade diversion from extraregional to intraregional trade within ASEAN. This diversion is likely to be facilitated by the recent evolution of a pattern of regional division of labour and intra-industry specialization and by the implementation of the ASEAN Free Trade Area.

ASEAN Free Trade Area

The compulsion to form a free trade area within ASEAN was partly a response to growing protectionism by the European Union towards third parties. In addition, with the creation of NAFTA (see Chapter 6), ASEAN countries feared that Mexico's membership in a free trade agreement with the US and Canada, and the possibility of NAFTA's expansion further south, would divert US trade and investments away from the ASEAN region. There was also the threat of increasing competition for trade and export-oriented investments from other developing countries including China, India and the newly emerging economies of Eastern Europe. Such fears are not without justification. For example there was a considerable fall in foreign commitments to Indonesia and Malaysia in 1992 and 1993 which is partly attributed to investment diversion to China and to a lesser extent, Vietnam.

AFTA was made possible by the changing dynamics in the region. During the eighties ASEAN leaders were forced to undertake economic reforms in response to ever-increasing external competition and falling commodity prices. Their replacement of inward-looking import-substitution policies by outward-oriented industrialization and liberalization policies has strengthened the economic structures of the individual ASEAN countries (except the Philippines and to some extent, Indonesia) and increased their competitiveness. It has also given their leaders more confidence in the free trade concept encouraging them to undertake additional liberalization measures including further tariff reductions. Even Indonesia, which has tended to protect itself with a high tariff wall, dropped its average tariff rates from more than 30 per cent in 1980 to about 20 per cent in 1990 (Naya and Imada, 1992).

ASEAN leaders believe that subscribing to multilateral free trade agreements as espoused by the General Agreement on Tariffs and Trade (GATT) and its successor, the World Trade Organization (WTO), will help to counter the growing protectionism of regional blocs like NAFTA and the EU. Cooperation through AFTA is seen as a first step in reducing tariff and non-tariff barriers regionally before being exposed to the wider international arena on a most-favoured-nation basis in the spirit of GATT. It is also seen as making the region more attractive to foreign investors.

At the Fourth ASEAN Summit Meeting in Singapore in January 1992 ASEAN leaders signed an agreement to achieve an ASEAN Free Trade Area within 15 years with implementation commencing in January 1993. This is to be achieved through reductions in tariff and non-tariff barriers within the region and the establishment of a common external tariff for non-members. The Common Effective Preferential Tariff (CEPT) is to be the means for achieving this goal. CEPT stipulates reductions in regional tariffs on all manufactured products, including capital goods and some processed agricultural goods, but provisions are made for safeguard measures against 'serious injury' to domestic producers. Certain items are excluded from tariff reductions and these will be reviewed after eight years while unprocessed agricultural goods and those with security implications are also excluded.[1]

Quantitative restrictions on products under the CEPT scheme, such as prohibitions, quotas and restrictive licensing, are to be eliminated when tariff rates reach 20 per cent while other non-tariff barriers are to be gradually eliminated, within five years following the benefit of concessions.

Using an *ex ante* model Imada (1993) has attempted to forecast the effects of an ASEAN free trade area by estimating future imports from both partners and non-partners. Two different approaches to trade liberalization are considered, viz. (a) total trade liberalization within ASEAN,

(b) a 50 per cent preferential tariff cut over five years within ASEAN. Under assumption (a), it is shown that intra-ASEAN imports will increase sharply (by 25 per cent) at the expense of imports from the rest of the world and total imports will increase between 2 to 5 per cent. The increase of exports however is not at the expense of exports to the rest of the world. Under assumption of partial trade liberalization (case b) also, intraregional trade will expand sharply.[2]

Many authors believe that AFTA does not go far enough. The reduction in tariffs to 5 per cent would yield insignificant customs revenue and protection compared with the high administrative and compliance costs, so it would make sense for tariffs eventually to be reduced to zero. Chia (1994, p. 59) notes that 'AFTA needs deepening and widening to reap greater economies of scale, exploit economic complementarities and improve bargaining leverage *vis-à-vis* the rest of the world'.

According to Ariff (1992), the items on the CEPT fast-track list which account for nearly 40 per cent of intra-ASEAN trade flows should give AFTA a 'jump start'. However, if viewed as a percentage of total ASEAN merchandise trade, they represent only 6–7 per cent. This, combined with the fact that the agreement excludes raw agricultural goods, services and investments, means that the CEPT is unlikely to contribute to a significant increase in intra-ASEAN trade. However, it is a beginning.

Failure to begin the CEPT implementation on schedule indicates a certain reticence towards the scheme. In late 1993, the commencement date was pushed to January 1995. A serious problem with the CEPT scheme is the time frame for tariff reductions. Chia (1992) points out that since the Uruguay Round has agreed a ten-year time frame for tariff reductions, AFTA's 15-year time frame becomes irrelevant. Pressure for tariff reductions within APEC (of which ASEAN countries are members) could accelerate the process by ASEAN countries. Perhaps in recognition of the problems with such a long time frame, ASEAN ministers meeting in Thailand in late 1994 agreed to complete the implementation of AFTA five years ahead of schedule (by the year 2003) as well as to broaden the coverage of the plan to include trade in agriculture in addition to manufactures.

Undermining the objectives of AFTA is the long list of 'sensitive products' temporarily excluded from tariff reductions. No criteria have been laid down to determine a product's sensitivity and there is no yardstick to measure whether a member is being reasonable or not in identifying which products qualify as 'sensitive'. The existence of such lists provides ample scope for protectionist loopholes. This was a failing with the ASEAN PTA, except that the latter agreed on specific product categories for an exclusion list. Despite this, the list of excluded items was so long as to make a mockery of the PTA provisions. It is, therefore, surprising that the CEPT 'sensitive products' are not more clearly defined so as to avoid the abuses experienced under PTA.

CEPT implementation is on a *quid pro quo* basis, that is, a member will not be eligible to avail of the preferences granted by the other members until its own tariffs are reduced to 20 per cent. Pupphavesa, Poapongsakorn and Grewe (1994) suggest that, as the CEPT schedule now stands, very few items will achieve a common tariff by the year 2000. As preferences will be largely bilateral rather than regional, AFTA will fail to provide the dynamic effects on which its success depends.

A particularly thorny issue for AFTA will be the enforcement of rules of origin. For some of the 15 items earmarked by CEPT for accelerated tariff reduction, tariff rates range from 0 per cent in Singapore to 100 per cent in countries like Thailand or Indonesia. Such disparities mean that strict enforcement of rules of origin would be necessary to prevent extraregional imports entering the region through the low-tariff countries. At present, to qualify as an ASEAN product, 40 per cent of its content must originate from an ASEAN country. Enforcement of rules of origin poses enormous problems especially in a region rife with 'rent seeking' practices. Besides, a dispute over the origin of an import could cause delays in customs clearance. Increasing globalization of production also complicates rules of origin requirements as components of a single product might be produced in a number of different countries both within and outside the region.

AFTA seems to differ from other free trade areas in that it has more of an outward orientation in line with the region's dependence on its extraregional trade and investment. The purpose of other free trade areas is mainly to enlarge the domestic market by removing trade barriers; AFTA's primary objective, in view of the small internal market, is to create an integrated area in order to achieve greater global competitiveness. The gradual CEPT approach is in line with ASEAN's tradition of caution so as to give business and political and economic interests time to adjust and restructure. It also makes the scheme more palatable to those members with higher tariffs and protectionist regimes. This being said, its limited coverage and time frame for tariff reductions to 0–5 per cent by all members might undermine its goals given the rapid pace of economic liberalization in the competing economies of China and, more recently, India. This could pose serious challenges to ASEAN's continued competitiveness in the global arena.

Prospects for AFTA

While there has been some progress in industrial complementarity in the region, it has not gone far enough to boost intraregional trade. Thus ASEAN's extraregional trade linkages continue to remain stronger than those within the region. AFTA is unlikely to change this in the near future unless member countries go further in their commitment to free trade. First of all, the CEPT accelerated list is too narrow. It should include a number of items that feature high on the list of intra-ASEAN trade such as sugar, fish, iron and steel, petroleum and vehicles. The present CEPT listings would not redistribute the gains from freer trade among countries of the region as it does not change the existing configuration of trade relations within ASEAN; of the accelerated CEPT listings, textiles and electronics, which are the largest contributors to intraregional trade, are exported mainly by Malaysia to Singapore. Thus, the Singapore–Malaysia trade relationship will continue to remain dominant in the region.

The disparities in tariff levels between Singapore, Malaysia and Brunei on the one hand and Indonesia, the Philippines, and Thailand, on the other hand, pose several problems. Singapore has virtually no tariff controls, its average import tariff being only 0.3 per cent, Malaysia's amounts to about 14 per cent while the remaining ASEAN countries apply *ad valorem* tariffs ranging between 18 per cent (Indonesia) and 31 per cent (Thailand). Non-tariff barriers (NTBs) are a significant obstacle to an open trade regime. Even the so-called 'open economy' of Singapore is marked by significant quantitative restrictions, mainly in the shape of licensing requirements on imports of cereals, agricultural raw materials and chemicals. Indonesia and the Philippines apply extensive NTBs to primary commodities and manufactures while Malaysia and Thailand are restrained in the application of NTBs except to imports of cereals (DeRosa, 1995). There is a perception among the high-tariff countries that those with already low tariffs will benefit the most from the agreement in that their gains from better access to the region's markets will not be reciprocated by offers of any additional advantages to their partners. Some members believe that Singapore should offer concessions in areas of services such as telecommunications links and management expertise or provide additional support in the form of logistical or statistical activities in return for better access to ASEAN partners' raw material and labour markets.

Sree Kumar (1992) suggests that an increase in intraregional trade may hinge on other measures than tariff reduction, such as a better coordination of monetary policy to reduce the divergence of exchange rates and improving the climate for private companies. In a survey of companies, most of them listed the major obstacles to intraregional trade as: lack of market sophistication, inelastic demand for reputable and high-quality products; existence of major markets outside the region; and a lack of credibility in the AFTA initiative, borne out by the fact that soon after the agreement was signed, certain industries in Thailand and Malaysia began to call for protection measures at least in the short term.

Countries such as Indonesia, the Philippines and Thailand are likely to resist cutting tariffs owing to the loss of revenue this would entail. For example, in the Philippines, taxes on international trade transactions accounted for 21.5 per cent of total government revenue in 1988 (Akrasanee and Stifel, 1992). Some ASEAN countries resist liberalization as they believe their interventionist policies have been successful, particularly their use of infant-industry protection for nurturing new industries.

Barriers such as bureaucratic delays, inefficient customs practices, subsidy schemes for domestic producers and consumers, and rent-seeking practices by the authorities, have discouraged many exporters. Other NTBs such as licensing requirements and the monopoly status of state enterprises have further prevented trade expansion. If it is to be taken seriously, AFTA will need to establish an institutional mechanism for monitoring and enforcing the dismantling of NTBs. It would also need to establish a dispute-settlement mechanism.

The ASEAN region remains heavily dependent on its external trade linkages – extra-ASEAN trade accounts for about 85 per cent of total ASEAN trade – which leads one to question whether a free trade agreement would not be more meaningful if it were extended beyond the region. Some scenarios suggest a free trade linkage with the East Asian economies and/or the Australia–New Zealand CER Agreement (Closer Economic Relations trade agreement of 1983). Others argue in favour of a Pacific-wide FTA. However, there is considerable doubt about the feasibility of an FTA among such a large and disparate group of countries at very different levels of economic development as those comprising APEC (see Chapter 5).

Viewed as a means of promoting intraregional trade, AFTA may not prove very successful owing to its small internal market, low intraregional trade, uneven protection levels and limited coverage of the CEPT scheme which forms the basis of the agreement as discussed above (see also Panagariya, 1994). However, AFTA puts a certain amount of 'peer pressure' on member countries to liberalize at a faster pace than they might in the absence of such an agreement. If AFTA is viewed as a means of promoting efficiency of production, improving the regional investment climate and the group's ability to negotiate more forcefully both with other groupings and at the multilateral level, it will serve ASEAN well in meeting some of the challenges associated with globalization.

Foreign Direct Investment (FDI)

Foreign direct investment (FDI) inflows into ASEAN have made important contributions to the economic development of the region. In fact the ASEAN experience shows that FDI can promote both industrial growth and the export capabilities of the host countries through the creation of intraregional and extraregional linkages.

From the early sixties to the mid-eighties, investment into ASEAN countries was motivated first by the need to secure access to petroleum and other raw materials and later by their lower wage, lower-cost locations for labour-intensive production. The import-substitution type of industrialization pursued by the ASEAN countries also led the US, Europe and later, Japan to locate some production there to serve local markets. In addition, protectionism in the OECD countries may have forced the Japanese and other investors to invest within the region (for example, Indonesia, Thailand and the Philippines) to take advantage of quotas, such as those governed by the Multi-Fibre Arrangement, in order to maintain market shares.

The eighties saw a rapid increase in FDI flows into the East and Southeast Asia region. Initially, there were significant FDI inflows into the rapidly industrializing economies of Korea, Taiwan, Singapore and Hong Kong. However, the single most important event which led to a sudden surge of FDI into ASEAN was the appreciation of the Japanese *yen* and Asian NIEs' currencies in 1985–6. This, combined with rising labour costs there, led many Japanese, Korean and Taiwanese export manufacturers to seek cheaper locations in the ASEAN developing economies in order to maintain their export competitiveness. In addition, as the NIEs graduated from the status of developing to that of newly industrializing countries, they lost US GSP (Generalized System of Trade Preferences to developing countries) privileges which made them less attractive for investments into GSP-related sectors of export-oriented manufacturing. This was also a factor leading to a shift in investments to those ASEAN countries that still benefit from GSP. By the latter half of the eighties, Japan and the Asian NIEs had overtaken

Table 4.4 Shares of foreign direct investment in GDP and gross fixed capital formation in ASEAN and SAARC members (percentages)

	Gross fixed capital formation[1]			*Gross domestic product*[2]		
	1984–89 (Annual average)	*1991*	*1994*	*1985*	*1990*	*1994*
ASEAN						
Brunei	–	–	–	0.9	1.1	1.9
Indonesia	1.6	3.6	3.6	28.6	36.6	26.5
Malaysia	8.8	23.8	16.1	27.2	33.0	46.2
Philippines	5.1	6.0	9.6	4.2	4.7	8.3
Singapore	28.3	33.5	23.5	73.6	86.6	72.8
Thailand	4.4	4.9	1.1	5.1	9.3	10.1
SAARC						
Bangladesh	0.1	0.1	0.3	0.7	0.7	0.7
India	0.2	0.3	1.1	0.5	0.5	0.9
Nepal	0.2	0.7	1.2	0.1	0.3	0.8
Pakistan	2.0	3.3	4.7	3.3	4.3	6.0
Sri Lanka	2.3	2.4	5.3	8.6	8.5	10.4

Source: UNCTAD (1996). 1 = FDI inflows; 2 = Inward FDI stock; – = not available.

the US and Europe as major investors in ASEAN partly owing to sluggish growth in the western economies but also because the latter began diverting their investments into Latin America and Eastern Europe respectively.

During 1985–90, the magnitude of FDI into ASEAN increased 5.7 times compared with world inward FDI which increased 3.3 times. The share of ASEAN in world inward FDI increased from 2.5 per cent in 1985 to 4.3 per cent in 1990, at a time when the share of developing countries in world inward FDI was on the decline (Urata, 1993a). This spurt of FDI share is attributed not only to currency realignments, but also to the rapid growth of the ASEAN economies and their increasing openness in an emerging global economy (see Alburo, Bautista and Gochoco, 1992). Most of them had begun to switch over from strategies of import substitution to export-led growth and many had liberalized their investment policies to promote growth and exports.

The investment boom has promoted economic growth in Asian developing countries by contributing to physical capital formation and human resource development, particularly in ASEAN, and more recently, in China (Okamoto, 1995). Table 4.4 gives trends in FDI as a proportion of GDP and gross fixed capital formation. Malaysia and

Singapore stand out as more open economies with relatively larger FDI shares.

During 1986–91, Singapore was the single largest recipient of FDI among non-OECD countries accounting for 14.2 per cent of FDI to the developing world (Chia, 1994). At the other extreme, in the Philippines the share of FDI in gross fixed capital formation was consistently the lowest, at barely one per cent, but it registered a sudden increase of over 5 per cent during 1986–91. A possible explanation for this increase is that the other ASEAN countries' industrial growth has led to their loss of comparative advantage in some labour-intensive industries and a shift of FDI in those industries to the Philippines and other developing countries. Malaysia's share of FDI has been declining although it is still higher than that of the other ASEAN countries except Singapore. (See Table 4.4).

The pattern of investment and production in ASEAN has thus followed the 'flying geese' pattern of evolving comparative advantage which characterises the East Asian region. Also, investments have shifted in line with industrial growth. We have noted that initially FDI aimed at exploiting ASEAN countries' comparative advantage of cheap labour. However, these countries succeeded in attracting new investments or reinvestments into new industries after their relative wage advantage deteriorated.

There has been a noticeable increase in FDI in manufacturing, hotels, commerce and other services. Automobiles and automobile parts have also seen increased FDI. This is partly due to increased demand for automobiles within the rapidly growing ASEAN countries, and also because this is a highly protected sector which implies that FDI is the only means of getting a foothold into the local market (the case of 'tariff jumping' FDI). The ASEAN Brand-to-Brand Complementation Scheme has further encouraged automobile manufacturers to set up integrated production facilities through a network of affiliates.[3] Such production patterns will be given further impetus if the successful implementation of AFTA leads to the elimination of barriers to intra-firm trade in intermediate inputs. This would not only strengthen ASEAN firms but also attract additional foreign investors who plan to produce regional goods (Akrasanee and Stifel, 1994).

What is unique in ASEAN seems to be that FDI has not merely effected a once-and-for-all change in industrial activities there, but ongoing upgrading. It is thus largely responsible for the increasing value-added content of manufactures. This in turn has promoted the export competitiveness of these countries by bringing in new technologies. It has thereby enabled the ASEAN countries to sustain their exports to industrialized countries despite protective measures and growing market penetration by other countries in the Pacific.

Urata (1993a) notes the high export propensity of foreign firms in ASEAN, particularly in the case of Malaysia and Singapore where foreign firms account for as much as 88 and 60 per cent of their respective exports of manufactures. He also shows how foreign firms have contributed to the developing host economies by expanding their sales and procurement networks.

The success of the ASEAN countries in continuing to attract FDI and multinationals is due largely to their economic and financial liberalization measures. Fiscal incentives include exemptions from import duties on intermediate goods used in export production, accelerated depreciation allowances, and tax holidays. In addition, export processing zones and industrial estates offer appropriate infrastructural provisions. The creation of AFTA is intended to provide a further incentive in terms of a large single market to foreign investors (as noted above). However, these measures may not be enough to compete against the emerging economies of China and Vietnam. Since 1991, the surge of FDI inflows into these countries has corresponded with a decline in FDI inflows into ASEAN (Petri, 1995) which would seem to indicate investment diversion. Investments in Thailand and Malaysia, in particular, have declined as a result of overheated economies.

Intra-ASEAN Investments

So far we have considered only extraregional investments. But intraregional investments in ASEAN are also increasing. Singapore is the major investor from within the region. The development of 'growth triangles' is a more recent manifestation of intraregional investments in sub-regional economic cooperation within ASEAN. Largely investment driven, economic cooperation in the triangles is being implemented through the private sector with strong government support. The growth triangle concept aims at exploiting economic complementarities between geographically contiguous regions. An example is the SIJORI growth triangle encompassing Singapore, the south Malaysian state of Johor and the west Indonesian province of Riau, including the island of Batam. Singapore provides the investment capital, entrepreneurial and managerial skills from both domestic sources and from the large concentration of multinational enterprises based there. It also provides ready access to financial services, and efficient entrepôt facilities and air, sea and telecommunications links with the rest of the world. Johor and Riau have land, natural resources and relatively lower-wage labour supply. These complementary resources are directed towards promoting industry, resource development and tourism as well as skill formation. New investments have been directed at infrastructural projects and property development.

Despite some social, political and distributional issues, SIJORI (Singapore, Johor and Riau growth triangle) is proving an overall success in terms of its main goal of attracting investments. For example, Johor accounted for 22 per cent of the total number of investment commitments in Malaysia in 1990, up from 12 per cent a decade earlier. (Kumar, 1994). Similarly, investment in Batam has grown significantly since the creation of SIJORI with Singapore being the largest investor there. Batam accounted for 2.2 per cent of total foreign investment in Indonesia in 1992 compared with only 1.4 per cent in 1988 (Naidu, 1994).

For Singapore, the growth triangle has provided a stepping stone for the internationalization of its industries and services. By being able to exploit the comparative advantage of the participating areas, specialization of production has enabled these industries to remain globally competitive. As for Johor and Batam, SIJORI has accelerated the pace of industrialization and the development of trained and skilled labour with consequent growth in GDP and employment. Traditional low value-added and labour-intensive industries such as textiles are being replaced by higher-value added manufactures such as electronics, automobile parts, consumer product assembly, chemicals, and metal products.

The SIJORI experience led ASEAN leaders meeting in Singapore in 1992 to endorse this form of cooperation as supporting overall regional economic cooperation. Other triangles in the offing in the ASEAN countries involve Indonesia, Malaysia and Thailand; and Brunei and contiguous areas of Indonesia, Malaysia and the Philippines. Their experiences could lead to multiple and overlapping growth triangles in ASEAN and their eventual merger under the wider AFTA (Chia and Lee, 1994).

Role of Multinationals

Multinational enterprises are largely responsible for the growth of trade and investment in the ASEAN. They have played an important role in the evolution of comparative advantage in the region through the introduction of new industries in ASEAN countries, for example, electrical machinery and parts, precision machinery and chemicals, all of which are strongly export-oriented. The speed of upgrading from exports of primary products (food, minerals, fuels and petroleum) to manufactured goods has been specially impressive for Malaysia. It showed a high share of 36 per cent for machinery in its total exports owing largely to the presence of multinationals engaged in the machinery industry there (Urata, 1993). The ASEAN economies support such export-oriented production. Their liberalization of FDI attracted foreign capital inflows resulting in expansion and diversification of production capacity intended for export. The high share of exports by multinationals in the total exports of some ASEAN economies in the latter half of the eighties testifies to the success of the liberalization.

The growing trend towards regionalism discussed in Chapter 2 seems to have encouraged these multinationals to regionalize their strategies. A sample survey of a limited number of multinationals with regional headquarters in Singapore indicated two types namely, those that concentrate on foreign markets (for example, electronic companies) and those that concentrate on domestic markets. In order to service customers from proximity and in view of the high growth and expanding markets of the ASEAN region, export-oriented enterprises which hitherto exported to Japan, Europe and the United States, are more and more inclined to export to the ASEAN market (see Pangestu *et al.*, 1992).

There is some fear that multinational enterprises might divert some investments towards other regions and groupings like NAFTA. For example, American enterprises based in Singapore may find it attractive to shift some investments to Mexico to cater for the US market, particularly following the NAFTA agreement (see Chapter 6). Similarly, some European enterprises may be tempted to shift investments towards Eastern Europe. However, the above survey (though based on a rather small sample) suggests that investment diversion may not occur at least in the near future. ASEAN continues to be more attractive because of its relatively higher growth (with the exception of the Philippines), better infrastructure and political stability. Furthermore, the scope for relocation of investments will also vary from one product group to another. Generally, bulkier products require investment proximity more than lighter products such as electronic components. The major competition is likely to come from China, Indo-China and South Asian countries with abundant labour, lower wages and increasing skills. China's export-processing zones are also providing the necessary infrastructural incentives.

ASEAN's record of economic cooperation may have been limited so far, but this is not to deny that by creating a politically stable climate in a region fraught with bilateral conflicts, it has enabled member countries to concentrate on their economic development and provided the necessary regional stability for promoting trade and investment. The bloc's extensive programme of consultations and dialogues on social, economic and political issues has permitted the group to develop shared perspectives on development *vis-à-vis* the rest of the world and given the group more clout in the multilateral arena as well as in its dealings with major trading nations and blocs.

Recent initiatives like AFTA are intended to bolster members' ability to compete for global trade and investments. However, given the fact that ASEAN's major trade and investment links are with Japan, the NIEs and the US, it cannot rely on AFTA alone for assuring sustained growth and competitiveness. It will need to adopt a three-pronged approach: assuring the success of AFTA; promoting ASEAN interests within APEC; and promoting free trade at the multilateral level to counter increasing protectionist trends by NAFTA and the European Single Market.

SOUTH ASIAN ASSOCIATION FOR REGIONAL COOPERATION (SAARC)

The South Asian Association for Regional Cooperation (SAARC) comprises the seven developing countries of Bangladesh, Bhutan, India, the Maldives, Nepal, Pakistan and Sri Lanka. The region is of special significance as it contains about 20 per cent of the world's population but has a low per capita GNP which in 1994 ranged from US$200 for Nepal to US$300 for India, US$430 for Pakistan and US$640 for Sri Lanka (see Table 4.1).

In a bid to promote and strengthen collective self-reliance through joint action, the countries of the region joined together to form the SAARC in 1985. However, in the absence of any strong political or economic motivations that have driven many other countries to form regional blocs, progress in regional cooperation within SAARC has been modest. This is not surprising given the political differences and chronic economic problems that have plagued the countries of the region.

They are all mainly producers of primary agricultural products with this sector employing about 75 per cent of the workforce. Until the late eighties, all the countries of the region had been pursuing import-substitution strategies with a high degree of protection for infant industries which has led to inefficient industries and production structures and inhibited external trade and investment links. Apart from the pressures of dense population on scarce resources, the countries of the region have also experienced deteriorating terms of trade, a mounting debt burden, and acute shortages of foreign exchange resources. It was only in the early nineties that South Asian countries began to undertake liberalization measures and open up their economies, albeit gradually, to trade and investment opportunities. As latecomers to liberalization they have lagged behind other Asian countries, such as ASEAN which opened up much earlier to trade- and investment-led growth.

There is a long history of bilateral disputes between the larger neighbouring countries within the region (notably, the long standing Indo-Pakistan dispute over Kashmir, and the Bangladesh–India disputes over cross-border migrations) and a persistent fear of Indian domination of the region by its smaller neighbours. The latter have sought to counter such domination by promoting closer relationships, including trade links, with China and other Asian countries, policies which have irked India.[4] India's dominance makes the smaller countries of the region wary of a possible 'centre-periphery' relationship in the region. SAARC has provided a forum to allay such fears as it creates the opportunity for dialogue where each country has an equal voice regardless of its size.

Initial regional cooperation has aimed more at people-to-people contact and the pooling of resources and know-how to combat socioeconomic problems such as drug trafficking, and improving the conditions of women and children. The cornerstone of SAARC regional cooperation is an 'Integrated Programme of Action' covering the following broad areas: agriculture and forestry, health and population activities, metereology, rural development, telecommunications, transportation, science and technology, postal services, sports, arts and culture, women in development, drug trafficking and abuse, anti-terrorism, control of environmental degradation and disaster management, food security and audiovisual exchange. But the vital sectors of trade, finance, services, manufacturing and energy had, until recently, been excluded from any regional agreements even though these had been recognized by members at the time of the establishment of the grouping as important areas of regional cooperation.

Intra-SAARC Trade

Neither the political nor economic climate within the region has been conducive to promoting intraregional trade and investment linkages.

To begin with, the economies of the member countries, along with their infrastructure, were developed along North–South lines whereby they served as primary producers for the markets of their colonizers. This meant that they developed little if any complementarity in production patterns. Intraregional trade has been fairly stagnant during the eighties but rose somewhat in the nineties. The share of intraregional trade to total SAARC trade rose from 3.2 per cent in 1980 to 4.0 per cent in 1995. The share of SAARC countries' intraregional exports to their total exports declined from 4.9 per cent in 1980 to 4.4 per cent in 1995, while their share of intraregional imports to total imports over the same period rose from around 2 per cent to 3.8 per cent (IMF, *Direction of Trade Statistics Yearbooks*).

These figures, however, do not reflect the high share of intraregional trade for the smaller SAARC economies (Aggarwal and Pandey, 1992). For Bhutan, which trades mainly with India, most of its imports and exports are intraregional. In 1995, the region accounted for about 9 per cent of Nepal's total exports and about 17.5 per cent of its imports. At the other end of the scale, the intraregional share of Pakistan's exports and imports were 3 per cent and less than 2 per cent respectively, while for India intraregional exports and imports represented 5 per cent and less than 1 per cent respectively of its global trade (IMF, *Direction of Trade Statistics Yearbook*, 1996).

In an attempt to explore the potential of intraregional trade expansion within SAARC, we estimated trade intensities for the SAARC members individually and for the region as a whole using the formula and the data sets cited in Chapter 2. These are presented in Table 4.5 which indicates high values of the index in 1970, 1975 and 1980, but these values have been declining since 1980 for all the countries within the SAARC region except India which showed a higher intra-SAARC trade intensity in 1994 than in previous years. The increase in the index for India between 1990 and 1994, despite an increase in trade with the rest of the world, seems to be due to trade reforms as part of economic reforms and an increase in the rate of economic growth after a dive in 1991. The declining values for other countries suggest continuing low complementarities, trade expansion with the rest of the world especially industrialized countries and continuing barriers to intra-SAARC trade.

The dominant constraint to intraregional exports of various minerals and industrial raw materials is the limited absorptive capacity and a lack of user industries. Similarly, with low regional demand for the intermediate goods and technology produced by India and Pakistan these countries have had to turn to lucrative markets in the Middle East.

Table 4.5 Indices of intraregional trade intensity for SAARC members

	1970	*1975*	*1980*	*1985*	*1990*	*1994*
BANGLADESH						
India	–	2.15	1.38	3.77	1.91	1.59
Maldives	–	–	–	–	–	–
Nepal	–	–	3.75	21.31	20.94	–
Pakistan	–	–	26.53	13.34	6.40	3.49
Sri Lanka	–	8.63	5.99	0.19	6.11	1.71
Total SAARC	–	2.20	7.78	6.23	3.57	2.42
INDIA						
Bangladesh	–	10.57	9.19	5.00	15.65	18.61
Maldives	–	–	23.61	4.46	6.87	–
Nepal	64.58	65.67	62.54	43.02	11.06	–
Pakistan	–	–	0.08	0.56	1.11	1.24
Sri Lanka	13.83	6.47	11.06	8.20	7.20	11.27
Total SAARC	6.35	6.82	6.67	4.75	6.38	9.31
MALDIVES						
Bangladesh	–	–	–	–	–	–
India	–	–	–	–	–	–
Nepal	–	–	–	–	–	–
Pakistan	–	–	18.73	–	–	–
Sri Lanka	–	–	207.08	174.36	172.07	–
Total SAARC	–	–	20.87	13.08	12.16	–
NEPAL						
Bangladesh	–	–	8.40	–	4.54	–
India	3.75	34.21	31.01	31.71	9.68	–
Maldives	–	–	–	–	–	–
Pakistan	60.80	9.91	16.32	3.62	–	–
Sri Lanka	–	–	4.72	24.36	–	–
Total SAARC	6.26	22.25	23.28	21.17	6.55	–
PAKISTAN						
Bangladesh	–	16.51	15.63	16.06	17.54	14.86
India	–	1.91	3.53	1.74	1.27	1.01
Maldives	–	–	7.78	3.92	4.44	–
Nepal	–	0.45	0.87	0.15	0.89	–
Sri Lanka	11.98	27.57	14.00	14.98	15.75	8.61
Total SAARC	0.19	6.70	6.16	4.96	4.44	3.87
SRI LANKA						
Bangladesh	–	3.59	2.82	7.42	4.81	2.30
India	0.13	0.08	4.23	0.59	1.46	1.46
Maldives	–	–	76.86	140.08	87.72	–
Nepal	–	–	–	0.31	–	–
Pakistan	5.36	27.34	11.72	6.58	7.50	5.77
Total SAARC	0.37	6.68	5.83	3.15	3.37	2.94

Source: Our estimates based on data from IMF, *Direction of Trade Statistics Yearbook*.

As with ASEAN countries, concessional aid and credit usually binds the recipients to purchase from the donors. SAARC countries' trade links therefore, have also tended to be oriented to donors outside the region.

It is understandable that the SAARC countries such as India and Pakistan follow an export-oriented strategy aimed at exporting much more to the rest of the world than to other countries within SAARC. There is weak demand in the region because of low incomes and slow growth. As most SAARC countries continue to suffer from low foreign exchange reserves, their exports need to be aimed at industrialized countries which pay in hard currency.

Trade between India and Nepal, which was traditionally quite high, declined between 1985 and 1990 which may explain a decline in the intensity index. During this period Nepal's trade with China expanded significantly, with exports rising from US$2 million in 1985 to US$5 million in 1990 and imports rising from US$19 million to US$46 million during the same period.

Trade is also low, particularly between the two largest economies of the region, Pakistan and India. Political hostilities have restricted trade relations between the two countries.[5] If trade between the two countries were to be liberalized, Indian exports to Pakistan are estimated to amount to about US$2.5 billion a year (*The Economist*, 27 January, 1996). Provisions of an agreement signed by Pakistan with the WTO in 1995 commit it to ending discriminatory trade practices against 106 countries, including India. However, many interest groups in Pakistan fear that cheap Indian imports could hurt Pakistan's protected consumer and engineering industries.

India has trade surpluses with all its regional partners, except Pakistan, a fact which reinforces their fear of Indian domination of the region. However, as Panchamukhi (1995) points out, this skewed relationship needs to be viewed in a wider perspective. For example, Bangladesh has trade deficits not only with India but also with Korea, Singapore, Hong Kong, and China in the Asian region. Similarly, Nepal has much larger deficits with China and the ASEAN economies than with India while Sri Lanka's trade deficit with India is lower than its deficit with Japan and some ASEAN countries. Between 1980 and 1992, India's exports to Bangladesh, Nepal and Sri Lanka were mainly food items, raw materials and intermediate and capital goods. The items which India is exporting to the deficit countries are cheaper than if they were imported from countries outside the region which means that the importing countries run up lower trade deficits than if they were to import from outside the region. In addition, their imports from India constitute essential inputs both in terms of meeting basic needs and in helping their industrialization process. The only way for these countries to reduce their deficits is for them to start diversifying their production base to enable them to produce goods for export to India and other countries.

Import-substitution policies of the past (which have now been abandoned by all members) led to the establishment of similar industries in consumer goods while diseconomies of scale in manufacturing resulted in excess capacity and uneconomic production in most of South Asia. Persistent trade deficits experienced by most of the SAARC members required strict import controls in the shape of high tariff and non-tariff barriers.

In respect of manufactured goods, (for example, iron and steel, cement, fertilizer, paper and newsprint and basic chemicals) the main constraint to trade within the region is the inadequacy and unreliability of supply. The countries of the region have a limited capability to expand and diversify their industrial bases owing to resource constraints. New efforts to attract foreign direct investment into the region may improve prospects for expansion of productive capacity for export (see below). Recent economic liberalization measures in an open economy framework are intended to improve efficiency through competition and exploiting of comparative advantage.

The ASEAN experience shows that trade liberalization measures tend to favour the economically stronger members of the grouping. In South Asia the pattern is similar. India, and to a lesser extent, Pakistan are in a better position to take advantage of market opportunities created by the opening up of the region as they are relatively more advanced industrially and possess more advanced technological skills and know-how. The smaller economies within SAARC fear that regional trade liberalization would adversely affect their infant industries which are unable to compete against well-established industries in India and Pakistan.

The larger SAARC members have large domestic markets and a diversified economic base which makes them less dependent on trade for economic growth. On the other hand, the smaller economies like the Maldives, Sri Lanka and Bhutan have to rely on external markets to stimulate expansion of their industrial base. Bhuyan (1988) has argued that SAARC could help alleviate this excessive vulnerability of dependence on trade through regional trading arrangements which, while bringing only marginal benefits to the larger members of SAARC, would provide significant gains to the exporting small economies. This presupposes the willingness of the larger economies to make the necessary structural adjustments to accommodate the imports of smaller members. With the process of globalization and the opening up of the multilateral trading system, this is not likely to occur in the absence of a comprehensive regional preferential trading arrangement as large countries like India would be more inclined to import from the cheapest source (see discussion on SAPTA below).

Several areas of cooperation which might have a marginal impact on India, the major SAARC partner, could have far-reaching effects on the smaller partners such as the Maldives, Nepal, Bhutan and Bangladesh – for example, regional promotion of tourism, establishment of linkages in the service and infrastructural sectors, a regional clearing union arrangement and joint research and development schemes. Also, rather than their competing in certain commodities such as rubber, jute, tea and textiles, the SAARC members might consider cooperation in the production, marketing and transportation of these commodities. Similarly, there would be an advantage in intraregional transfer of technologies through the creation of regional joint ventures and joint or sub-regional training schemes.

Until the regional political climate improves, there is unlikely to be free interaction between individuals and firms in the private sector. However, as each SAARC member has a state trading organization, there is scope for expanding intraregional trade and long-term contract arrangements through these organizations.

SAPTA

At the SAARC Summit held in New Delhi in April 1995, all the countries unanimously agreed to the launching of the SAARC Preferential Trading Arrangement (SAPTA) by November 1995. This should, in principle, lead to a gradual reduction of tariff and non-tariff barriers and the opening up of national markets to goods from other member countries. Members have promised to offer each other a 10–25 per cent preferential cut in tariffs on a range of goods. As a start, the seven members of SAARC exchanged lists of goods on which preferential tariffs would be offered. The list contains 106 items from India, 35 items from Pakistan, 31 items from Sri Lanka and 12 items from Bangladesh. However, non-tariff barriers on the exchange of goods are likely to persist, particularly between India and Pakistan.

As with ASEAN's initial tariff reductions under PTA (Preferential Trading Agreement), SAPTA's tariff reductions are also being implemented on a product-by-product basis, rather than on sectoral or across-the-board basis. This is a slow process implying that the small level of reductions achieved is not likely to have a noticeable impact on intraregional trade. As with the ASEAN PTA, there is a tendency to restrict the offer list to items of little trade significance in order to avoid erosion of the market by liberalizing trade in major products. Even if the scheme were to be widened, it is unlikely to improve intraregional trade unless other schemes of regional cooperation are also introduced, aimed at creating greater complementarity among the economies of the region, improving their supply capabilities (that is, investment and production partnerships, such as regional/bilateral joint ventures), and creating efficient infrastructural linkages, especially in terms of transport and communications and information exchange. Moreover, for SAPTA to be effective members' tariff reduction offers would need to be greater than those made under multilateral trade agreements including their WTO commitments.

It has been suggested (Panchamukhi, 1995a) that in order to accelerate the pace of regional trade liberalization, it might be preferable to adopt two tracks – one being the region-wide slower track, and the other, a series of bilateral agreements between the more advanced countries within the group. There are already some bilateral initiatives between India and Sri Lanka, India and Bangladesh and India and Nepal. Sectoral cooperation, such as a SAARC Textile Council, could also boost economic and trade relations within the region. Panchamukhi points out that this is a priority sector as developing countries will no longer benefit from preferential quotas when the Multi-Fibre Arrangement is disbanded in the year 2005. The textile sector, an important component of SAARC country exports, will need to rise to the challenge of open competition. SAARC producers will more likely achieve this if they pool their design, marketing and technological resources.

It is clear from the ASEAN experience discussed above that the main beneficiaries of a preferential trading agreement in South Asia would be the industrially more advanced countries like India and Pakistan as their level of industrial development enables them to best take advantage of the larger market created by a free trade regime. PTA measures would not contribute significantly to intraregional trade in South Asia at its present stage of development, owing to the constraints already noted.

Judging from the ASEAN experience, developing country preferential or free trade arrangements cannot contribute significantly either to improved intraregional trade or rapid growth in the member countries. ASEAN countries' extraregional trade and investment linkages with the industrially more advanced countries of Japan and the rapidly growing NIEs have enabled their structural adjustment and industrial upgrading. More importantly, we have seen how FDI has contributed to ASEAN countries' growth in exports and to a spontaneous market-led integration with the rest of the East Asian region. This has further enabled them to integrate into the global trading system. As SAARC is also a grouping of only developing countries, it will need to strengthen its extraregional linkages with the more industrialized countries, particularly those on the Western Pacific rim. This is all the more urgent as South Asia's share in world trade has not been increasing (see Table 4.2). Therefore, with the proliferation of regional trade blocs and free trade arrangements, the priority for South Asia should be less in terms of intraregional linkages than in seeking to forge extraregional linkages to find niches in the markets of other more advanced blocs.

Foreign Direct Investment (FDI)

It is estimated that about 25 per cent of global FDI has been directed towards developing countries, with up to 95 per cent of all FDI in the Asia Pacific region going to the East Asian NIEs and ASEAN countries during the period 1977–1983. Compared with ASEAN's share of 63.4 per cent, SAARC received only 3.5 per cent of all FDI flows to developing countries during this period. (Wadhva, 1994). The flows of FDI into SAARC continued to remain much lower than those into ASEAN right up to 1994 (see Table 4.4). This is due partly to relatively lower growth rates, import-substitution policies adopted till the late eighties, and strict controls on foreign investment by most SAARC countries, often on ideological grounds.

However, two major factors in the early nineties may encourage future flows of FDI into the SAARC countries. First, India and most other countries in South Asia have liberalized their industrial, import and foreign investment policies partly under pressure from the Bretton Woods institutions. In 1995, FDI inflows to South Asia doubled to an estimated US$ 2.7 billion mainly due to a tripling of inflows to India (UNCTAD, 1996, p. 52). It is reported that the value of foreign equity in joint ventures approved in the first seven months of 1992 was a little over US$1 billion, which is three times greater than total investments in the whole of 1991. (UNCTAD, 1993, p. 47). But while increasing, foreign investments in India are far lower than those in China and other East Asian economies. Investments by non-resident Indians in India are far less important than those by the overseas Chinese in China. It would appear that the Chinese reforms have given more credible signals to foreign investors than the Indian reforms which have not yet removed many controls and restrictions on FDI (see Bhalla, 1995). Secondly, with rapid growth in the ASEAN economies (except the Philippines), wages and labour costs have been rising considerably. SAARC countries need to adopt policies which would favour the relocation of some investments and labour-intensive production from ASEAN to SAARC countries particularly as the NIEs and Japan and even some ASEAN countries such as Malaysia and Thailand have become important sources of FDI in the past decade. All these ASEAN countries have a common interest with SAARC countries in creating trade-generating joint ventures. As India became an ASEAN 'dialogue partner' in 1992–3, it is likely that the ASEAN countries view India as a long-term potential market, a view which India should exploit by facilitating and encouraging private-sector contacts with ASEAN entrepreneurs. So far, the US has been India's largest trading partner and investor. Several hundred US firms are already in India since its moves towards liberalization, with total investments estimated at about US$5 billion (Siv, 1995).

However, it is not clear whether SAARC countries will be prepared to open up their economies to the extent of offering incentives to attract FDI in the way the ASEAN economies have done. For example, India's economic reforms could well stall with growing political instability following the defeat of the ruling Congress Party in the 1996 elections. The opposition parties, which now govern most major States in India, oppose unrestricted inflows of foreign investment for fear that it will provide tough competition to local business. Also poor and badly maintained infrastructure dampens foreign investors' enthusiasm to invest in India and other SAARC countries.

CONCLUDING REMARKS

Both ASEAN and SAARC are weak forms of regional economic cooperation. The origins of both were based more on political than on economic compulsions. It is for this reason that neither of them has so far shown much success in intraregional trade or investment cooperation. It is only recently that both SAARC and ASEAN have agreed on the gradual creation of free trade areas through reduction of tariff and non-tariff barriers. These agreements have been induced more by exogenous factors such as the creation of APEC (Chapter 5), NAFTA

(Chapter 6) and the European Single Market (Chapter 7) than internal compulsions. It remains to be seen how effectively the recent agreements on SAPTA and AFTA will be implemented. Having practised import-substitution for very long periods, SAARC countries are much more protectionist than ASEAN countries with the exception, perhaps, of Indonesia.

With a much longer history, ASEAN has developed better intraregional and extraregional linkages than has SAARC. Indeed, as we noted above, until recently SAARC excluded from its activities trade and investment cooperation for fear that bigger members like India and Pakistan would be the beneficiaries. Also ASEAN has more effectively set aside territorial disputes in an effort to promote trade and other forms of economic cooperation. This has not yet been achieved by SAARC which remains bogged down by political disputes dominated by the one between India and Pakistan.

ASEAN economies are far more open than those of SAARC, thanks to their long-followed policies of export promotion and international competitiveness. Foreign investment inflows into ASEAN have been far more significant and instrumental in raising the productivity and competitiveness of the private sector through the introduction of newer technologies and marketing know-how. Thus ASEAN is much more integrated into the global economy than SAARC.

SAARC, on the other hand, has so far made little contribution to either regionalism or globalization. There is hope, however, that with SAPTA, SAARC members have taken a first step towards regional trade cooperation. But in order to benefit from globalization, SAARC will need to agree on a clear policy towards foreign investment as a vehicle of productivity growth and competitiveness, the two essential prerequisites for ensuring access to global markets. This, along with market liberalization and open trade, will facilitate the region's integration with the global trading system.

5 APEC: A Case of Open Regionalism

The Asia-Pacific Economic Cooperation (APEC) Forum is one of the most recent and potentially significant cooperation initiatives. Established in 1989, this forum consists of 18 members from both developed (Australia, Canada, Japan, New Zealand and the United States) and developing countries (Brunei, Chile, China, Hong Kong, Indonesia, Malaysia, Mexico, Papua New Guinea, Philippines, Republic of Korea, Singapore, Taiwan, Thailand). Owing to its large membership, the fact that it includes the world's leading economic powers, the US and Japan, and the world's most rapidly growing newly industrializing economies (NIEs) of East Asia, it is likely to become an important influence in shaping the future of multilateral trade and globalization.[1] APEC's diverse group of economies accounts for more than half of world GDP, almost 40 per cent of world trade (compared with the EU-12 share of about 41 per cent) and about 65 per cent of intra-APEC exports which is higher than the EC share of intraregional exports (Elek, 1992; Yamazawa, 1996).

APEC is a consultative grouping unlike regional blocs such as NAFTA, the EU or ASEAN. The second Report of the APEC Eminent Persons' Group (APEC, 1994, p. 3) stated:

> 'Without any reservation whatsoever, we strongly oppose the creation of a trading bloc that would be inward-looking and that would divert from the pursuit of global free trade.'

Although APEC is not a trading bloc, it deserves separate treatment in view of its economic and political clout as well as the seriousness and speed with which it is promoting global free trade.

The basic economic indicators of the different members of APEC show wide variations in terms of GNP per capita and imports and exports as a percentage of GDP (See Table 5.1). Some economies are much more open (in terms of export shares) than others. Besides these economic differences, the region is characterized by different environments, cultures, and historical and colonial relations. These differences

Table 5.1 Basic economic indicators of APEC members

Country/Group	*GNP per capita (US$) (1994)*	*Average annual growth rate of per capita GNP (%) (1985–94)*	*Share of industry in GDP (%) (1994)*	*Population (millions) (mid-1994)*	*Export to GDP ratio (%) (1995)*	*Import to GDP ratio (%) (1995)*	*Share in world exports (%) (1995)*	*Share in world imports (%) (1995)*
I. Developed Countries								
United States	25880	1.3	–	260.6	11.1	12.4	11.6	15.1
Japan	34630	3.2	40	125.0	9.4	7.9	8.8	6.6
Canada	19510	0.3	32[1]	29.2	37.4	34.9	3.8	3.3
Australia	18000	1.2	30	17.8	19.6	21.0	1.03	1.2
New Zealand	13350	0.7	30[1]	3.5	31.4[1]	29.2[1]	0.3	0.3
II. Newly Industrializing Economies								
Hong Kong	21650	5.3	18	6.1	114.0[1]	123.0[1]	3.4	3.8
Taiwan, China	11930	–	36[3]	21.0	–	–	2.2	2.0
Korea, Republic	8260	7.8	43	44.5	33.2	34.2	2.5	2.6
of Singapore	22500	6.1	36	2.9	139.0	138.0	2.3	2.4
III. Developing Countries								
Brunei	14240	–	–	0.28	–	–	–	–
Malaysia	3480	5.6	43	19.7	89.8[1]	91.3[1]	1.5	1.5
Indonesia	880	6.0	41	190.4	26.0	25.2	0.9	0.8
Philippines	950	1.7	33	67.0	36.2	44.0	0.3	0.5
Thailand	2410	8.6	39	58.0	41.4	48.4	1.1	1.4
Papua New Guinea	1240	2.2	38	4.2	48.6[2]	39.6[2]	0.04	0.02
China	530	7.8	47	1190.9	23.8[1]	20.9[1]	2.9	2.5
Mexico	4180	0.9	28	88.5	24.0	21.1	0.9	1.1
Chile	3520	6.5	–	14.0	29.2	27.3	0.3	0.3

Sources: World Bank, *World Development Report*, 1996 for GNP per capita, population and share of industry in GDP; IMF, *International Financial Statistics*, Nov. 1996 for import and export shares, and ratios of exports and imports to GDP, and Asian Development Bank, *Key Indicators of Developing Asian and Pacific Countries*, 1996.

[1] = 1994; [2] = 1993; [3] = 1995; – = not available

have influenced their bilateral and multilateral relationships. They have also contributed to intraregional complementarities which the members have successfully exploited to promote regional specialization of production and trade linkages. The inclusion of the powerful economies and markets of Japan and the United States and the rapid industrialization of the developing economies of the region have contributed to increasing competitiveness within the APEC region.

The idea of Pacific cooperation dates back as early as the sixties when Japanese politicians, followed by academics, first mooted the concept of a pan-Pacific organization to promote Asian economic development and cooperation. However, sceptics in neighbouring countries, still sensitive about Japan's role during the war, saw this as an attempt to promote Japanese hegemony in the region. Successive proposals were put forward, including a Pacific Free Trade Area (PAFTA), which would embrace the five developed Pacific countries (Australia, Canada, Japan, New Zealand and the United States), to promote integration and trade expansion among them, but they gained little support in the absence of close dialogue and linkages at the time.

In 1967, an Australia–Japan private-sector initiative launched the Pacific Basin Economic Council (PBEC), comprising the national committees of the five developed Pacific countries, to study issues concerning regional trade and investment and to promote cooperation between public and private interests. Another initiative followed in the form of a series of Pacific Trade and Development Conferences (PAFTAD) organized among academics in the region. They served as an important vehicle for articulating ideas on Pacific economic cooperation but failed to garner support for a PAFTA. Many believed that obstacles to realising the region's full potential for economic cooperation and growth stemmed from a failure of mutual understanding between the countries of the region as a result of their many differences. A process of consensus-building involving inter-governmental dialogues was set in motion through the Pacific Economic Cooperation Conference (PECC).

The motivation to form a regional forum was a response to developments both within the region and outside it. Within the Asia Pacific region, rapid economic growth during the seventies and eighties was leading to an intensification of trade and investment linkages along the lines of comparative advantage. In Chapter 4, we referred to the 'flying geese pattern of development' or tiered development, which represented the changes occurring in the factor endowments (labour, capital and technology) of the different countries. Simplistically, the pattern of development can be presented in terms of Japan and the US representing the first tier, Canada and the Asian NIEs, the second tier and the ASEAN group of countries, the third. This led to increasing economic interdependence as a result of regional specialization of production. The spontaneous economic integration gave the countries of the region a certain sense of community.

Meanwhile, there were also external factors which revived interest in enhanced cooperation in the Asia Pacific region: the increasingly competitive trade and investment climate in the world, a trend towards regionalism in other parts of the world, and growing protectionism. The EEC's Common Agricultural Policy (CAP), its role in the Multi-Fibre Arrangement (MFA) and its use of non-tariff barriers (NTBs) to protect its steel and textile industries were all contributing towards what Arndt (1994) refers to as the 'internationalization of protection'. Trade friction between the major players – Japan, the United States and Western Europe – gave an impetus to protectionism and discriminatory trade practices. This, along with the threatened breakdown of the Uruguay Round of multilateral trade negotiations which revealed a weak GATT, prompted a serious move to strengthen regional cooperation.

APEC was launched at a meeting in Canberra, Australia in November 1989 as an intergovernmental forum. It works closely with private cooperative initiatives in the region such as the Pacific Trade and Development Conference (PAFTAD), the Pacific Basin Economic Council (PBEC) and the Pacific Economic Cooperation Council (PECC).

Given the need to accommodate the global interests of the major participants – the US and Japan – there was a strong commitment to keeping participation in Pacific economic cooperation open. APEC, therefore, complemented existing bilateral, regional and global mechanisms.

OPEN REGIONALISM IN ASIA PACIFIC ECONOMIC COOPERATION (APEC) FORUM

APEC has deliberately chosen the path of 'open regionalism'. In addition, APEC endorses a process of unilateral liberalization by its members in recognition of the different levels of development of individual economies and the differences in their economic and political regimes. This enables some countries to undertake economic and trade liberalization measures earlier than others and to a greater or lesser degree than others.

At the first ministerial meeting in Australia in 1989, members had noted the potential threat of regional imbalances which could impede growth and stability in the region. Considering their heavy reliance on export-oriented growth, they recognized the importance of cooperation in pursuing structural changes within the region including joint actions to liberalize trade and strengthen the multilateral trading system.

Initially, APEC was conceived as a loose consultative body working through Ministerial Meetings and Senior Officials' Meetings. Task forces working in close cooperation with the semi-official organization of PECC, undertook various work projects in the following areas: trade and investment data review, trade promotion, investment and technology transfer, human resource development, energy cooperation, marine resources conservation and fisheries, transportation, telecommunications and tourism.

In its formative years, APEC played a passive role, working through the governments of member countries to achieve its main objectives of: creating and maintaining a favourable climate for stimulating trade creation; averting regional trade wars and protectionism; and, promoting regional cooperation. It has adopted a gradual consensus-building approach to tackling an ever wider range of economic issues, an approach aided by giving every member an equal opportunity to influence the forum.

It was not until the Seattle summit in November 1993, that APEC in effect graduated from a merely consultative body to an institutional arrangement with agreements on a concrete agenda for economic cooperation and trade liberalization. This agenda included first, agreement on an extensive package of trade liberalization offers which greatly reinforced the Uruguay Round negotiations, helping to bring them to a successful conclusion. Second, there was agreement to hold annual summit meetings. This is likely to accelerate the pace of cooperation and community building in the region. High-level political representation at APEC meetings assures that regional economic, political and security interests will be incorporated into national policy making. In addition, as APEC meetings are conducted in different member countries, the host country, which chairs the meetings, has an opportunity to shape the direction and priorities of the grouping in line with its own agenda. At the same time peer pressure forces countries to show progress in attaining the goals set by APEC. Third, it was agreed to develop a voluntary, non-binding investment code for adoption at the next summit in 1994. Declining investment flows in the region had heightened interest in initiatives of this sort to attract foreign investors, including the setting up of a Trade and Investment Committee. The leaders welcomed the idea of achieving a free trade area in the Asia Pacific, but fell short of an actual commitment to a specific plan or timetable for achieving this.

Following the Seattle Summit, a proliferation of meetings of finance, trade and industry ministers in the region have been working out details of cooperation on several trade related issues: mutual recognition of product standards, domestic testing and monitoring procedures; cooperation in national competition (including anti-dumping) policies, tackling problems arising out of rules of origin provisions in various sub-regional agreements (including NAFTA); annual review of the trade facilitation programme. Also, an *ad hoc* group to examine economic trends and issues and an informal group for regional trade liberalization were established. The Seattle Summit thus set regional cooperation on a more substantive footing. In addition, a modest secretariat was established in Singapore.

One of the main achievements of the Bogor Summit in 1994, was agreement on a timetable for realizing the goals of free and open trade and investment within APEC – by 2010 for the developed countries that account for 85 per cent of regional trade, by 2015 for the newly industrializing economies (NIEs) and by 2020 for the other developing-country members. The APEC partners agreed to start lowering trade barriers from the year 2000. However, the Declaration does not indicate which countries are developing. In the absence of a clear definition there is potential for confusion and conflict. To take advantage of some concessions many countries will seek to remain in the developing-country category. Also, developing countries need to be viewed in a dynamic sense. For example, the Republic of Korea may be a NIE now but a developed country by 2010. Malaysia sought a safeguard in the form of an addendum to the Declaration stating that the date of 2020 was not binding and might change depending on the stage of development at that time.

While the Bogor Declaration agreed on the goal of free trade, it failed to indicate the mechanisms through which to achieve it. Over the course of this conference differences surfaced over the specifics of plans to liberalize trade and investments within the region. The proponents of rapid liberalization – Australia, Canada and the US – conflicted with those opposed, including China, Korea, Malaysia and Thailand. In addition, the non-binding investment code agreed by APEC governments was of limited scope.

The Osaka summit (November 1995) developed on the Bogor summit by agreeing to a 15-point 'Action Agenda' with implementation to begin in January 1997. Agreements were reached on key 'trade facilitation' issues including cutting tariffs, liberalizing services, public procurement and investment, harmonizing industrial standards; and customs harmonization and simplification. Member countries made individual commitments to liberalization.[2]

A number of stumbling blocks to the Osaka agreement (for example, the US inability to guarantee free market access to China on a MFN basis and the reluctance of China, Japan, Korea and Taiwan to liberalize such sensitive sectors as agriculture) point to certain limitations in creating a free trade area among very diverse economies at different stages of development.

Disparities in commitment to free trade were brought into sharp focus at the APEC Summit in the Philippines in November 1996. The US bid to obtain a free trade agreement in information technology (IT) (which represents an annual total of around US$500 billion and is expected to double by the end of the century) got a mixed reception among APEC members. The US hoped that an endorsement by APEC leaders would help achieve worldwide agreement at the WTO negotiations to be held the following month in Singapore. However, developing-country members of APEC – notably Malaysia, China, Indonesia and Chile – fear that their infant computer and telecommunications industries would not be able to survive competition from the established American and Japanese producers in a free trade environment. They also believe that advanced countries will gain disproportionately from such a free trade agreement due to their comparative advantage in information industries. The final APEC agreement was therefore watered down. It called for members to 'substantially eliminate' within three years tariffs on most IT products. This allows the developing economies to negotiate exceptions and delays to protect sensitive industries.

At the previous APEC summit in Osaka each country was expected to prepare individual action plans specifying how they intended to achieve the free trade targets by 2010–20 for presentation to the 1996 summit meeting. In addition, collective action plans to facilitate trade and investments in the region were to be prepared and submitted for approval in the Philippines. However, most members did not seem willing to go beyond commitments to measures already listed in the Uruguay Round agreement. The sensitive sectors of agricultural production, textiles and clothing continue to elude the free trade agenda.[3]

Intellectual property is another highly contentious issue that confronts APEC members. In May 1996, the US threatened China with trade sanctions over issues of copyright while the latter promised to retaliate. Such trade friction will likely dampen the trade and investment climate in the region.

There has been considerable discussion about extending APEC's role beyond a tariff-cutting exercise to promoting trade and economic co-operation in other ways. Examples cited by Elek (1992) include, information exchange about the pattern and trend of regional trade (APEC has already established an Electronic Data Interchange Project to facilitate exchange of trade documentation in the region), investment and tourism which would pinpoint the need for timely investments so as to avoid infrastructure bottlenecks; product labelling and environmental and safety standards; and the standardizing of customs documentation and clearance procedures. Additional proposals include improvements in transport and communications to reduce transaction costs, and a dispute settlement procedure. However, any form of supranational authority, such as a dispute settlement mechanism, tends to be resisted by the ASEAN group of countries. In any case, as the WTO already has a dispute settlement procedure, they believe a regional one to be unnecessary.

More delicate, but perhaps necessary, if APEC is to prove effective in promoting regional trade and investments in an increasingly competitive environment, is the need for regional harmonization both in investment rules and competition policies. The formulation of standardized investment rules would preclude the need for protracted bilateral negotiations concerning investments. Harmonization of competition policies would facilitate access to markets and reduce allegations of unfair competition.

The western developed countries, in particular Australia and the United States, are strong supporters of a free trade area within APEC since this would offer them the opportunity of expanding markets for their goods. They argue that tariff cuts under APEC could go further and faster than those under the GATT. Countries such as Japan and Thailand, on the other hand, would prefer to see the new WTO set the pace for trade liberalization (*The Economist*, 19 November 1994). They are acutely aware of selective liberalization which ignores certain forms of protectionism, such as anti-dumping practices or import quotas, pursued through regional arrangements outside the GATT. They therefore continue to be strong proponents of open regionalism for APEC. If APEC were to go the way of the NAFTA or the EU, both of which have tended to undermine GATT through their discriminatory trade practices (see Chapters 6 and 7), the resulting regional fragmentation of trade would usher in an era of trade conflicts and a breakdown in the GATT/WTO multilateral trading system.

In order to understand further the compulsion for APEC to remain

Table 5.2 Shares of APEC members in world trade (%)

	1980	*1985*	*1990*	*1995*
Australia	1.14	1.30	1.19	1.12
Canada	3.35	4.60	3.69	3.56
Japan	7.00	8.25	7.70	7.70
New Zealand	0.28	0.31	0.28	0.28
United States	12.43	15.33	13.41	13.40
Brunei	0.13	0.09	0.05	–
Chile	0.27	0.18	0.24	0.32
China	0.98	1.87	1.70	2.75
Hong Kong	1.09	1.61	2.42	3.63
Indonesia	0.85	0.78	0.70	0.85
Malaysia	0.61	0.75	0.87	1.50
Mexico	0.90	0.97	0.84	0.94
Papua New Guinea	0.06	0.05	0.03	0.04
Philippines	0.36	0.27	0.31	0.45
Republic of Korea	1.03	1.65	1.99	2.56
Singapore	1.12	1.32	1.68	2.40
Taiwan	1.02	1.36	1.80	2.12
Thailand	0.41	0.44	0.83	1.25
Total APEC	33.03	41.13	39.73	44.87

Source: Our estimates based on IMF, *International Financial Statistics Yearbook*, 1995; and IMF, *International Financial Statistics*, November, 1996.

– = not available.

an open regional grouping, it is necessary to examine the trade and investment patterns in the region as well as the significant roles and activities of multinationals there.

TRADE PATTERNS IN THE ASIA PACIFIC REGION

The APEC countries accounted for nearly 45 per cent of total world trade in 1995, up from 33 per cent in 1980 and about 40 per cent in 1990. However,the largest share of this increase is due to a dramatic growth in world trade of the Asian NIEs and China, which more than doubled between 1980 and 1995 (see Table 5.2).

In particular, China's market-oriented reforms have opened it up to trade and investments. Its use of Hong Kong as an entrepôt (just as ASEAN countries have used Singapore as an entrepôt causing it to become the hub of ASEAN intraregional trade), could account largely for the dramatic increase in the NIEs' share of trade with that country which almost doubled, from 26.3 per cent in 1980 to 50.4 per cent in 1991. China and Hong Kong have become each other's most important trading partners although Hong Kong serves as the transit point for considerable trade flows to China from third countries or areas, notably Taiwan. In 1992, Hong Kong accounted for 43.5 per cent of China's exports and 25 per cent of its imports, the bulk of which represented entrepôt trade, while 33.2 per cent of Hong Kong's exports and 40.5 per cent of its imports were with China (Chia, 1994).

As we noted in Chapter 2 (see Table 2.3) the two most important groupings indicating high intraregional trade are APEC and the EC-12. Other economic groupings tend to trade more with non-members than with members. The share of intra-APEC trade in the region's total trade has grown from 53 per cent in 1980 to over 64 per cent in 1991 compared with the EC-12 whose share of intraregional trade in its total trade was almost 56 per cent in 1980 and about 61.4 per cent in 1991 (see Chapter 2, Table 2.3). Since then the figure has exceeded 70 per cent.

Intraregional trade among ASEAN members has not increased significantly (as we noted in Chapter 4) contrary to trends in trade between NAFTA countries (see Chapter 6). This would suggest that, apart from the intra-East Asian trade, stronger trade linkages among NAFTA countries (which are also members of APEC) may account for a significant increase in APEC's intraregional trade.

The high intensities of trade between ASEAN and the NIEs and Japan on the west side of the Pacific and between Canada and the US on the eastern side are due to proximity, familiarity, institutional arrangements and factors such as trade-linked investments and aid flows, as well as to complementarity.

Besides the increasing complementarity amongst the various economies and sub-regional blocs (that is, the NIEs and ASEAN) other factors promoting intraregional trade flows include: rapid economic growth, particularly in Japan and the NIEs which has generated high rates of consumption and high demands for investments; the appreciation of the *yen* and NIE currencies, leading to increasing regional specialization in production; in recent years growing signs of protectionism within the EC and sluggish growth in the economies of EC member countries; and policy reforms aimed at deregulation and liberalization, most recently in the developing but rapidly growing economies of China, Korea, Taiwan, Vietnam and ASEAN (excluding Singapore which has always had a liberal trade regime).

In Chapter 4, we noted how comparative advantage has changed both the composition and direction of trade in the region. This has created a 'triangular' pattern of trade. Japan has tended to export its capital goods mainly to the US, Western Europe, the Asian NIEs and ASEAN but its source of imports are mainly from the two latter groups. Similarly, the developing economies of the region, including the Asian NIEs, ASEAN and more recently, China, have been importing capital and intermediate goods and components from Japan and from each other to produce manufactures for the North American and West European markets.

This trend has resulted in huge trade imbalances. Japan's ability to maintain a competitive manufacturing edge largely through its FDI policies and the activities of its multinationals within the region has resulted in its experiencing persistent trade surpluses with its trading partners, which peaked to US$107 billion in 1992 (Chia 1994).[4] These huge trade imbalances, have become a growing source of friction, particularly between the two leading economies, the US and Japan. The Asian NIEs have been seeking new markets, particularly in the East Asian region, in order to reduce their dependence on the US and West European markets. The corresponding reduction of their surpluses with the US, has to some extent, enabled them to avoid the kind of trade friction that continues to plague Japan-US trade relations.

However, the US market continues to remain an extremely important one for the East Asian NIEs' exports as demonstrated by some policy simulations based on the world economy model of the Economic Institute of the Economic Planning Agency of Japan. According to these simulations, if the US were to reduce its fiscal expenditure by 1 per cent of its GNP every year over a three-year period, the resulting decline in US demand would cause a decline in import demand and 'a 4.5 per cent GNP decline in real terms in the particularly export-dependent NIEs, namely South Korea' (Watanabe, 1991). Despite the US trade deficits with Japan and the NIEs, it still has a large share of these markets for manufactures – its market share in Japan is nearly 30 per cent and in other East Asian countries it is 15.6 per cent (Petri, 1994a). It also shows a strong relative performance there compared with its performance in other parts of the world.

In the case of Australia, over 60 per cent of its merchandise trade until the early fifties was with western Europe and mainly the United Kingdom. Over the next 40 years this gradually declined, first in favour of the US, but then increasingly in favour of Japan. Japan's rapid growth and the high complementarity between Australia's resource rich economy and Japan's resource-poor but highly industrialized economy enabled trade expansion between the two countries. Japan became Australia's major trading partner throughout the seventies and eighties, a role it relinquished to the Asian NIEs by the early nineties. As export markets, the Asian NIEs became even more important for Australia than the US and the European Union combined. Australia's trade with the four major Northeast Asian economies rose by over 300 per cent in just a little over two decades (Hill, 1994). High growth in ASEAN countries and China have also stimulated trade with Australia in recent years to the extent that by the early nineties, ASEAN had become a more important export market for Australia than either the US or the EU.

REGIONALIZATION/GLOBALIZATION OF INVESTMENTS

Traditionally Japan and the United States have been the largest sources of FDI in the APEC region, especially in East Asia, each providing almost 30 per cent in the NIEs (Flatters and Harris, 1994). On the whole, the US has more investments than Japan in Indonesia and Korea while Japan has gained over the US in Hong Kong and Thailand. Notwithstanding the recent surge of East Asian investments within their own region, the US remains an important investor there.

In the pre-1960 period, FDI was linked to resource exploitation; in the sixties and seventies, as many economies in the region tended to pursue import-substitution strategies, FDI served to promote manufactures linked to these strategies partly to gain access to local protected markets. It shifted to manufactures for export by the eighties particularly after the 1986 appreciation of the *yen* forced Japanese firms to go offshore to the developing economies of East Asia for production in order to maintain their competitiveness.

Of Japan's investments in developing countries, 90 per cent flowed to Asian NIEs and ASEAN. However, more recently, China, India and Vietnam are also beginning to attract Japanese investors. Japan's investments in the NIEs were largely in manufactures such as chemicals, electronics and electrical goods, while in Hong Kong and Singapore they tended to be in the service sectors including finance and commerce. In the ASEAN-4 (that is, excluding Brunei and Singapore), they were aimed at natural resource exploitation to secure supplies and then at labour-intensive operations in electronics and electrical goods production, chemicals and textiles, and more recently, in automobiles and their parts (as ASEAN protectionism prevents imports of automobiles, investments are one way of gaining entry into this growing market), in order to capitalise on lower production costs.

The surge of Japanese investments overtook US investments which had traditionally been the highest in the region. More recently, the sluggish performance of the US and West European economies has led Japan and the Asian NIEs to further diversify their investments into ASEAN and China and other developing countries. In fact, the NIEs are emerging as major investors within ASEAN – in 1991 they contributed nearly 28 per cent compared with 20 per cent by Japan and over 10 per cent by the US (Flatters and Harris, 1994, p. 127).

FDI by the Asian NIEs in the developing countries' textile manufactures has largely been motivated by the desire to take advantage of the latter's MFA textile quotas and benefits under the Generalized System of Preferences (GSP) to which they themselves are no longer entitled. More recently with rising labour costs in some ASEAN countries, investments are shifting to lower-cost locations in China, India, Vietnam and the Philippines. At the same time, Asian NIEs are attracting FDI into high-tech industries and processes as well as service activities, such as finance, commerce, tourism and infrastructural development.

As noted in Chapter 4, FDI has played a pivotal role in the export-led industrialization of the East Asian economies, particularly in the ASEAN countries, through technology transfer and upgrading of industrial production. These countries have offered a variety of incentives to attract foreign direct investment into export-oriented manufactures while at the same time assuring that the investing multinational enterprises do not compete against domestic infant industries (Okamoto, 1995). Conditions that have attracted FDI inflows into the Asian NIEs and ASEAN, and more recently, into China and Vietnam include: opening up of the economies with growing liberalization in trade and investment rules, low labour costs in manufactures, export-oriented industrialization, rapid growth and therefore growing demand in the domestic markets, made all the more attractive as they enjoy certain degrees of protection from external competition, for example, the automobile industry. Policies aimed at attracting FDI include: relaxation of restrictions on foreign ownership, investment and tax incentives, exemptions from import duties, the creation of industrial parks and export-processing zones with a well-developed infrastructure. Deregulation and privatization policies are also being pursued aggressively by countries of the region in a further bid to compete for FDI.

China has been one of the most successful APEC members in attracting FDI inflows which tripled between 1992 and 1994, and reached

US$38 billion in 1995 (UNCTAD, 1995a, p. 54 and UNCTAD, 1996, p. 53). Foreign affiliates are known to have become a major channel for Chinese trade, particularly in labour-intensive manufacturing exports.

A major feature of intraregional FDI is Hong Kong's pivotal role in directing investments into China – as much as US$25.1 billion. In 1992 investments from Hong Kong represented 63 per cent of China's inward FDI, much of it constituting Taiwanese or Western investments (Petri, 1995). Hong Kong's importance as an FDI source will likely diminish as China becomes more open and accessible to other countries. Another 'tiger economy', Singapore is a major investor as well as recipient of FDI, accounting for 14.2 per cent of FDI to developing countries and 23.7 per cent of FDI flows to NIEs of East Asia. It was the largest recipient of FDI among non-OECD countries during 1987–91 (Chia, 1994). Initially, other main beneficiaries of FDI were Thailand and Malaysia but by 1991, investor interest shifted towards Indonesia and the Philippines.

Rapid growth in Japanese and East Asian FDI into the US has added a new dimension to trans-Pacific economic linkages. Japan and the NIEs have increasingly directed investments in manufacturing towards the US (and Japan to the EC) in order to overcome potential trade barriers. For example, North America (mainly the US) was a recipient of as much as 60.5 per cent of Taiwan's FDI and 43.8 per cent of Korea's between 1987 and 1989 (Petri, 1994a). This is motivated by the need to diversify their assets, penetrate the US market to find a way around potential protectionist measures and gain access to technology. In 1985, 44 per cent of Japan's FDI went to the US compared with 11.6 per cent to South and East Asia; whereas in 1994, the figures were 42 per cent and 23.6 per cent respectively (OECD, 1996).

Multinationals and Regional Integration

Structural adjustment throughout the Pacific region has been an ongoing process with manufacturing industries shifting successively from lower to higher levels of production first in Japan and the United States followed by the Asian NIEs and then ASEAN and more recently China and Vietnam. The region's firms adopted global production strategies through extensive intra-firm division of labour. Two types of enterprises have promoted industrial transfer: local enterprises in the developing countries which have received industrial and technology transfer, and multinational enterprises in the developed countries which are the sources of industrial transfer. Unlike textile and steel production which tends to be locally driven, multinationals tend to play a more important role in chemical, electrical and electronic industries as they are more dependent on FDI and technology upgrading and transfer. Further, if there is a limited domestic market for these products, these industries are export driven and therefore more heavily reliant on the marketing networks and skills of the MNEs (Yamazawa, 1992). Through FDI, receiving firms in host countries gain access to foreign firms' marketing networks and to their networks of supplies for the purchase of capital and intermediate goods for production.

In their bid to remain competitive following the appreciation of the *yen*, Japanese firms in the latter half of the eighties had to adopt simultaneous strategies of globalization, rationalization and diversification of production (Urata, 1993). They resorted to offshore production in the NIEs and ASEAN for a number of electrical and electronics goods such as televisions. These firms have been responsible for providing large employment in the host countries and there is evidence of a high export propensity of foreign firms. The share of exports by multinationals in the total exports of some of the East Asian countries in the latter half of the eighties and early nineties is revealing: Hong Kong (24 per cent), Indonesia (22 per cent), Korea (29 per cent), Malaysia (57 per cent), the Philippines (34.7 per cent), Singapore (91 per cent) and Taiwan (17 per cent) (Urata, 1993; Ramstetter, 1994). The magnitude of sales and procurement by Asian affiliates of Japanese manufacturing firms appears to have increased substantially during the eighties. The share of exports in total sales of the affiliates remained roughly the same throughout the eighties at 36 per cent, increasing to 40 per cent in 1990 (Urata, 1993). Japan absorbed a larger share of these sales, particularly in electrical machinery, but also in textiles, nonferrous metals and machinery.

In sum, the expanding trade and investment linkages within the Asia Pacific region have developed more out of private-sector initiatives responding to market forces, than out of any formal institutional arrangements. Comparative advantage and market access factors have forced multinationals to go offshore for various stages in the production process in order to diversify risks, minimize costs and maximize performance. This has led to regional specialization as is evident by increasing intra-firm trade within the region.

It is true that governments have played a facilitating role through regulations that encourage trade promotion and economic liberalization and, in the case of the ASEAN countries, promoting stability and forcing the pace of liberalization and cooperation through, albeit, not very successful institutional measures. But such measures have at least provided a framework for the inevitable structural adjustments that member countries need to undertake in the face of growing pressures to liberalise their economies in order to sustain their trade and investment linkages in the future.

Thus trade and investment in the region have progressed in an upward spiral. Increased trade linkages have promoted intraregional FDI and this in turn has boosted trade. Ahmad, Rao and Barnes (1996) show that a 10 per cent increase in total direct investment stock increases trade flows by 6 per cent a year among APEC member economies. Through their diffusion of new technologies and skills, multinationals have enabled expansion of exports into advanced industrial economies. For example, some companies that control Japanese markets can now import into Japan from their subsidiaries abroad. The APEC region thus represents dynamic linkages at different levels: through trans-Pacific, intra-East Asian and North American integration.

A PACIFIC FREE TRADE AREA (PAFTA)?

There are some concerns that if APEC were to develop into a Pacific Free Trade Area, trade discrimination against non-member countries would result in trade diversion from the rest of the world. This is likely to create interregional rivalries, provoke retaliatory protectionist tendencies by the EC and other excluded regions and countries and thereby undermine the multilateral trade liberalization process advanced by GATT/WTO. However, a PAFTA seems improbable for the following reasons:

- Too many countries on the Pacific rim, including the US, Japan and the East Asian NIEs have important extraregional trade and investment linkages which they would not want to risk compromising by adherence to a discriminatory free trade arrangement;
- US interests in Latin American countries are likely to lead to demands from a PAFTA for special arrangements and exceptions to accommodate these interests. These would weaken PAFTA while antagonising those excluded from any form of preferential treatment;
- Many policy-makers in the US fear that a free trade agreement would not change many of the invisible barriers such as government policies and business procurement practices, raised by countries like Japan and Korea which block international trade and investment in the

region. They fear that those with high informal barriers would gain at the expense of the more open trading countries. Frequent bilateral trade disputes between the US and Japan and the US and China, due partly to serious trade imbalances (both China and Japan have large trade surpluses with the US) have caused US policy-makers to reconsider their support for the concept of unconditional and free trade. (Drysdale and Garnaut, 1989, 1993).

- The diversity of size, economy, structure, factor endowments, technology, and firm behaviour suggests that what appears a beneficial policy for one country may not be so for another. In fact, similar policies could have very different effects from one country to another. This makes some APEC members wary of the inevitable inequitable gains which would accrue from a free trade arrangement, with the stronger economies likely to benefit the most. However, according to a study by Martin *et al.* (1994), most of the gains from Pacific-wide liberalization would accrue to China and the ASEAN economies (that is, those with the highest initial level of protection) and the United States would actually be worse off.[5]
- Given the different levels of economic development of the APEC countries, any Pacific-wide free trade area would necessitate a series of special arrangements to accommodate some of the developing economies. Such arrangements, combined with trade imbalances, risk exacerbating existing tensions in relations with the developed-country partners;
- The removal of trade restrictions would require wide intersectoral adjustments which would meet with considerable political resistance in many member countries. Strong vested interests have long been used to protection which they are unlikely to give up (as is indeed shown by the experience of the European Union with its Common Agricultural Policy discussed in Chapter 7). Developing countries would seek continued protection for their infant industries; countries such as China, Malaysia, Thailand and the Philippines with a number of infant industries necessary for industrialization are reluctant to lower barriers quickly. Even US textile producers will resist lowering of protective barriers;
- It is hard to imagine the diverse economic and political systems within the APEC region subscribing to a supranational authority or binding agreements which a discriminatory free trade area would necessitate;
- China, a growing economic force in the region, and other developing countries in the Pacific, are unlikely to be prepared to implement

trade liberalization programmes on the scale which a free trade area would necessitate. ASEAN countries' difficulties in implementing AFTA and their slow pace of tariff reductions despite AFTA is evidence of this (see Chapter 4). However, to exclude China and some of these other developing countries from PAFTA would not only stall their economic growth, but in doing so, would also reduce their ability to liberalize their trade and investment policies. This would have a considerably negative impact on the present momentum of regional growth and integration, and reduce the opportunities for increasingly profitable intra-Pacific trade. Even assuming that China continues rapid economic growth despite exclusion from PAFTA, the free trade area without an economically strong China would be the loser in the long term. Similarly, the exclusion of the ASEAN bloc of countries which have developed strong complementary trade and investment relationships with other countries in the region, would reduce the impact of a free trade area;
- PAFTA would weaken its members' ability to respond to new markets outside the region, especially the emerging markets of the Eastern European countries. These markets are of little significance to the Asian economies at present, but they represent a huge potential market both for trade and outward investments
- The region's economic institutions cover a wide range from legalistic market systems to oligarchic and highly bureaucratised or interventionist systems. It is unlikely that such differences could be overcome rapidly enough to eliminate all internal barriers which GATT requires of a free trade area.

Given all these considerations, it seems unlikely that APEC trade liberalization would eventually lead to the formation of another regional bloc like the European Union or NAFTA. However, whether APEC evolves in the spirit of multilateralism will depend on how regional trade liberalization is achieved. The protagonists of open regionalism within APEC have proposed the following three-stage approach towards trade liberalization:

(i) in the first stage, unilateral trade liberalization will be carried out by the APEC members;
(ii) in the second stage, APEC as a group will reduce its trade barriers to outsiders;
(iii) in the final stage, APEC should treat non-members in the same way as members, provided non-members make similar concessions

as APEC's members (the US position), that is, on a reciprocal basis. The East Asian position does not insist on the condition of reciprocity.

The US condition of reciprocity is aimed at avoiding 'free riders' who would benefit from APEC regional trade liberalization without offering APEC members similar benefits. The East Asians, however, believe that if a Pacific free trade area were to remain open and non-discriminatory, it would have the effect of accelerating movement towards trade liberalization on a MFN basis (that is not discriminating against non-APEC countries). Countries both within and outside the region would then compete to provide the best possible conditions for promoting trade and investment opportunities, thereby promoting WTO goals.

On the other hand, it can equally well be argued that the condition of reciprocity could serve as a bargaining chip with the European Union and other groupings to lower their protective barriers. It could thus put pressure on non-members to liberalize.

In principle, free trade within the APEC region should expand markets for American goods, particularly, automobiles, in the region. Tariffs imposed by the East Asian countries are some of the highest for import of automobiles. In the past, tariff and non-tariff barriers have been kept high in order to expand domestic industries under import substitution. Trade liberalization within the region will require these countries to lower such tariff barriers. Although tariff barriers in general are being lowered in a number of countries they remain high and it will take several years before a zero-tariff regime is adopted.

CHALLENGES AND PROSPECTS

The future evolution of APEC and whether it detracts from or contributes to the process of trade multilateralism, will depend to a large degree on the manner of implementation of the Uruguay Round accord. It will also depend on the direction taken by the expanded European Union (since January 1995 it consists of 15 members and many more countries are hoping to join). There is a danger that the Single European Market's trade preferences to EFTA and Eastern European countries will divert trade from East Asia (see Young, 1993a and Chapter 7). The trade conflict between APEC's two most powerful members, Japan and the United States, has cast a shadow on trade and investment relations within the region as has the US threat of trade sanctions against

China owing to its failure to observe intellectual property rights. With the Republican majority in both houses of Congress in the US, growing protectionism by NAFTA cannot be ruled out (see Chapter 6).

In this case, the APEC's East Asian economies might well threaten retaliation by the creation of an inward-looking regional bloc composed of the NIEs, ASEAN, Japan and China. China and Malaysia have been pushing for an East Asian grouping but in the face of US objections, their proposal has been reduced to an East Asian Economic Caucus (EAEC) which has formal status as a Standing Committee of APEC. While Japan alone would not be in a position to compensate in terms of market size and investments for the loss of a US market, an East Asian grouping would be able to turn to China's big potential market as an obvious attraction. The growing markets of the Indian sub-continent and of the former Soviet Union could also offer increasing possibilities for trade expansion.

There seems little chance of a successful Asian regional grouping without the participation of Japan. But at present, Japan does not regard regionalism as the only or the best way to achieve global multilateralism; and many in ASEAN fear Japanese domination without the US to provide a counterbalance. At present, therefore, a Japan-centred regional bloc is not seen as necessary or even desirable (Hodder, 1994). Since approval of the Uruguay Round accord Japan has favoured global as opposed to regional liberalization and favours the more open regionalism of APEC as contributing to this process. Nevertheless, the threat of East Asian counter-protectionism could well deter NAFTA from becoming protectionist.

APEC has deliberately chosen a flexible form of cooperation in order to accommodate the vastly different economies of the Pacific rim. The challenge for the APEC process in the years to come will be to sustain the momentum of trade and investments in the region by assuring that the different economies of the region implement the goals set in Bogor and Osaka. It remains to be seen whether APEC's flexibility and the absence of institutional arrangements will promote or inhibit the achievement of these goals.

Unlike NAFTA or the EC, APEC's agreements are implemented on a voluntary, non-binding basis. The APEC style of consensus-building through extensive dialogue and gradual evolution modelled on the ASEAN's approach has so far been the only way to progress for as disparate a group of nations as those within APEC. In this way, it has succeeded in avoiding the often rancorous, confrontational negotiations that characterize some of the EU agreements. The growing antagonism towards the Brussels bureaucracy by the constituents in the EC countries serves as a lesson against a top-down approach. APEC countries are determined to liberalize at their own pace without being pressured and only when they are politically and economically ready for the inevitable structural adjustments involved in trade liberalization. This voluntary process may result in slow progress, but it is steady progress and for that reason might prove less destabilising and more enduring.

Under APEC's flexible approach, it is possible for some members to enter into cooperative agreements faster than others. Drysdale and Elek (1995) suggest some countries may be ready to adopt compatible standards for accounting, disclosure and auditing based on mutually acceptable criteria with each government responsible for monitoring adherence to their own domestic standards. The potential gains from participating in this form of cooperation, namely additional investments and integration of production processes, would provide the incentives for enforcement at a national level without the need for a supranational body to monitor and enforce compliance. And the demonstration effects of such gains would encourage others to join. In order for this to be possible, such cooperation would have to be transparent and without discrimination among firms by location or ownership.

The absence of institutional arrangements makes the APEC process slow but even a forum is better than no arrangement at all as it helps to accelerate cooperation in many ways:

- The collective process of liberalization enables some governments to overcome narrow vested interests through 'peer pressure'. If many governments present commitments to liberalize and these are widely publicised in the region, the more reluctant members are fearful of being left behind, particularly if agreements on targets and guiding principles are announced in joint declarations (even if such declarations have no binding effect); however, the converse is also possible, namely, that if some members slow down in their commitments to liberalization as indeed appeared to be the mood at the Philippines Summit in 1996, others might also be encouraged to follow suit;
- Demonstrable gains from certain policies resisted by vested interests in other countries, make it easier for the latter to appeal to public opinion over resistance by these interests;
- It has been demonstrated (Drysdale and Elek, 1995 and Drysdale and Garnaut, 1994) that while deregulation and market opening benefits most those economies that are implementing them, they also bring benefits to other economies linked to them – a process described by

Drysdale and Garnaut as a game of 'prisoner's delight'. Thus, all the Asia Pacific economies gain in terms of income growth and employment when reforms are undertaken by a few of them. This improves their capacities and willingness to accept structural adjustments in their own strategies. This process thus generates a momentum of its own.

By allowing for the fact that integration will take place more rapidly in some trading relationships and sub-regions than in others, APEC manages to accommodate different sub-regional arrangements such as ASEAN, NAFTA, the CER Agreement between Australia and New Zealand or the sub-regional growth triangles that are rapidly developing between neighbouring countries within the region. The ways in which these sub-regional arrangements evolve will have a direct impact on the future of APEC. They could either serve as building blocks to promote integration on a small scale before extending it to a Pacific-wide scale or they could fragment regional relationships.

A discouraging sign is the development of discriminatory trade practices by NAFTA and the USA's growing tendency to forge bilateral trading arrangements which imply preferences. These run counter to APEC's underlying principle of non-discrimination and could threaten to damage its prospects as a cohesive group. The mushrooming growth triangles in China, Hong Kong, Taiwan and some of the ASEAN countries also involve preferential arrangements which could further fragment economic cooperation in the region, the very tendency which APEC aims to counter. On the other hand, it can be argued that growth triangles are a first step in promoting integration. By effecting integration on a small scale with the resultant improvement in industrial competitiveness, they enhance the capabilities of the participating countries to take part in a wider regional integration process.

APEC *VIS-À-VIS* THE URUGUAY ROUND

APEC open regionalism attempts to reconcile the two apparently contradictory notions of regionalism versus global trade within the framework of the Uruguay Round accord (Aggarwal, 1993). As all non-member countries are eligible for APEC's most favoured-nation-status, and as all members follow export-oriented policies, the grouping does not follow rigidly the principle of reciprocity. On the other hand, in the case of the Uruguay Round accord, the members exchange trade concessions on a directly reciprocal basis. The Uruguay Round also provides safeguards: these involve restrictions to trade under specific cases of actual or potential damage to markets for products of a particular country. At present there are no such safeguards provided under APEC. But as Aggarwal (1993) notes, this may simply be because of 'the nascent character of (the APEC) regime'. As many members of APEC have been known for unilateral government interventions which have affected trading patterns, there is a possibility that they might tend to press for safeguards and restrictions in a more institutionalized APEC.

A factor that is likely to ensure compatibility between APEC and the world trading system under WTO is APEC members' contribution to growth in world trade. Trade relations among the Pacific rim economies are so inextricably linked that it is in their mutual interests to maintain and encourage a *free and open* trading system that concentrates not merely on trade liberalization, but also on the removal of invisible barriers to market access. For example, there would be serious consequences for FDI throughout East Asia if a US–Japan trade war occurred. Restrictions by the US on imports from Japan could affect Japanese MNEs with offshore production facilities throughout East Asia and thus on Japanese investments in those plants. Thus a practical approach to further APEC trade facilitation would be to select sectors where a majority of APEC members are interested in further liberalization and willing to apply this to non-members on an unconditional MFN basis. Priority areas concern trade-related investment measures (TRIMs), trade-related intellectual property rights (TRIPs), and services, all of which could not be covered by the Uruguay Round negotiations owing to lack of time. Successful liberalization in these areas would increase momentum for further liberalization thus improving prospects for multilateral agreements in these areas under WTO. As FDI has been a leading mechanism behind the rapid growth of APEC countries, they seem predisposed to concluding an Asia Pacific Investment Code which would go beyond the mere framework agreement reached during the Uruguay Round negotiations. Such an Investment Code would best fit open regionalism as it is in the interests of host governments to provide the best conditions for investment both by member and non-member firms (Yamazawa, 1994).[6]

6 The Americas: NAFTA and MERCOSUR

The North American Free Trade Area (NAFTA) consisting of Canada, Mexico and the United States, which came into effect in January 1994, is the first developed–developing country or rich–poor trade arrangement. In South America, MERCOSUR, the Common Market of Argentina, Brazil, Paraguay and Uruguay is also a grouping of unequal partners, but with nothing like the different levels of economic development found among members of NAFTA (Table 6.1 shows the vast differences in GDP per capita of the members); none of the MERCOSUR economies is industrialized. The per capita GNP and population data in Table 6.1 suggest that NAFTA is one of the biggest free trade areas in the world. The United States is clearly the richest and the largest of the three members. Between 1970 and 1990, all three members have, however, grown significantly in terms of absolute GNP and GNP per capita.

In this Chapter, we discuss the motivations behind the creation of NAFTA and MERCOSUR, the likely impact of these two groupings in terms of intra-bloc trade creation, trade and investment diversion, and multinationals' strategies in response to regional integration. The scope for a Western Hemisphere integration arrangement is also examined since such integration could affect multilateralism by diverting trade and investment.

NORTH AMERICAN FREE TRADE AREA (NAFTA)

The creation of NAFTA aroused passionate debate particularly in the US. And such an agreement would have been unthinkable in Mexico, or for that mattter, in any South American country, even a decade ago. Despite considerable opposition, a number of factors prompted NAFTA's creation:

(i) The emergence of an enlarged European Union with rising protective barriers threatening to make it into a 'fortress Europe',

Table 6.1 Basic economic indicators of NAFTA and MERCOSUR members

Grouping/ Country	*Per capita GNP (US$) (1994)*	*GNP per capita average annual growth (1985–94) (%)*	*Population (mid-1994) (millions)*	*Share of industry in GDP (%) (1995)*	*Export to GDP ratio (%) (1995)*	*Import to GDP ratio (%) (1995)*	*Share in world exports (%) (1995)*	*Share in world imports (%) (1995)*
NAFTA								
United States	25,880	1.3	260.6	–	11.1	12.4	11.6	15.1
Canada	19,510	0.3	29.2	32[1]	37.4	34.9	3.8	3.3
Mexico	4,180	0.9	88.5	28	24.0	21.1	0.9	1.1
MERCOSUR								
Argentina	8,110	2.0	34.2	30	6.7[2]	9.2[2]	2.4	0.4
Brazil	2,970	−0.4	159.0	39	8.4[2]	7.3[2]	0.9	1.0
Paraguay	1,580	1.0	4.8	22	34.8	51.2	0.02[2]	0.04[2]
Uruguay	4,660	2.9	3.2	23	19.4	19.4	0.04	0.06

Sources: Exports and imports data are from IMF, *International Financial Statistics*, Nov. 1996. GNP, population and share of industry data are from World Bank, *World Development Report*, 1996.

[1] = 1993; [2] = 1994; – = not available

and regional integration in Asia inevitably drew a North American response (see Grinspun and Cameron, 1993; Hufbauer and Schott, 1993).

(ii) The existing high level of trade between the United States and Mexico prior to the agreement and the view that the agreement would legitimise the illegal cross-border smuggling of goods, facilitated negotiations on NAFTA.

(iii) A major 'social' consideration concerned Mexico's proximity to the United States and a vague hope that a regional arrangement would help stem illegal immigration into the US.

(iv) Canada was concerned that a separate agreement between the US and Mexico would adversely affect its exports and it might become less attractive for FDI. Reducing dependence on the US market and increasing trade with Latin America were other reasons for Canada to participate in the creation of NAFTA (See Lipsey, Schwanen and Wonnacott, 1994[1] and Lipsey and Meller, 1997).

(v) Mexico was similarly concerned that CUSFTA would hurt its exports to the US and that FDI might be diverted away from Mexico as a result of CUSFTA, the SEM and the opening up of Eastern Europe (see Gestrin and Waverman, 1994).

(vi) Mexico's trade liberalization policies in the eighties and early nineties (preconditions for starting negotiations with the US) encouraged it to participate in NAFTA to guarantee access to the US market. All the more so as the US had been resorting to increasing use of protectionist measures such as anti-dumping measures and countervailing duties (see Waverman, 1994).

The NAFTA builds on the Canada-US Free Trade Agreement (CUSFTA) which came into effect on 1 January 1989. It is therefore useful to examine the CUSFTA provisions and their impact. CUSFTA serves to consolidate the traditionally close links between the two geographically contiguous economies of the United States and Canada. It aims to remove all tariffs between the two countries over a ten-year period. Other elements of the CUSFTA include: removal of some non-tariff barriers, but others concerning textiles, beer and agricultural products remain in place; the right of establishment of service industries in each other's country; allowing for cross-border bids for government procurement of some items; allowing of temporary access to paid employment, for a period of two years for some categories of occupations; liberalization of investment; and the establishment of a Dispute

Settlement Mechanism to review anti-dumping and countervailing duties imposed under each country's domestic laws.

Since the implementation of the CUSFTA, trade between the US and Canada has increased. It is estimated that between 1988 and 1993, Canadian exports to the US rose 45 per cent while during the same period exports to other destinations fell: to Europe by 2.2 per cent, to Japan by 3.9 per cent and to Southeast Asia, by 11 per cent (see Lipsey, 1995; Schwanen, 1994). Furthermore, and contrary to public expectations, the gains in exports to the US were concentrated in high value-added manufactures rather than in resource industries, despite the high value of the Canadian dollar and a sluggish US economy at that time.[2] It is not clear to what extent the above increase was in the form of intra-firm and inter-firm trade. As intra-firm trade between Canada and the US is quite significant (see Eden, 1994; Seebach, 1993), trade expansion could simply be the result of restructuring of production on a continental basis. It is likely that such restructuring was made possible by the liberalization of foreign investment rules (see below).

The impact of CUSFTA, particularly on Canada also reflects, to some extent, the short-term impact of the wider NAFTA in terms of trade creation/diversion and employment. As industry begins to respond to the trilateral free trade provisions, dislocations caused by inter-industry adjustments and massive plant closures call for policies to reinforce competitiveness by encouraging industrial investment, productivity gains, wage restraints and other intra-industrial measures. So far this has not been happening and Canada is paying the price with continuing job losses. Since the advent of the CUSFTA, Canada has lost 18 per cent of its manufacturing jobs while the rest of the economy experiences net job losses of only 2.9 per cent. It is difficult to estimate how much of these job losses are due to the FTA. Several other factors have also been at work: the economic recession, high interest rates and the resulting appreciation of the Canadian dollar, global restructuring and relocation of industry and technological change, for example (see Lipsey, 1995).

Mexico, like Canada, has strong trade links with the United States. Beginning in 1984, Mexico started introducing import-liberalization measures by relaxing import-licensing requirements and by reducing tariffs. Between 1982 and 1990, the import tariff coverage was reduced to only a few items and the import license coverage (as percentage of import value) was reduced from 100 per cent in 1982 to only 18 per cent in 1990. Apart from import liberalization, the Mexican government also placed much greater emphasis on export promotion, competitiveness and modernization of technology and liberalization of foreign investment. The poor performance of its non-oil exports in the first half of the eighties was a major reason for this shift in industrial and export policies.

Vested interests in the US (and for that matter, in Canada and Mexico) opposed a free trade arrangement, mainly on social and economic grounds (see Hufbauer and Schott, 1993; McConnell and MacPherson, 1994). A major concern was the effects on income and employment of free trade with a country where wages average about one-eighth of those in the US. Unions feared that some labour-intensive industries and hence jobs might shift to Mexico. The worst affected in the US and Canada would be low-skilled workers. In conditions of free trade and open competition, lower wages in Mexico might depress wages and living standards in the other two rich members. Also, NAFTA detractors feared that Mexican health and safety standards and use of child labour would put them at a competitive disadvantage. Environmentalists argued that increased industrialization in Mexico and its lower environmental standards would cause environmental damage.

There is no clear agreement on the likely employment and wage effects of the formation of NAFTA. Hufbauer and Schott (1993, p. 21) note that 'based on the 1990 composition of trade, the median weekly wage associated with US exports to Mexico and US imports from Mexico were practically the same: about US$420 to $425 per week'. They therefore conclude that Mexican exports to the US are unlikely to displace low-skilled US jobs.

Of course, there is no doubt that any trade liberalization scheme, which leads to increasing competition, necessitates industrial restructuring involving job gains and job losses depending on which industries decline, shut down or relocate and which ones expand. It may well be that in the short run, especially in conditions of slow economic growth, jobs lost might be greater than the jobs created. In the long run, higher rates of growth are likely to compensate for the adverse effects on employment of industrial restructuring and rapid increases in labour productivity.[3]

The US is likely to enjoy long-term, if not short-term, gains of a free trade agreement with Mexico. Mexico is a substantial market for US merchandise exports, the third largest after Canada and Japan and a positive correlation is shown to exist between growth in Mexican GDP and growth in US exports to that country (see Weintraub, 1992).[4] It is therefore in US interests to help boost Mexican growth which a free-trade agreement could accomplish. Another reason why a NAFTA makes sense from the point of view of the US, is that its suppliers dominate Mexican and Canadian imports. Increased US imports from these two countries are likely to result in a reciprocal increase in US exports to them.[5] US interest in securing political stability in Mexico and in the region as a whole may also have provided a strong motivation for it to support NAFTA.

Objectives and Content

The NAFTA's objectives, according to Article 102 of the text of the Agreement include: elimination of trade barriers and facilitating of cross-border movement of goods and services among the member countries leading to the establishment of a free trade area; promotion of fair competition; promotion of investment opportunities in the member countries; provision of adequate and effective protection and enforcement of intellectual property rights; establishment of a framework for further trilateral, regional and multilateral cooperation to expand and enhance the benefits of the Agreement.

The NAFTA accord covers the main instrument of the Agreement and two supplemental or side agreements on labour and environment. According to the main agreement, within ten to 15 years all customs duties will be abolished among the three member countries, thus leading to the creation of a free trade area. No common external tariff has been agreed to for non-members and the members will continue to maintain an independent trade policy.

However, the inclusion of 'rules of origin' in the Agreement, which are quite stringent, implies some discrimination against third parties. For example, special rules of origin apply to such goods as garments, textiles, automobiles and certain agricultural products. For other goods, the local content requirement is either 50 per cent of the net cost or 60 per cent of the transaction value originating in North America (see Lipsey, Schwanen and Wonnacott, 1994). Apart from discriminating against non-members, rules of origin can also hurt NAFTA producers by requiring them to source from less efficient suppliers from within the region. This reduces their international competitiveness (Hufbauer and Schott, 1993; Drysdale and Garnaut, 1993a).

The Agreement covers a number of sectors, viz. agriculture, manufacturing, telecommunications and banking and insurance services. Different schedules have been accepted for tariff reduction in each of these sectors. Within the next five years, Mexico will abolish import duties on 65 per cent of its agricultural and industrial imports originating in Canada and the United States; all tariffs will be lifted over the next 15 years; tariffs on textiles, garments, automobiles and spare parts will be gradually phased out. Duties on automobiles and spare parts imported into Mexico will be reduced by 50 per cent. On the condition that at least 62.5 per cent of the spare parts and vehicles are manufactured within the NAFTA region (domestic content clause), three-quarters of spare parts will be traded duty-free in five years' time and vehicles in eight years' time.

In agriculture, Mexico will abolish the existing system of import licenses on agricultural products over a period of 15 years; 57 per cent of agricultural tariffs will be lifted at once whereas tariffs on US corn and Mexican peanuts, oranges and sugar will be gradually phased out.

The NAFTA partners have liberalized their national investment regimes. Rules regarding discrimination against foreign investors, transfer of funds and expropriation have been relaxed and appropriate dispute settlement procedures introduced. NAFTA goes beyond CUSFTA in liberalizing investment. Mexico has reduced restrictions on US and Canadian investors in several sectors including financial services. It has also agreed to prohibit the use of performance requirements as an instrument of investment regulation, to adopt a separate forum for settlement of investment disputes, and to pay full and fair compensation for expropriated investments (see Rugman and Gestrin, 1994; Weston, 1994). By the year 2000 investors from Canada and the United States will be free to invest in the Mexican telecommunications industry as well as in banking and insurance industries. With the exception of US airlines and radio communications industries, Canadian culture industry and Mexican energy and railways industries, foreign investors from NAFTA member countries will be treated like domestic investors. The US and Canada also eased FDI inflows during the eighties, although in the US, Congressional pressures led to an amendment to the 1988 Trade Act under which the President could prohibit a foreign takeover on grounds of national security (Safarian, 1992). The above investment liberalization measures have led some scholars (for example, Aspe, 1991; Ros, 1992; Waverman, 1994) to consider NAFTA as an investment rather than a trade pact.

The trade union and environmental lobbies in Canada and the United States insisted on the inclusion of provisions on labour conditions and environmental protection in the NAFTA agreement. As there was no unanimous agreement between the three governments and their business communities and trade unions, a side agreement on each of these two issues was negotiated as a compromise.

Other issues covered by the NAFTA agreement are intellectual property rights, trade in services, government procurement and dispute settlement procedures (for details, see Hufbauer and Schott, 1992; 1993).

Intra-NAFTA Trade

It is too early to measure the concrete impact of NAFTA (which came into force only on 1 January 1994) on the economies of the member countries. However, trade between the United States and Mexico, which was already high prior to the Agreement, has expanded further. US exports to Mexico rose from US$41.6 billion in 1993 to US$45.4 billion in 1995; its imports from Mexico rose from US$40.7 billion in 1993 to US$62.7 billion in 1995. US exports to and imports from Canada also increased: between 1993 and 1995, US exports rose from US$100 billion to US$126 billion whereas imports rose from US$113.6 billion to US$148.3 billion. Canada's trade with Mexico, though relatively small, has also grown; Mexico exports more to Canada than it imports. Canada accounted for US$599 million worth of exports in 1993 and US$786 million in 1995. Its imports from Mexico increased from US$2.9 billion in 1993 to US$4.1 billion in 1995 (IMF, *Direction of Trade Statistics Yearbook*, 1996).

The composition of intra-NAFTA trade has also changed in favour of manufactured goods, notably machinery and transport equipment. Although Mexican exports remain concentrated in a few products, over the years they have changed from oil to such non-oil manufactured exports as passenger cars and parts, telecommunications and information processing equipment which account for about 60 per cent of total exports (Unger, 1994).

Table 6.2 on intraregional trade intensity indices of NAFTA members shows that US trade with Mexico was the highest in 1980 and 1985 after which it has declined. These results are somewhat surprising considering that US exports to Mexico rose significantly in the nineties. In principle, therefore, the intensity index should be relatively high, not low. But Mexico's major devaluation in 1994 made Mexican imports from the US more expensive and exports cheaper. The Mexican trade intensities were influenced in the seventies by the high international price of petroleum and its impact on Mexican exports and in the eighties and nineties by the *maquiladora* ('in-bond' assembly operations similar to export processing zones) phenomenon discussed below.

Several factors contributed to the increase in Mexican exports (non-oil manufactured goods) during the eighties: a decline in real wages, a fall in domestic demand after 1982, favourable exchange rates (massive

Table 6.2 Indices of intraregional trade intensity of NAFTA members

	1970	*1975*	*1980*	*1985*	*1990*	*1993*	*1994*
Canada							
Mexico	0.63	0.74	0.75	0.45	0.44	0.31	0.30
United States	3.94	4.55	4.34	3.57	4.78	4.72	4.73
NAFTA	3.98	4.46	4.25	3.67	4.56	4.34	4.53
Mexico							
Canada	0.02	0.33	0.23	0.40	0.24	2.41	2.48
United States	0.38	4.28	4.74	2.98	4.56	7.52	7.97
NAFTA	0.30	3.38	3.98	2.65	3.75	6.49	7.20
United States							
Canada	21.65	21.11	17.36	26.27	21.41	14.17	13.45
Mexico	4.06	4.99	7.43	7.58	7.32	5.89	5.98
NAFTA	3.94	4.26	5.09	4.80	5.54	5.15	5.60

Source: Our estimates based on data from IMF, *Direction of Trade Statistics Yearbook.*

devaluations) and massive new investments in such export-oriented sectors as automobiles, chemicals, computers, and steel. In the early nineties, Mexican exports suffered owing to both a demand factor (US recession) and a supply factor (capacity constraints).

Canada's trade with its main partner, the US, has been significant since the seventies; after some decline in the trade intensity index in 1985, the value of the index has increased in the nineties. Canada's trade with Mexico is low and the value of its trade intensity with Mexico was higher in 1970 and 1975 than in 1993 and 1994.

Would regional trade have expanded in the absence of NAFTA? A continuous expansionary trend in trade between Mexico and the US, over several years before the agreement was signed, suggests that this might well have been the case. Between 1987 and 1991, Mexico's two-way trade with the US rose to about US$50 billion which represents a 100 per cent increase; its trade with Canada had risen to over US$2 billion (McConell and MacPherson, 1994, p. 164). Even if a positive correlation is established, tariff reductions and the removal of non-tariff barriers are not likely to have an immediate effect. Furthermore, factors other than the trade agreement such as domestic macroeconomic reforms in Mexico, and the higher Mexican growth rate and inflow of foreign capital, may have influenced the positive results more than trade *per se.*

Trade Diversion?

There is no doubt that trade creation has taken place since the NAFTA agreement. But both trade creation and trade diversion can occur at the same time, as we noted in Chapter 2. Some studies show that trade diversion will be negligible (see Brown, Deardorff and Stern, 1992; Shiells, 1995). This finding is plausible since NAFTA members are natural trading partners and their current trade barriers are low. It does not appear that tariff cuts under NAFTA will have a significant effect as 60 to 70 per cent of Mexican products had already been entering the US market tariff free prior to NAFTA under the US Generalized System of Preferences (GSP) and the Harmonized Tariff Schedule (HTS).[6]

As we noted in Chapter 4, there is some fear on the part of ASEAN countries that the discriminatory attitude of NAFTA against non-member countries might hurt their exports to the US. The NAFTA rules of origin may be designed precisely to discriminate against non-members (see Smith, 1993; Young, 1993a) particularly as these rules are more stringent for textiles and clothing than under CUSFTA. Some trade diversion may therefore occur in specific products such as labour-intensive manufactures (for example, textiles and clothing).

Kim and Weston (1993) note that if selected East Asian countries' exports to the US are grouped according to the level of tariffs actually applied to Mexican exports to the US, 54 per cent of exports from China, 41 per cent from the Republic of Korea and 30 per cent from the Philippines are in product categories where trade diversion is most likely to occur.

Textiles and clothing have been traditionally protected by Canada and the US. Under the rules of origin, NAFTA's 'yarn forward' rule gives regional preferences to items produced from yarn made in a NAFTA country. Otherwise the high MFN (Most Favoured Nation) barriers apply. Mexico already benefited from preferences in textiles before NAFTA but the free trade agreement goes even further in discriminating against Pacific Basin suppliers. Particularly affected will be the Republic of Korea. Nearly half of its exports to Mexico in 1990 were textile products for use in Mexican exports to the US. However, if NAFTA had not affected East Asian textile exports, the eventual worldwide dismantling of the Multi-Fibre Arrangement under the Uruguay Round Accord would have some impact.

The rules of origin under NAFTA also discriminate against the Caribbean Basin and Central American countries whose clothing industry is quite significant, employing 200 000 people and accounting for 24 per cent of the region's total exports (Hufbauer and Schott, 1993, pp. 45–46). The World Bank (1994a) estimates that 36 per cent of the Caribbean exports to the US will be subject to potential NAFTA displacement (also see Bernal, 1994).

In the automobile sector, the NAFTA has imposed tight rules of origin – the minimum North American content is set at 62.5 per cent for passenger cars, light trucks, engines and transmissions and 60 per cent for other vehicles and parts. This could block access of developing countries to the rapidly growing, though as yet small Mexican market. In addition, it may divert North American producers from purchasing parts and components from the Pacific Basin countries. It will confer preferential access to US and Canadian auto makers and parts suppliers in the potentially large Mexican automobile market.

Indirectly, by encouraging competition among producers within the free trade area, NAFTA will make them much more competitive than the East Asian producers such as China, Malaysia and Thailand. On the other hand, as we noted earlier, trade diversion under FTA may involve a shift to higher-cost US sources which may reduce the competitiveness of US suppliers in East Asian markets. In general, whether the NAFTA producers can outcompete the East Asians will depend *inter alia*, on complementarity or substitution between goods exported, the comparative advantage of the economies in question and the existing level of trade barriers between members and non-members in competitive markets. In order to test the hypothesis that NAFTA would hurt exports from China and Hong Kong, Zhan (1993) undertook a sectoral and industry-specific quantitative analysis which shows that the effect of tariff and non-tariff barriers on third countries such as China is likely to be very small, considering that the existing barriers are already low in industry groups in which Chinese exports compete. Furthermore, there is a fair amount of complementarity between Chinese exports and those of NAFTA members, which suggests that only sectors like footwear, travel goods and handbags are likely to be adversely affected.

What would be the impact of NAFTA on exports from SAARC countries like India and Pakistan, for example? Like the East Asians these countries are also producers and exporters of such manufactured goods as textiles, garments and footwear which might in principle be adversely affected. But tentative simulations and projections suggest that the impact on SAARC exports of these goods might be marginal. Exports from SAARC countries are likely to be displaced by NAFTA members like Mexico only if they do not suffer from supply constraints.

However, in the past Mexico has clearly faced domestic supply constraints (see Bannister and Low, 1992) which suggest that despite preferential treatment within NAFTA, Mexico may not be able to displace SAARC exports such as textiles and garments at least in the near future. Thus, this factor could have the effect of lowering the trade losses of SAARC countries.

Simulations based on the UNCTAD/World Bank partial equilibrium trade projection model, show that NAFTA-induced trade losses of all SAARC countries' core export products average about 1 per cent of the 1989 value of exports, with the combined losses on all goods ranging from one-half a per cent (India) to eight-tenths of a per cent (Pakistan and Sri Lanka) of total exports to the United States (Safadi and Yeats, 1994, p. 207 and p. 209). A comparison with the World Bank estimates of trade gains resulting from the successful completion of the Uruguay Round and resulting trade liberalization suggests that these gains are far more substantial than the trade losses that might be induced by the creation of NAFTA.

One needs to bear in mind the restrictive assumptions of the above estimations; they consider only short-term effects on changes in trade barriers and ignore longer-term economy-wide effects such as changes in capacity utilization and investment flows, and they neglect supply constraints as noted above.

In most instances, regional integration in NAFTA complements multilateral liberalization with the notable exceptions of the stringent rules of origin requirements and industry-specific provisions designed with reference to their possible extension to additional countries. However, there seems little likelihood of this free trade bloc extending beyond the present three members as the US begins to backtrack in negotiations on trade liberalization issues. For instance, US negotiators are increasingly incorporating labour and environmental issues, and foreign policy and human rights issues as preconditions for further agreements on trade liberalization. These may not be acceptable to other countries.

A successful implementation of the Uruguay Round Agreement including major cuts in global MFN tariff and non-tariff barriers – such as Voluntary Export Restraints (VERs) on textiles, clothing and steel exports and stronger multilateral rules on countervailing and anti-dumping duties will go a long way in countering some of NAFTA's more restrictive trade practices and thus removing some of its adverse effects on third countries. The emergence of China as an important market for East Asian exporters will further reduce their dependence on the US market for trade and investments. The East Asian Economic Caucus and ASEAN could be pushed into bargaining for improvements in trade policies by the NAFTA countries.

Role of Foreign Direct Investment

Foreign direct investment (FDI) played an important role in economic relations between Canada and the US and the US and Mexico even before NAFTA. Like trade, it also represents a hub-and-spoke type of relationship with clear dominance of the US as the hub. In 1994, over half of FDI inflows into Mexico originated in the US, whereas 95 per cent of Canada's FDI was in the US (OECD, 1996). Liberalization of investment under NAFTA discussed above is likely to integrate these three economies even further. For example, in future there will be greater scope for Canadian and US investments in the Mexican financial services and telecommunications industries which have been liberalized. In general, investors will be attracted to Mexico with lower labour costs and well-qualified human resources. Furthermore, in conditions of free capital mobility, capital will flow to where its profitability is the highest. As capital is more scarce in Mexico, rates of interest there are much higher which should further attract investments from Canada and the US.

1. Magnitude of FDI Over Time

Figure 6.1 shows FDI inflows into Canada, Mexico and the US between 1985 and 1995 and FDI outflows from Canada and the US for the same period. It reveals a number of interesting features. First, for the US during the eighties FDI inflows were far more significant than FDI outflows. The situation was reversed in the nineties. Secondly, in both Canada and the US FDI inflows declined considerably between 1990 and 1992 owing to the recession worldwide, but thereafter started rising. This rising trend coincides with the creation of NAFTA and may have been partly owing to the attraction of a larger NAFTA market.

US FDI outflows by destination are shown in Figure 6.2. The EC accounts for the highest share. It is interesting to note that since 1993, the shares for NAFTA, Latin America and the Caribbean and South and East Asia have been rising whereas those for the EU have been declining. This suggests that the creation of NAFTA had some positive effect on the FDI inflows as did the expanding markets in the other two regions.

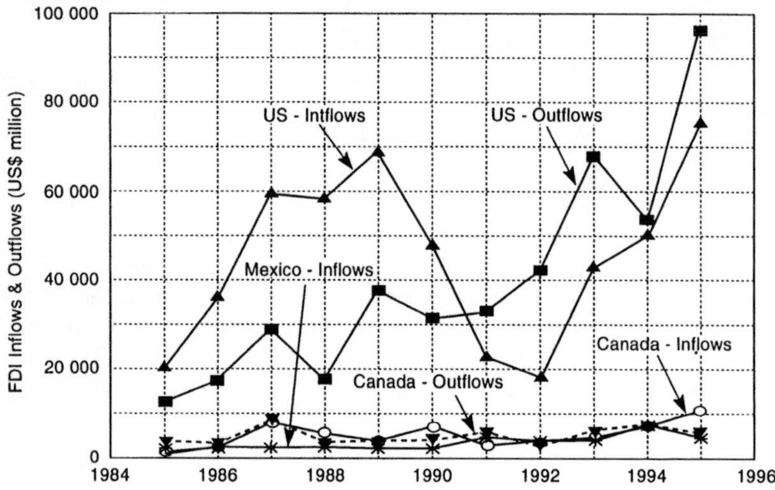

Figure 6.1 FDI Inflows and Outflows: NAFTA Countries

Note: There are no data on Mexico's FDI outflows.

Source: Based on data from OECD (1996).

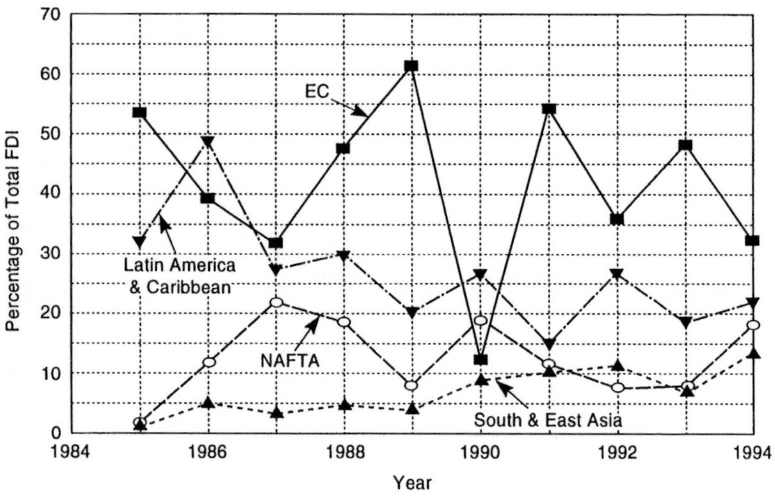

Figure 6.2 United States: FDI Outflows to NAFTA and Other Regions

Source: Based on data from OECD (1996).

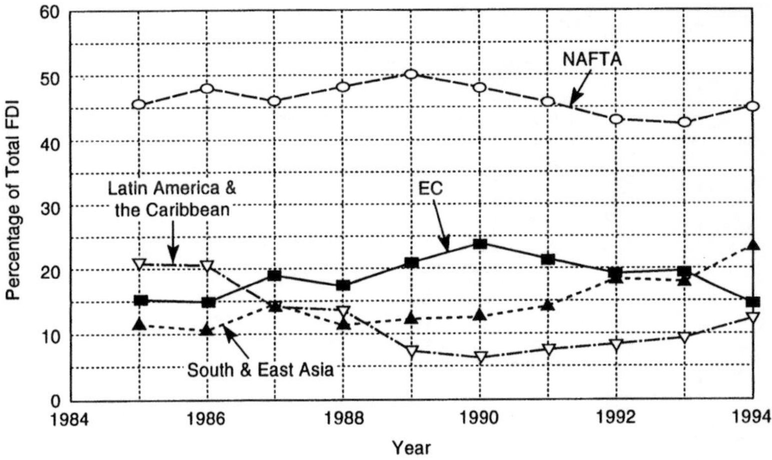

Figure 6.3 Japan: FDI Outflows to NAFTA and Other Regions

Source: Based on data from OECD (1996).

Amongst FDI inflows into the US, Japanese investments are the most significant (see Figure 6.3). These investments need to be considered in the light of such factors as the globalization of Japanese manufacturing MNEs. Their strategy is a response to the intensification of global competition and globalization of production elsewhere, resulting partly from the revolution in information technology. The highest share of total Japanese FDI goes to NAFTA countries (particularly the US), followed by the EC, South and East Asia and Latin America and the Caribbean. Within Latin America, the share of MERCOSUR (Argentina and Brazil) is quite small.

While Japanese investments in the US are directed towards manufacturing and commerce, banking and finance and are oriented to the local market, those in Canada are in such sectors as mining and lumber and pulp in order to supply the Japanese market. In Mexico, Japanese investments are in mining, metals and transport equipment (see Edgington and Fruin, 1994).

Japanese investments in the US are geared primarily for the local market as a means of reducing trade frictions; those in Canada and Mexico, particularly in the automobile industry, are intended more for the NAFTA

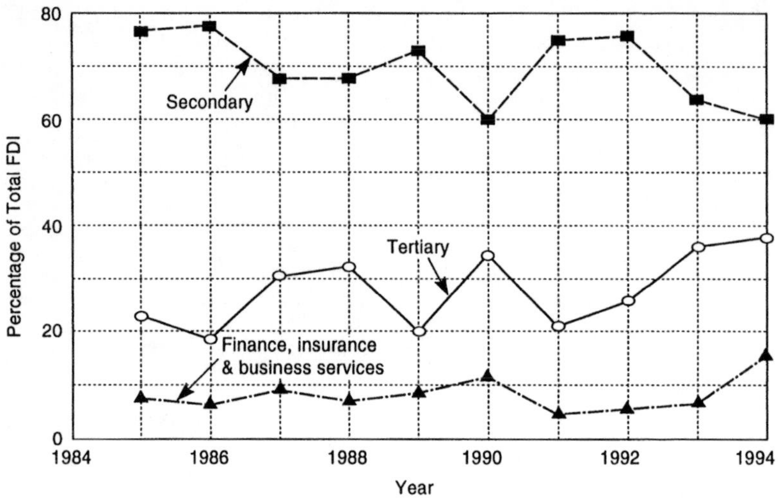

Figure 6.4 Mexico: FDI Inflows by Sector

Source: Based on data from OECD (1996).

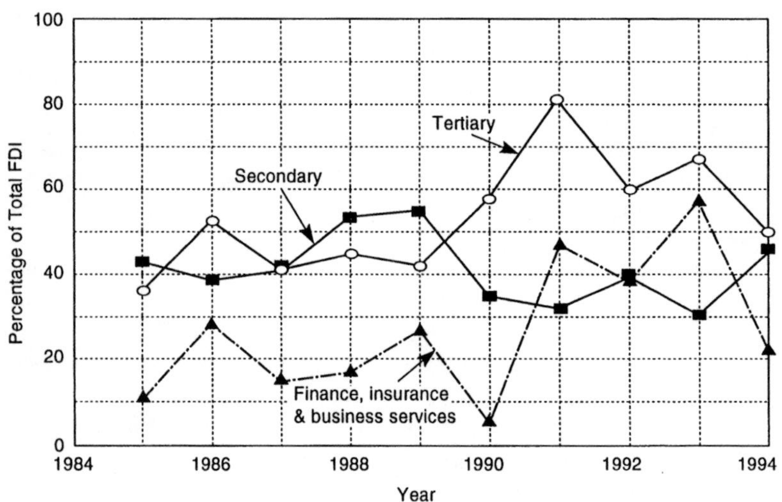

Figure 6.5 United States: FDI Inflows by Sector

Source: Based on data from OECD (1996).

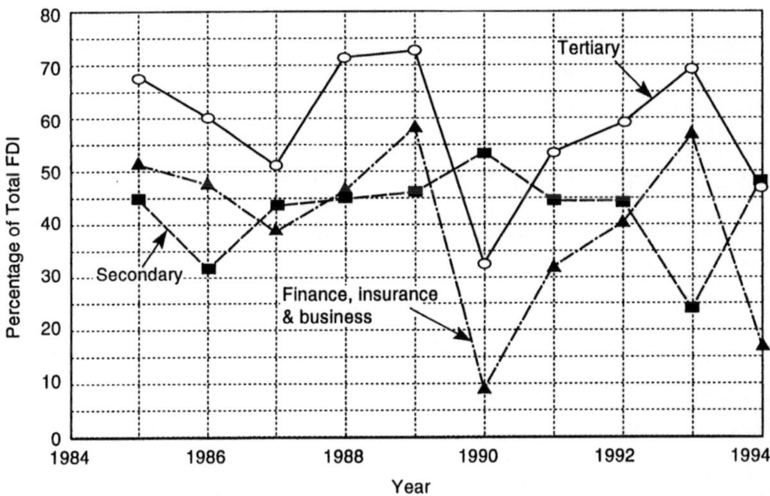

Figure 6.6 United States: FDI Outflows by Sector

Source: Based on data from OECD (1996).

continental market. The Japanese automobile plants in the *maquiladoras* in Mexico for example, supply cheaper components to Japanese industries located in Canada and the US. This rationalization of Japanese investments is necessitated by considerations of efficiency and competitiveness.

US investments in Mexico (about 51 per cent of Mexico's FDI inflows in 1994) are far more important than Japanese investments there (8.5 per cent) (see OECD, 1996). The bulk of US investment is in the service sector; generally an extension of service chains established in Canada and the US. FDI is particularly important in Mexico's financial services: it rose by US$3 billion from 1989 to 1993 (Ortiz, 1994). Figure 6.4 on Mexican FDI inflows by sector shows that since 1992 the share of FDI going to the secondary sector started declining whereas that of the tertiary sector (including finance, insurance and business services) started rising. On the other hand, FDI inflows into the US show a decline in the tertiary sector and a rise in the secondary sector since 1993 (see Figure 6.5). However, in the case of US FDI sectoral outflows, the tertiary sector has generally been more significant than the secondary sector (see Figure 6.6). This predominance of FDI in services corresponds to the rapid growth of trade in services suggesting linkages between trade and FDI.

Investor confidence in Mexico has been encouraged by the country's economic reforms, liberalization of rules and regulations towards foreign investment, privatization of state enterprises and trade liberalization. These policies, combined with economic recession in the OECD countries particularly in the US, and a decline in US interest rates, are some of the other factors which explain massive capital inflows into Mexico.[7]

Liberalization of foreign investment included both FDI and short-term flows through foreign borrowing and purchase by non-residents of stocks and bonds. While the surge of capital inflows into Mexico in the early nineties has been impressive, representing more than 8 per cent of GDP (Ffrench-Davis and Agosin, 1995, p. 5), FDI accounted for only 1.4 per cent of GDP. As the bulk of these inflows were accounted for by portfolio investments, very little productive capacity is likely to have been created. Clearly, short-term speculative investment in the stock market tends to be very volatile and destabilizing whereas longer-term direct investment creates new productive capacity in industry and services. This was evident in the financial crisis of December 1994 involving a major devaluation and capital flight out of the country.[8]

2. *Investment Diversion?*

Like possible trade diversion considered above, there is also scope for investment diversion. Wonnacott (1993) notes that investment diversion may simply be a reflection of trade diversion since diversion of import purchases may also involve diversion of investment to produce these goods. The ASEAN countries and some Asian NIEs, which rely heavily on FDI to promote their export-oriented industries, will find Mexico a strong competitor for US FDI, particularly since Mexico has relaxed restrictions on FDI from Canada and the US. In future, US multinationals might redirect their foreign investments from East Asia (for example, Singapore) to Mexico as we noted in Chapter 4. In fact, US foreign investment in East Asia has already declined in importance relative to that of Japan.

The stringent rules of origin may also discourage FDI flows from non-members to NAFTA countries. NAFTA rules of origin are particularly discriminatory against new investments of firms located outside the region since these firms tend to source from their home country more than long-established firms within the region (Graham, 1994). Kim and Weston (1993) believe that NAFTA will deter East Asian investments in Canada and Mexico. Japan and the Republic of Korea in particular had been increasing their FDI to Mexico in recent years, especially in the Mexican *maquiladora* industries along the US-Mexican border. These industries enjoy favourable US tariffs and Mexican government policies which encourage investments (for example, duty-free imports of inputs and machinery, 100 per cent foreign ownership). But the US and Canada have proposed that Mexico's *maquiladora* incentives be ended under NAFTA which could diminish the attractiveness of the programme to NIE investments, particularly if the exports do not meet the NAFTA requirements of rules of origin for preferential access to the US market. In general, the discriminatory nature of rules of origin is likely to determine investment decisions more on the basis of market factors than those of production cost and efficiency.[9] Japanese investment into the other NAFTA countries may also be restricted unless members negotiate bilateral concessions to attract investments from outside NAFTA into such industries as financial services which remain heavily protected against third parties (see Dobson, 1994).

3. Multinationals' Strategies and Trade and Investment Linkages

Global industrial restructuring and US corporate initiatives to manufacture offshore in Latin America (including Mexico) in order to compete against the East Asian exports to the US have influenced trade and investment linkages in NAFTA. A detailed examination of US imports of automobiles, electronics and garments reveals that Mexico and the Caribbean countries (garments and electronics are produced mainly in export processing zones) are gaining market shares at the expense of East Asian exports of these goods.[10]

US multinationals have played a significant role in Latin American industrialization particularly in such sectors as transportation equipment, electrical and non-electrical machinery and chemicals. Mexico and Brazil are the two main countries accounting for the bulk of sales of US multinationals in the region. In the case of Mexico, the *maquiladora* account for a sizeable proportion of the total sales of US multinationals.[11]

The programme accounts for 60 per cent of Mexico's non-oil exports to the United States which grew particularly rapidly during the eighties. Such exports were given a boost by the devaluation of the *peso*. In 1993, foreign affiliates in Mexico alone are estimated to have 'produced more than a half of all exports by foreign affiliates among the top 200 exporters from the region'. (UNCTAD, 1995a, p. 75).

However, the impact of NAFTA on Mexican exports of foreign affiliates should not be overstated. Even before the creation of NAFTA, these affiliates had started expanding exports by raising product quality through industrial restructuring and replacement of inefficient local suppliers of inputs by imports. It is reported that during 1982–89, four-fifths of the foreign affiliates were able to increase their exports as a proportion of their total sales (UNCTC, 1992, p. 79).

FDI inflows into Mexico are also linked to an increase in imports; the import content of production by multinational subsidiaries has gone up. Rather than importing entire lines of production, the multinationals often import from other plants with excess capacity (a case of intra-firm trade).

Multinationals are known to have planned and structured production on the basis of the enlarged NAFTA market in order to benefit from economies of scale. The multinationals in the automobile industry, in particular, have been pursuing regionalization strategies in order to rationalize production. Molot (1995) notes that this continental organization of production by the multinationals started accelerating since the implementation of CUSFTA in 1989. The implementation of NAFTA is likely to accelerate this process further as evidenced by US multinationals which have located to lower-cost production sites in Mexico in order to compete more effectively in the US market (Mortimore, 1995). The NAFTA rules on investment, liberalization of FDI rules by the member countries and gradual tariff reductions will facilitate the adoption of such a regional strategy. Private-sector support for NAFTA and free trade is in part motivated by a desire to protect investments.

Large US multinationals such as Ford, Chrysler and General Motors were involved in Canada and Mexico even before CUSFTA and NAFTA. In Mexico during the import-substitution phase of industrialization, multinationals also played an important role by producing mainly for the protected domestic market. In this case, FDI substituted for trade. In the export-liberalization NAFTA phase, trade and foreign investment have become complementary and the multinationals' strategy has shifted from the domestic to the regional market in response to growing competition and the need to exploit economies of scale.

Significant intra-firm trade between the parent companies and their affiliates in the three partner countries further reflects regional strategies. One estimate shows that in 1990, nearly 36 per cent of total US merchandise exports and 44 per cent of US imports were between affiliates of the same enterprise. In the case of Canada, 43 per cent of Canadian merchandise imports from the US and 45 per cent of Canadian exports to the US were intra-firm (see Eden, 1994, p. 12).

Eden (1994) notes that the strategic responses of multinationals to NAFTA will vary depending on whether they are veteran insiders, outsiders or domestics. The firms already well established within NAFTA countries will be more inclined to exploit economies of scale and scope resulting from the enlarged market and the elimination of intraregional barriers. The rationalization of automobile production in North America discussed above supports this argument. Other industries are likely to follow the approach adopted by the automobile industry. Thus, plants producing only for the Mexican national market will gradually diminish in importance. The firms which are currently outside the area may be induced to locate plants within NAFTA, attracted as they will be by the size of the market. But as we noted above, rules of origin and other non-tariff barriers will be important deterrents.

NAFTA will be only one of the factors influencing multinationals' strategies which are influenced equally by the future growth prospects of the partners, the rapidity and costs of structural adjustment in response to technological change and their interests and investments in other regions such as the European Union and Southeast and East Asia.

COMMON MARKET OF THE SOUTHERN CONE (MERCOSUR)

Like NAFTA (which followed a bilateral trade agreement between Canada and the United States), MERCOSUR was also preceded by a bilateral trade agreement between Argentina and Brazil (1986) which later culminated into a bigger grouping when Paraguay and Uruguay joined. MERCOSUR, created in March 1991 by the Asunción Treaty, is a regional arrangement between the two rather large-sized economies of Argentina and Brazil and the two small economies of Paraguay and Uruguay which are much less developed (see Table 6.1).

With a total population of 200 million, MERCOSUR represents a large market particularly for the small economies of Paraguay and Uruguay. Apart from access to this market, the smaller economies are also likely to benefit from economies of scale in production and cost reductions attractive to both producers and consumers. Also Paraguay felt that a reduction in tariff barriers would help its industrialization by attracting foreign investment and would discourage contraband border trade. However, there is also a possibility that the economies of the smaller and less developed members, (whose industrial sectors are characterized by small and medium enterprises) may fail to withstand competition from Argentina and Brazil at least during the period of structural adjustment (Breuer, 1995). Despite this fear of a possible negative effect of regional integration, the entry of Paraguay and Uruguay into MERCOSUR was inevitable considering their close trading relationships with both Argentina and Brazil.

Argentina and Brazil are two rather sophisticated and naturally complementary economies in South America. Economic and trade cooperation between them makes sense for both economic and geographical reasons. While Argentina is traditionally agriculture-based, the economy of Brazil is more industrialized and diversified. It was believed that in a combined market of the two countries Argentina's highly competitive agricultural and agro-industrial production could help lower prices of consumer products in Brazil thus raising social welfare. Furthermore, Argentina's abundant scientific and engineering manpower would contribute towards more efficient skill-intensive production for the combined market (Chudnovsky, 1992). MERCOSUR provided an opportunity for rationalising production and reducing costs. Combined with this, the common problems of external and fiscal imbalances and debt crises in both Argentina and Brazil, and the difficulties faced by Argentinian agricultural exports in the US protectionist market, opened the doors for bilateral collaboration in trade, technology and industrial restructuring (see Chudnovsky, 1994).

The failure of the Latin American Integration Association (LAIA) to promote intraregional trade may have reinforced the creation of MERCOSUR. But bilateral trade negotiations between Argentina and Brazil started when the two countries had political rivalries, suffered from macroeconomic instability and traded little with each other. The question then arises: what led them to believe that regionalism, which did not succeed in the sixties and seventies, would offer better results in the late eighties and nineties? Several factors seem to have led to the renewal of regional economic cooperation in the Southern Cone.

First, the political process of democratization in the partner countries has facilitated the process of economic integration. The need to strengthen 'infant democratic regimes' seems to have brought the four partners to the negotiating table. The survival of democracy in Paraguay during disturbances in early 1996 was in no small part due to the intervention of the three MERCOSUR partners. Secondly, unilateral trade liberalization, structural economic reforms and deregulation of the economies in Latin America and elsewhere created a more favourable environment. Unprecedented economic growth and trade expansion of East Asia as well as the success of economic reforms in Chile may have spurred the MERCOSUR partners to a dialogue. Thirdly, negotiations among Canada, Mexico and the United States for the creation of NAFTA and the changed world economic environment may have had a domino effect. Particularly for Brazil which competes with Mexico in several goods in the US market, the creation of MERCOSUR may have been a defensive reaction (see Hurrell, 1994).

Objectives and Content

The Treaty of Asunción provided for the creation of a common market by January 1995. Between 1991 and 1994, the transitional period, agreements were reached regarding rules of origin of goods, safeguard clauses, dispute settlements and a time-table for the reduction/elimination of tariff and non-tariff barriers to trade by the end of 1994 and the establishment of a free trade area by 2000. Two bodies were established: a Council of Foreign and Economy Ministers and an executive body directly responsible for the implementation of the Treaty. However, as of March 1996 decisions were still to be made about the creation of a permanent secretariat (which the Uruguay government is keen to host) and other bodies in the post-transition period.

Temporary exemptions to the tariff and non-tariff reductions have been allowed at a differential rate for different member countries (for example, four years for Argentina and Brazil and five years for Paraguay and Uruguay). The exemption list includes such goods as automobiles, sugar, capital goods, informatics and telecommunications. For example, in the automobile industry, Brazil had a high import tariff of 85 per cent on automobiles in 1990. Argentina imposes a three-tier import regime to protect the domestic market for automobiles. Under the first tier, established manufacturers are entitled to import finished vehicles and parts at preferential tariff rates. Under the second tier, consumers can import vehicles on payment of 20 per cent tariff. The third tier imposes a quota which in 1994, was 10 per cent of the domestic output. In addition, Argentinian regulations require local content of 60 per cent from firms wishing to invest in the automobile industry (see Bouzas, 1995).

Until recently bilateral trade between Argentina and Brazil in the automobile industry was governed by Protocol 21 (which is no longer in force) under which trade in automobiles was duty-free but quotas were established for bilateral trade between the two countries.

The creation of a customs union required an agreement on a common external tariff (CET) by all four partners against the rest of the world. Products in the exemption list noted above are also excluded from CET which means that on these goods national tariffs will continue to be imposed during the transition period. These exemptions from CET necessitated agreement on rules of origin (60 per cent of value added test and change in tariff heading) to ensure that goods are not imported into high-tariff MERCOSUR partners via the low-tariff ones.

Brazil has the highest tariffs and Paraguay, the lowest. In 1992, it was agreed to establish an external tariff ceiling of 20 per cent for the majority of goods. In 1994, for computers and telecommunications external tariffs were established at a maximum of 16 per cent whereas for capital goods they were 14 per cent. The most advanced members (Argentina and Brazil) are expected to converge by 1 January 2001, whereas the less developed members (Paraguay and Uruguay) are allowed until 2006 to do so. Brazil and Argentina will have to reduce their external tariff whereas Paraguay will have to increase it. In the case of Uruguay, there will be little change.

The reduction in tariff and non-tariff barriers has not been an easy task. As a global trader, Brazil depends less on the South American market than other partners. Its large number of domestic capital goods producers (protected by high tariffs) have opposed bids to lower or remove barriers to trade. In 1995, Brazil slowed down the liberalization process by raising tariffs on imports of cars (to a high level of 70 per cent) and imposing quotas without consulting its MERCOSUR partners and without exempting them from these quotas. This nearly led to the collapse of MERCOSUR. Brazil feared an increase in car imports would worsen its trade deficit. On the other hand, Argentina, which is not a major capital goods producer and had zero tariffs on the import of capital goods needed to modernize its industry. In March 1995, Argentina raised import tariffs on capital goods to 10 per cent. It has also made extensive use of quotas and anti-dumping duties. In April 1996, Brazil again changed its rules on textile imports and required that the import duties be paid in 30 days instead of six months. Although the decision has since been reversed, it is estimated to have cost Uruguay up to US$ 40 million in lost exports (*The Economist,* 29 June 1996). In 1993 and 1994, Argentina imposed specific duties and quotas on selected paper and textile products in response to rapidly rising imports from Brazil. Thus, both Argentina and Brazil have adopted stop-go trade policies and practices in violation of the Asunción Treaty's goal of tariff reduction and trade liberalization.

The MERCOSUR experience contrasts with that of NAFTA which is known to be more investment-led. In the case of MERCOSUR, FDI inflows have not been significant (see below) whereas the process of trade liberalization has been subject to the vicissitudes of government trade policy. Unlike NAFTA, the Asunción Treaty provides for the coordination of such macroeconomic and sectoral policies as monetary and fiscal policy related to trade, land transportation, maritime transportation, industrial and technological policies, agricultural policy, energy policy, and industrial relations, employment and social security. Such policy coordination is more meaningful among partners at a similar stage of development than among North-South partners of NAFTA which might be harmful for southern countries (see Panagariya, 1996). However, so far little progress has been made in this direction. Macroeconomic instability in Argentina and Brazil, unstable bilateral real exchange rates and the Mexican crisis have hindered such policy coordination.

Intra-MERCOSUR Trade

Trade between MERCOSUR partners has expanded significantly between 1991 and 1995, the transition period to the creation of the common market. Brazil, a global trader, now trades more with Argentina and other partners. Its exports to Argentina went up from US$ 1.5 billion in 1991 to US$ 4.0 billion in 1995; its imports from Argentina increased from US$ 1.7 billion to US$ 5.6 billion during the same period. Brazil's trade with Paraguay and Uruguay has also increased from a rather small base: exports to Paraguay rose from US$ 496 million in 1991 to US$ 1.3 billion in 1995, whereas imports rose from US$ 223 million to US$ 514 million. Brazil's exports to Uruguay rose from US$ 337 million in 1991 to US$ 812 million in 1995, whereas its imports rose from US$ 446 million to US$ 737 million. Argentina's trade with Paraguay and Uruguay has also increased significantly. Argentina's exports to Paraguay rose from US$ 178 million in 1991 to US$ 657 million in 1995 whereas its imports rose from US$ 40 million to US$ 76 million. Its exports to Uruguay rose from US$ 311 million in 1991 to US$ 650 million in 1994 and imports rose from US$ 166 million in 1991 to US$ 789 million in 1994 (IMF, *Direction of Trade Statistics Yearbook,* 1996). However, trade between the small partners, Paraguay and Uruguay, is small. Therefore, the increase in intra-MERCOSUR trade is largely explained by bilateral trade between Argentina and Brazil.

Intraregional trade intensities for MERCOSUR countries (Table 6.3) show high values for Paraguay and Uruguay. As is to be expected, trade intensities for Brazil, which has a large domestic market, have much lower values. The intensity indices also show that trade among

Table 6.3 Indices of intraregional trade intensity of MERCOSUR members

	1970	*1975*	*1980*	*1985*	*1990*	*1993*	*1994*
Argentina							
Brazil	8.10	4.30	7.41	7.80	17.65	28.55	24.54
Paraguay	39.50	57.31	88.53	36.75	34.43	68.17	–
Uruguay	20.33	20.07	26.66	31.49	54.72	62.01	58.89
MERCOSUR	9.63	5.57	10.14	9.71	20.44	32.87	29.89
Brazil							
Argentina	11.79	8.92	9.90	10.53	17.30	20.80	19.13
Paraguay	18.55	61.18	75.60	37.96	34.81	62.01	–
Uruguay	14.41	14.61	17.69	14.50	24.01	31.80	22.95
MERCOSUR	12.31	11.58	13.60	13.54	21.82	25.00	24.01
Paraguay							
Argentina	48.89	59.09	44.21	27.61	48.61	19.80	–
Brazil	1.75	1.95	10.13	26.12	49.90	39.63	–
Uruguay	54.10	19.23	37.98	56.61	32.19	15.40	–
MERCOSUR	21.01	14.95	21.05	27.57	48.86	31.33	–
Uruguay							
Argentina	4.79	15.93	24.84	36.48	41.05	42.42	40.17
Brazil	5.56	10.22	14.08	22.17	45.84	29.73	30.94
Paraguay	31.65	44.16	51.94	30.56	10.26	24.39	–
MERCOSUR	5.63	11.83	17.77	25.31	43.61	34.19	35.34

Source: Our estimates based on data from IMF, *Direction of Trade Statistics Yearbooks*.

MERCOSUR partners expanded even during the pre-MERCOSUR period but it has grown even more for both the smaller and larger partners particularly after its creation in the early nineties. This would suggest that regional integration and relaxation of trade restrictions (despite the stop-go measures noted above) had a role to play in trade expansion.

Trade liberalization has created local markets for such manufactures as automobiles and auto parts, chemicals and machinery, and has increased intra-MERCOSUR trade in these goods. The bulk of this trade is of an intra-industry nature which results from specialization facilitated by larger market size and economies of scale. However, rationalization necessary to make industry competitive within the region does not seem to be taking place on any significant scale. The MERCOSUR treaty does not contain any provisions for enabling such rationalization so essential during a period of industrial adjustment. In general, production within MERCOSUR continues to be organized vertically rather than horizontally. Yet for raising competitiveness of industry, product specialization along horizontal lines and complementarity in national production systems is required. Complete trade liberalization in automobiles, for example, would not have allowed any location of plants in Argentina with a much smaller market than that of Brazil. Intra-industry trade in automobiles may have resulted more from a system of managed trade (through a sectoral agreement between Argentina and Brazil) than trade liberalization (see Filippo, 1995).

Behar (1995) estimates the effects of trade liberalization through tariff reduction using data for a selected number of industrial sectors in Argentina, Brazil and Uruguay. Preferential tariff reductions within MERCOSUR are incorporated through a diminution of trade costs and changes in relative prices. Three sets of effects were estimated: (a) in output, (b) in average costs and (c) in welfare in terms of a sum of consumer surplus, profits and government tariff revenues.

A number of conclusions of the above study are worth noting. First, a reduction of trade barriers leads to an increase in output and a reduction in average cost in all industries. This may be the result of economies of scale in production. It also leads to an increase in welfare. However, for individual member countries, while output goes up and average cost goes down in most cases in Argentina and Brazil, in Uruguay which is a less developed partner, the output of pharmaceutical products, electrical machinery, electrical household appliances and motor vehicles goes down. This is to be expected since competition within MERCOSUR is likely to increase in the wake of trade liberalization, and inefficient firms in Uruguay are likely to be weeded out.

One needs to be cautious about interpreting the above results because the underlying model is based on a number of restrictive assumptions. As a partial equilibrium model, it does not capture the economy-wide effects. Secondly, the sample of industries covered is quite small. Thirdly, the Behar estimates are limited only to trade liberalization effects, and do not take account of the dynamic effects of domestic and foreign direct investments which may result from the creation of an enlarged MERCOSUR market (see below).

Unlike NAFTA or the European Union, all MERCOSUR partners are medium-income developing countries without any rich partner. Therefore, it is believed that there is no room for a regional policy à la European Union under which rich partners subsidize poor ones. The head of the Uruguayan delegation to MERCOSUR noted (in a personal interview) that difference in size rather than wealth was the major factor in negotiations. He argued that Brazil is a large country but it is

Table 6.4 Estimates of trade diversion in MERCOSUR

	Trade Diversion		
	Number of product groups	*Relative magnitude of diversion*	
		In intrazonal exports(%)	*In total exports (%)*
Argentina	21	25	4
Brazil	98	77	8
Paraguay	–	–	–
Uruguay	3	3	1

Source: Baumann (1993).

not rich; indeed northeast Brazil is quite poor. However, one can just as well argue that the per capita incomes of the central and southern regions of Brazil compare favourably with those of some developed countries. Indeed, there is an ongoing debate in Brazil that MERCOSUR may make these regions richer thus widening the already serious income inequalities.

Trade Diversion?

Intra-MERCOSUR trade is likely to increase at the expense of the rest of the world, especially after the completion of the common market process. Trade diversion will occur because the reduction of tariffs within the region leads to a reduction in prices of imports from within MERCOSUR relative to those of imports from outside. However, it is difficult to estimate the magnitude of trade diversion. We know of only one estimate by Baumann (1993) for 1989, based on such assumptions as homogeneous traded goods, absence of supply constraints, perfect substitution between goods demanded by MERCOSUR members and the rest of the world, and absence of any substitution effects in domestic production. Furthermore, only first-round effects on trade flows are considered. Simulation undertaken considered export products being diverted to MERCOSUR from the rest of the world, and other products continuing to be imported from third parties because MERCOSUR members could not meet the demand. These static effects of trade diversion are given in Table 6.4. As is to be expected, trade diversion is more significant for major exporters, Brazil with high tariff barriers, and to a lesser extent, Argentina.

We noted above that preferential trade liberalization within

MERCOSUR has raised intraregional trade in automobiles, chemicals and transport equipment. These are capital intensive goods being produced under protectionist conditions. They may not, therefore, be competitive in the world markets. Thus intraregional trade may have been expanding at the expense of interregional trade (see Yeats, 1996).[12] This is also suggested by Table 2.2 in Chapter 2 which shows that in Latin America, the intraregional trade share has been increasing while the share in world trade has been declining. This contrasts with the situation in Asia where both shares have been rising.

Role of Foreign Direct Investment and Multinationals

1. Magnitude of FDI Inflows

In principle, the large size of the MERCOSUR market should encourage FDI into the region. Multinational enterprises are more likely to locate production in MERCOSUR countries so as to gain access to the larger market. However, FDI inflows into MERCOSUR are at present rather low and are accounted for mainly by Argentina and to a lesser extent, Brazil; FDI inflows of Paraguay and Uruguay are insignificant (see Figure 6.7).[13] Assuming that the inflows of Argentina and Brazil are representative of MERCOSUR as a whole, Figure 6.8 shows FDI inflows from EC-12, Japan and the United States. MERCOSUR FDI inflows from the EC are far more important than those from either Japan or the US. The inflows from the EC shot up since the creation of MERCOSUR which suggests that enlarged market size may have been the main motivating factor for this increase.

Poor FDI inflows into MERCOSUR countries may be explained by difficulties experienced in achieving economic stabilization and regional integration at the same time. This, combined with overvalued and fluctuating exchange rates, makes industrial specialization difficult and foreign investment risky. Moreover, the frequent stop-go policy of trade liberalization adopted by Brazil (and, to a lesser extent, Argentina) mentioned above, generates uncertainty which may reduce investor confidence. Finally, stringent rules of origin may also inhibit foreign investors. Competition between Argentina and Brazil for FDI inflows is also noticeable. This competition tends to hurt the smaller MERCOSUR partners. For example, in 1994 Toyota Corporation was exploring the possibility of setting up a plant in Uruguay, but Argentina offered better incentives and the plant was located in that country instead. (Personal communication with the Uruguyan Chamber of Industry in March

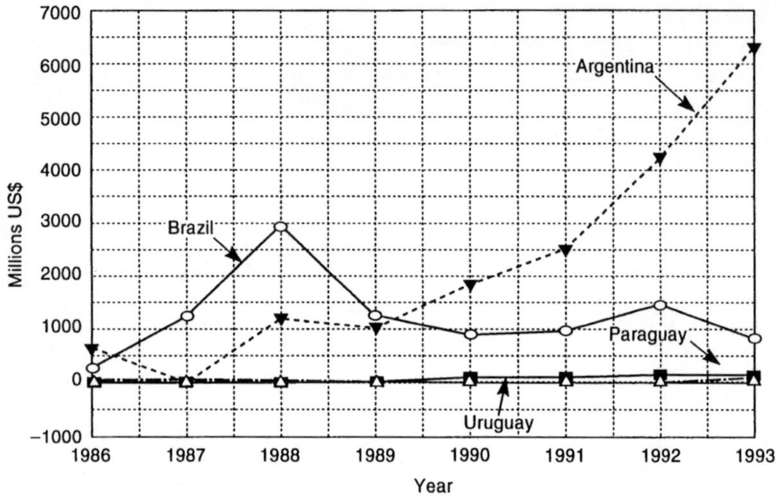

Figure 6.7 Total FDI Inflows into MERCOSUR Countries

Source: Based on data from ECLAC (1995).

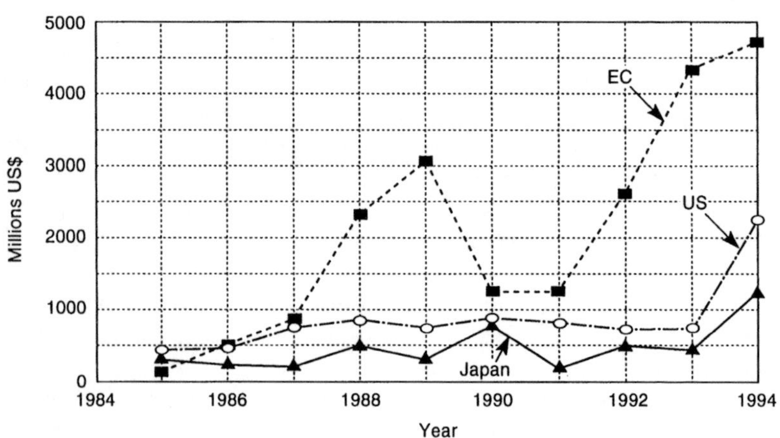

Figure 6.8 Inflows into MERCOSUR* from EC, US and Japan

Source: Based on data from OECD (1996).

Note: Based on data for Argentina and Brazil. FDI inflows into other MERCOSUR countries were insignificant.

1996). In future, Argentina and Brazil may have to compete with Mexico for US and Japanese foreign investments particularly since the NAFTA liberalization of investment regimes seems to be more marked than that of MERCOSUR.

Much FDI in the region has been associated with privatization programmes. The bulk of FDI in Argentina, for example, is accounted for by the privatization of public services and of the state petroleum company. In a historical context, there seems to have been a boom of FDI inflows into Argentina which are known to have continued even after privatization ceased.[14] FDI may be responding to the growing domestic market particularly in the case of the food-processing industry. On the other hand, in the Argentinian automobile industry FDI is induced by policy incentives. Apart from the increase in demand, there may be 'locational advantages' (presumably skilled manpower and good infrastructure) for multinationals to relocate production to the sub-region (Chudnovsky, 1992).

With the exception of the automobile industry which is integrated at the level of the MERCOSUR market (see below), FDI has not contributed to much export growth in Argentina. As FDI is oriented mainly towards the domestic market, it accounts for significant import content (see Chudnovsky, Lopez and Porta, 1995).

2. *Intra-MERCOSUR FDI*

Despite larger market size however, the intra-MERCOSUR flow of investment has not increased significantly. Since 1991, MNE subsidiaries based in the region have increased their bilateral and intra-firm initiatives which may account for some increase in intra-MERCOSUR investment flows. According to an official Argentinian survey, by late 1994, 215 such initiatives were identified. Of these, about 25 per cent were in the food and beverages industries and 12 per cent in car assembly and car parts production (Bouzas, 1995).

Brazil, as the biggest and the most industrially advanced member of MERCOSUR, is likely to play a major role in the expansion of both intraregional trade and investment flows. It is estimated that by the end of 1994, more than 300 Brazilian firms had made some commitments to invest in Argentina in different sectors. (cited in Bouzas, 1995). Another estimate by Goulart, Arruda and Brasil (cited in Bouzas, 1995) suggests that during 1990-94, of the 85 Brazilian investments in Latin America, 59 were in the MERCOSUR partners, notably Argentina.

The pattern of intraregional investments in MERCOSUR varies

between the large countries (Argentina and Brazil) and the two smaller partners (Paraguay and Uruguay). Argentina and Brazil have a much smaller proportion of FDI from within the region than Paraguay or Uruguay (see UNECLAC, 1994); most FDI inflows come from the US and Western Europe, although lately Chile's investment in these countries has also started rising.

In October 1996, Chile joined MERCOSUR as an associate member (full membership is not envisaged since Chile has a different tariff structure from that of the other member countries). This association will enable Chile's investors to expand investments in the MERCOSUR countries. Chile is already investing in Argentina and Uruguay. Labàn and Meller (1995) note that Chile's bilateral trade agreement with MERCOSUR also opens up the possibility of reducing or eliminating discrimination against foreign producers and investors.[15]

In future, the Colonia Protocol on intraregional investment signed in January 1994 should, in principle, contribute to the growth of intra-MERCOSUR investment flows. The Protocol provides for equal treatment for regional and national investors. It also eliminates restrictions on the repatriation of capital and profits in convertible currencies.

3. Multinationals' Strategies and Trade and Investment Linkages

Chudnovsky, Lopez and Porta (1995) note that there is no conclusive evidence at present to show that MNEs now exploit the economies of the larger regional market of MERCOSUR. In the past, under the import-substitution regimes, MNEs produced mainly for the rapidly growing domestic markets. However, two factors suggest that in future, multinationals' strategy may shift from the domestic to the regional market. First, intra-firm trade, particularly in manufactured goods, has been rising which would suggest an increase in trade through FDI inflows. In Argentina, a survey of 61 MNE subsidiaries showed that intra-firm exports rose from nearly 52 per cent in 1991 to nearly 59 per cent in 1992; intra-firm imports rose from 70 per cent to over 78 per cent during the same period (Kosacoff and Bezchinsky, 1994). In Brazil, foreign affiliates accounted for 44 per cent of manufactured exports in 1990. These affiliates are particularly important in the non-electrical machinery industry whose exports from Brazil rose from 15 per cent (US$0.3 billion) to 27 per cent (US$1.6 billion) during 1977–1989 (see UNCTAD, 1995a, p. 216). The World Investment Report (UNCTAD, 1995a, p. 83) notes that 'transnational corporations have led . . . intraregional trade boom, accounting for 65 per cent (US$4.2 billion) of intraregional manufacturing exports in 1993.' The bulk of this trade was between Argentina and Brazil. Secondly, a sudden recent rise in FDI inflows into such industries as food and paper, particularly into Argentina, may pave the way to production for the MERCOSUR market. Argentina has always been a major exporter of food. FDI into the industry is replacing domestic family-owned firms, and is most likely to cater for the expanded regional market.

There is evidence of some multinational enterprises adopting a regional rather than global strategy by locating in one of the MERCOSUR countries. This is the case of the automobiles and autoparts industry. For example, Toyota Motor Corporation has established a plant in Argentina to produce pick-up trucks for the regional market. Half of the production will be destined for the Brazilian market for which most of the spare parts will be imported from Brazil. Local parts suppliers are also beginning to regionalize. A Brazilian automobile parts supplier has started producing in Argentina to supply the local General Motors plant (UNCTAD, 1995a, p. 83). After the United States, Argentina has become the second largest supplier of spare parts to Brazil. Similarly, Brazil has become an important supplier to Argentina. However, other industries (for example, the Argentinian pulp and paper and agricultural processing industries) remain protected and continue to cater for the domestic market.

Protocol 21 on the automobile industry, mentioned above, is said to have made it easier for MNEs to design regional strategies since bilateral trade in the automobile sector was very low and the Brazilan and Argentinian markets were almost closed at the time of the signing of the Protocol. Chudnovsky believes that the Protocol, in a gradual and negotiated manner, increased opportunities for bilateral trade in automobiles and the integration of MNE operations in the Southern Cone region (personal communication).

The MNE strategies in MERCOSUR vary a great deal depending partly on the nature of the product and the industry and the national market conditions. For example, the survey of 61 multinational subsidiaries in Argentina noted above, identified three types, namely: (i) those which participate in the globalization strategy of the parent company, (ii) those operating mainly for the domestic market under the import-substitution model, and (iii) those which concentrate on goods which are intensive in natural resources. As is to be expected, the shares of intra-firm exports and imports are larger for type (i). These types of subsidiaries rely more and more on assembly for export based on imports rather than on domestic production for export.

PROSPECTS FOR WESTERN HEMISPHERE INTEGRATION[16]

A number of authors (for example, Hufbauer and Schott (1994); and McConnell and MacPherson (1994)) have considered the possible creation of a Western Hemisphere Free Trade Area (WHFTA) consisting of the United States and the whole of Latin America. McConnell and MacPherson (1994, p. 168) state that 'it would be a mistake to underestimate the importance, particularly to the US, of eventually extending the North American trade bloc southward to include central and South American nations'. The Enterprise for the Americas Initiative launched by former US President George Bush in 1992 provides a rough blueprint for a free trade area of the Western Hemisphere. It is believed that such an initiative would better exploit the market potential in the region by building on the already close linkages between the Latin American and US economies. Following the Bush initiative a number of Latin American countries have already entered into bilateral economic treaties with the US.

In December 1994, at a hemispheric summit in Miami (the first of its kind since 1967), the US and 33 countries of the Americas (excluding Cuba) agreed on the creation of a free trade area of the Americas by the year 2005. A trade ministers' meeting in Denver in June 1995 laid the groundwork for preparations towards this goal.

Brazil and the United States are the two key players but they have different perceptions of hemisphere integration. Brazil is a global trader and FDI inflows into Brazil come from different parts of the world, including the US and Western Europe. Because of these global economic interests, Brazil tends to lean towards multilateralism more than regionalism. It fears that the benefits from hemisphere economic integration may not compensate for the adjustment costs involved. Its three main worries about the Miami declaration on hemisphere integration are: (i) the unrealistic deadline of 2005; (ii) extension of the NAFTA model throughout the hemisphere, and (iii) the scope of the proposed agreement going beyond the Uruguay Round accord (Veiga, 1995).[17]

However, Brazil cannot ignore its regional economic and political interests. As a large country in South America, it is interested in playing a leadership role in both South America and in the Third World for which it needs US support. Its trade interests also require some negotiation with the US and NAFTA; Brazil's exports to the US will face stiff competition from Mexico which receives preferential treatment in the US market.

In 1994 Brazil championed the idea of a South American Free Trade

Area (SAFTA) which would presumably offer it an opportunity to dominate in the region and eventually negotiate more effectively with NAFTA and the United States. This idea has not met with much success so far and Brazil seems to be reconciled for the present, to support MERCOSUR. It has therefore passively embraced the regional approach and is inclined to move slowly with regard to both sub-regional integration through MERCOSUR and hemisphere integration. However, following agreements in 1996 by Chile and Bolivia to join MERCOSUR as associate members, similar negotiations are expected to start with Colombia, Ecuador, Peru and Venezuela later in 1997, followed by Mexico. In fact, one can argue that progress towards SAFTA is more significant today than towards WHFTA because of a greater interest in trade liberalization in South America than in the United States.

A few years ago, the concept of a free trade area of the Western Hemisphere would have been considered utopian. So what has changed that puts the concept within the bounds of reality in the future? Most Latin American economies today are engaged in the process of economic and trade liberalization on a unilateral basis in order to improve their competitive position in the world economy. Participation in a hemispheric free trade area with Canada and the United States is expected to strengthen the competitive position of Latin American countries, assure them access to Northern markets and offer them a share of the increased production potential to satisfy these growing markets. Furthermore, within the framework of open regionalism today, participation in regional groupings does not prevent individual countries and the region from expanding commercial and financial ties with other centres of growth in the international economy (Rosenthal, 1993, p. 17). Chile's participation in APEC and its recent application for the membership of NAFTA reinforces this argument (Chile signed a bilateral trade agreement with Canada in November 1996).

Despite such support for a region-wide free trade area, the fact remains that the less developed countries in the Latin American region are unlikely to benefit immediately from such an area. Also economic stabilization in Argentina and Brazil has not yet taken root (this has in the past been one factor explaining Chile's reluctance to join MERCOSUR). It may therefore be more prudent to follow a phased approach under which, as a first step, sub-regional groupings, which already exist, are strengthened. Economic diversity and different stages of development among Latin American countries suggest that conditions need to be created under which different countries might eventually all benefit from a region-wide free trade area.

Many Southern American countries have traditional economic, trade and cultural links with Western Europe which the European Union is exploiting by signing a trade agreement with MERCOSUR in early 1996. A number of Latin American countries trade more with the EU than with the US, and substantial trade restrictions in the EU may suggest that a free trade area with the EU rather than with US may be more beneficial to Latin America (see Panagariya, 1996).

Will NAFTA, MERCOSUR and a possible Western Hemisphere Free Trade agreement serve as building blocks towards an open world economy? Some fear that these groupings may become discriminatory and protectionist in the same way as the European Union. This is unlikely considering that all NAFTA members (Canada, Mexico and the United States) are also members of APEC, a forum committed to open regionalism. The amount of trade and investment diversion caused by NAFTA would be limited especially when all NAFTA members eliminate import quotas and reduce tariffs on most goods. However, there is no guarantee that discrimination through non-tariff barriers would be reduced (Bhagwati, 1992; Drysdale and Garnaut, 1993). NAFTA and MERCOSUR need to be outward-looking in order to stimulate trade and investment flows. MERCOSUR's agreement with the European Union is a positive step in this direction. Chile's application for membership of NAFTA can be considered a test of the seriousness of the US about western hemisphere integration. The real test of whether hemisphere-wide free trade will contribute to the growth of multilateral trade will also depend on how Europe and the Pacific region respond to the implementation of the Uruguay Round.

CONCLUDING REMARKS

This Chapter has discussed NAFTA as a free trade area and MERCOSUR as a customs union. There are obvious differences between the approaches of these two regional blocs. First, as a free trade area, NAFTA has no common external tariffs against third parties. But stringent rules of origin (as an instrument of protection) may have a similar effect on non-members as MERCOSUR's common external tariff. MERCOSUR has kept its common external tariff against third parties rather low. In both cases, however, the two instruments can lead to trade and investment diversion. We have shown in the case of NAFTA that such diversion may not be so significant considering that tariffs are already low. However, non-tariff barriers prevailing in both NAFTA and

MERCOSUR in future could lead to trade diversion. In the case of MERCOSUR both tariff and non-tariff barriers were much higher and stricter at the time of its creation. Therefore, more significant trade diversion from the rest of the world may be expected.

NAFTA and MERCOSUR also differ in respect of the significance of FDI inflows and in the response of multinationals to regional integration. While in the case of NAFTA multinationals are already on the road to a regional market strategy for efficiency seeking, in the case of MERCOSUR trade restrictions and long exception lists tend to distort efficient resource allocation. Despite the fact that FDI is more significant in NAFTA than MERCOSUR, in both cases, government policies have played an important role in dealing with multinationals as well as in the creation of the regional blocs.

How would the multinationals' strategies in future be influenced by the two different models of regional integration? Much will depend on the destination of FDI; if it is invested in services (which is more and more the case especially in NAFTA), their strategies may be based more on national markets since some services are non-tradeables. In the case of manufacturing investments, MNE strategies are likely to be governed more by regional and global markets.

7 Regionalism in Europe

The European Union (EU), the European Free Trade Association (EFTA) and the now defunct Council for Mutual Economic Assistance (COMECON) of the former East European communist countries, represent three examples of regional economic cooperation in Europe. These groupings are the subject of this chapter. Unlike other regional groupings examined in Chapters 3 to 6, the European Union is a unique example of deep integration. It is also the oldest and arguably the most effectively functioning case of economic integration (though, as we shall discuss, not necessarily the most conducive to the globalization of trade).

THE EUROPEAN UNION (EU)

The creation of the European Community by the Treaty of Rome signed in 1957 was motivated as much by security considerations as economic ones. The desire to ward off the communist threat and a vision of pan-Europeanism, including a wish to maintain a European sphere of influence, were the underlying political factors. However, on the economic and trade front, it was not until 1968, 11 years after its formation, that the six original members of the European Economic Community (France, the Federal Republic of Germany, the Netherlands, Belgium, Luxembourg and Italy) achieved the Treaty's goal of eliminating all tariffs and quotas within the region and introducing a common external tariff, making it in effect, a customs union. Regional free trade was also extended to agriculture. In addition, labour mobility was opened up to a large extent. However, sectoral harmonization was limited to the common agricultural policy (CAP) and the Coal and Steel Community. Supranational bodies such as the Council of Ministers and the European Court of Justice were also created.

The seventies and eighties saw a widening of the community membership with the UK, Ireland and Denmark joining the EEC in 1973, Greece in 1981 and Portugal and Spain in 1986. The accession of Austria, Sweden and Finland in 1995 has brought membership to 15. Both the enlargement of the EEC and the moves towards deeper integration in recent years have been driven by the desire to reinforce market democracies, the desire to stem immigration, a need to open up access to other markets, preferably on a preferential basis, and the need to compete for global trade and investment. There has also been pressure from non-members to be included in what is seen to be an increasingly powerful but protectionist bloc. These successive enlargements not only increased the political diversity of the EEC but inevitably diluted its cohesion. The original six favoured deep integration, both economically and politically, while the first batch of newcomers, particularly the UK and Denmark, preferred shallow integration, at an economic level (Baldwin, 1994). The acceptance of the poorer economies of Greece, Spain and Portugal was motivated largely by the desire to help these restored democracies remain democratic by bolstering them politically and economically. As Table 7.1 shows, there are wide variations among the members in respect of GNP per capita, export and import shares in GDP and shares in world trade. In terms of GNP per capita, Greece, Portugal and Spain are the poorest members. According to Baldwin (1994), the accession of these three countries, along with Ireland, drastically altered the shape of EC policies in that redistributive policies in the Community were increasingly required. The EU's unique Structural and Cohesion Funds were created to help narrow the gap between the rich and poorer members.

Unlike the two earlier enlargements, the most recent wave of accessions by some of the EFTA countries, Sweden, Finland and Austria, has not appreciably changed the character or politics of the Community. If anything, they are likely to reinforce existing Community policies with regard to supporting agricultural protectionism as embodied in the CAP as their own agricultural policies (except Sweden's) have been even more protectionist than the CAP.

In addition to the widening of the Community, the nineties have witnessed an accelerated process of deepening integration. The two landmarks in this process have been the Single European Market Programme (SEM) and the Treaty on European Union, also known as the Maastricht Treaty (since then the EC has generally been referred to as the EU). Introduced in January 1993, the SEM programme is expected to lead to the free movement of capital, goods and services as well as people through the removal of non-tariff barriers. This implies that prior to this, free trade had not been achieved within the common market owing to several barriers such as: border taxes, different technical standards and regulations, government procurement practices, varying degrees of compensation in agricultural production, production quotas, import quotas and restrictions on the right of establishment (Cline, 1994).

Table 7.1 Basic economic indicators of members of the European Union

Country	*Per capita GNP (US$) (1994)*	*Population (millions) (mid-1994)*	*Annual GNP per capita growth rate (%) (1985–94)*	*Share of industry in (%) (1994)*	*Export to GDP ratio (%) (1995)*	*Import to GDP ratio (%) (1995)*	*Share in world exports (%) (1995)*	*Share in world imports (%) (1995)*
Austria	24,630	8.0	2.0	34	37.8	38.7	1.06	1.28[1]
Belgium	22,870	10.1	2.3	–	72.6	67.7	3.23[1]*	2.92[1]*
Denmark	27,970	5.2	1.3	27	34.5	30.4	0.97	0.84
Finland	18,850	5.1	−0.3	32	37.9	29.3	0.77	0.55
France	23,420	57.9	1.6	28	23.5	21.2	5.70	5.40
Germany	25,580	81.5	–	–	23.0	22.0	10.09	8.72
Greece	7,700	10.4	1.3	31	17.2[1]	26.4[1]	0.21[1]	0.49[1]
Ireland	13,530	3.6	5.0	9	77.7	65.9	0.87	0.62
Italy	19,300	57.1	1.8	31	23.0[1]	20.2[1]	4.6	4.0
Luxembourg	39,600	0.4	1.2	–	89.0[2]	92.6[2]	–	–
Netherlands	22,010	15.4	1.9	27	52.9	47.0	3.8	3.4
Portugal	9,320	9.9	4.0	–	24.6[1]	36.3[1]	0.4	0.6
Spain	13,440	39.1	2.8	–	23.7	23.5	1.8	2.3
Sweden	23,530	8.8	−0.1	30	40.8	34.5	1.6	1.2
United Kingdom	18,340	58.4	1.3	32	28.2	28.9	4.8	5.2

Sources for GNP, population and share of industry in GDP, *World Development Report*, 1996; for export and import data, IMF, *International Financial Statistics*, Nov. 1996.

[1] = 1994; [2] = 1992; * = includes Luxembourg; – = not available

Liberalization of trade has already been expanded to cover liberalization of financial services including insurance. Customs borders are to be removed and all national trade policy measures are to be disbanded (for more details, see Wise, 1994).

The Maastricht Treaty, which entered into force in November 1993, aims at taking the European Common Market a step further by providing for the establishment of a monetary union leading to a single European currency by January 1999. This is intended to eliminate fluctuations of national currencies and is seen as necessary for the successful functioning of the single market. On the political front, the Treaty aims at a common foreign, security and defence policy, common citizenship and cooperation in justice and social affairs (WTO, 1995).

A major aspect of the Maastricht Agreement concerns the convergence criteria established for determining which countries would become eligible for monetary union. In effect this has created a two-track structure (Cline, 1994) whereby countries that perform well and meet the criteria will be admitted to the union while those that do not meet the criteria will remain excluded. The agreement places considerable pressure to improve fiscal performance as EMU members are subject to penalties, such as suspension of intra-EC lending, for regional development if they do not achieve fiscal targets.

The proposed economic and monetary union has been a hotly debated issue for a number of years. As it involves some loss of national autonomy and sovereignty, it is viewed with a jaundiced eye by some members of the European Union, particularly the United Kingdom. Differences of policy and public opinion in member states have slowed down the realization of the goal of a single currency. The interim measure of a system of semi-fixed exchange rates with national currencies moving against each other within an agreed range (the Exchange Rate Mechanism) has not functioned well, especially as the UK decided to withdraw from the system in September 1992. In August 1993, there was serious speculation against the French franc which was devalued along with the weaker currencies of Ireland, Italy, Portugal and Spain. The EU has failed to cooperate well in the face of international currency speculation.

Common EU standards in public health, environment, labour legislation, education, consumer protection and culture are also being developed. This is unique to the European Union; NAFTA has attempted to harmonise labour and environmental legislation but no common NAFTA policies have been formulated. However, despite provisions for joint action and common policies, individual members retain their national right to opt out of joint action. Indeed the UK has exercised this right by opting out of the social charter (Wise, 1994, pp. 96–7). In order to allay public fears of loss of national sovereignty, the Maastricht Agreement adopted the principle of subsidiarity. This provides that whatever political and economic responsibilities are not explicitly given to the Union reside with the national states.

Harmonization of foreign and defence policies has not been possible either despite the fact that peace and stability was a major political motivation for regional integration apart from the goal of economic prosperity. The EU's failure to act decisively or with one voice, notably on its policy towards the Croatian and Bosnian crises at its doorstep, has undermined its credibility. Issues involving the French nuclear tests in the Pacific, and more recently, the crisis over British beef exports as a result of mad cow disease have further tested EU solidarity.

The implications of the Single Market and European Monetary Union on international trade are significant. The elimination of internal barriers has inevitably led to the EU harmonizing its policies with regard to trade with non-members and this has tended to follow the lowest common denominator. For example, the imposition of voluntary export restraint agreements, particularly with regard to Japanese automobile exports to Europe, was prompted by the group of countries which had restrictive national quotas (France, Italy and the UK). The accession to the EU of the lesser developed countries like Spain, Portugal and Greece has given the countries of East Asia, which have similar industrial structures, particular cause for concern. An eventual absorption into the EU of Eastern European countries like Poland, the Czech Republic and Hungary, seems likely to create additional pressures for EU protectionism against goods from non-members. Even without such forms of protectionism, a more integrated Europe is bound to result in trade diversion away from exports by third world countries to the EU. This is mainly because lowering of internal barriers will make it harder for non-members which are subject to external barriers to compete in the Single European Market, in addition to the higher transport costs involved. Such trade diversion may not have an entirely negative impact if a more integrated Europe were to stimulate EU growth sufficiently to lead to trade creation of a magnitude that will offset trade diversion and thus stimulate overall world trade. However, so far the expected growth has not occurred.

Patterns of EU Trade

Table 7.2 shows trends in EC(12) shares in intra-EC and extraregional merchandise trade between 1958 and 1993. A number of features are worth noting:

(a) intra-EC trade increased steadily for both exports and imports.
(b) EC imports from the ACP countries and its exports to these countries, have been steadily declining;
(c) trade with Eastern Europe declined steadily between 1980 and 1990; but rose again between 1990 and 1993;
(d) trade with the Mediterranean countries has been declining although there is no clear trend for imports;
(e) imports from and exports to the rest of the world (both developing and industrialised countries) declined significantly and consistently during the past three decades.
(f) EC-12 trade with itself has expanded significantly over the years. This could signify trade creation as well as diversion (discussed later in the Chapter).

Intra-EU Trade

Intraregional trade within the EU (formerly EC) has expanded more rapidly and significantly than in any other regional bloc. As we showed in Chapter 2 Table 2.4, the regional trade intensities for the EU rose consistently between 1970 and 1994. This is further confirmed by Appendix Table A 7.1 which gives regional trade intensities for individual members of the EU. The Table shows that the trade intensities of each member country for its trade with the EU (EC) increased over time, although in the case of the United Kingdom they rose less than for many other countries such as Denmark, France and Germany.

What led to the significant increase in intraregional trade within the European Union? Tariff barriers on intra-EC trade were significantly reduced first for the original six members by the end of sixties and for additional members, subsequently. The common external tariff against the rest of the world, especially against Japan and the United States, may have had the effect of diverting trade to Europe. The intra-EC trade increase could also be attributed to the process of economic integration which has led to greater efficiency in production, higher income levels and lower prices.

Besides economic integration, factors such as changes in external

Table 7.2 The regional structure of EC-12 trade (as per cent of total EC-12 trade)

	Partners							
	Western Europe		*Eastern and Southern neighbours*			*Rest of the world*		
Year	*EC-12*	*EFTA*	*Eastern Europe*	*Mediterranean Countries*	*ACP*	*Developing Countries*	*Industrial Countries*	*Total*
				Exports				
1958	37.2	12.2	2.7	7.8	6.6	15.3	18.2	100.0
1965	49.6	13.0	2.9	4.8	4.4	9.4	15.9	100.0
1970	53.4	11.7	3.4	4.8	3.6	7.1	16.0	100.0
1975	52.4	10.6	4.9	6.7	3.6	9.6	12.2	100.0
1980	56.1	11.2	3.5	5.9	3.5	9.2	10.6	100.0
1985	55.2	10.0	2.8	5.2	2.3	8.7	15.8	100.0
1990	61.2	10.4	2.3	4.2	1.6	7.3	13.0	100.0
1993	57.3	9.4	3.7	4.7	1.4	10.3	13.2	100.0
				Imports				
1958	35.2	9.3	2.9	4.5	6.8	19.2	22.1	100.0
1965	44.9	9.0	3.4	4.7	5.2	12.7	20.1	100.0
1970	50.3	8.7	3.2	4.7	4.4	10.3	18.4	100.0
1975	49.5	7.9	3.5	3.8	3.8	16.3	15.2	100.0
1980	49.3	8.6	3.7	4.2	3.8	15.6	14.8	100.0
1985	53.4	9.4	3.9	5.1	3.5	9.8	14.9	100.0
1990	59.0	9.6	2.7	3.8	1.8	8.2	14.9	100.0
1993	56.3	9.8	3.6	3.5	1.3	10.5	15.0	100.0

Source: Sapir (1992). For 1993 data, EUROSTAT (Statistical Office of the European Communities), *Eurostatistics*.

trade policy and competitiveness *vis-à-vis* non-EU members have also affected changes in intraregional trade (see Lloyd, 1992; Sapir, 1992). This is most evident in the steady increase in the intra-EU share of processed agricultural products in trade thanks to the protectionist Common Agricultural Policy. On the other hand, the share of intra-EU imports of footwear and clothing has declined owing to its loss of competitiveness in labour-intensive products (Sapir, 1992).

Preferential Trade

The EU offers preferential treatment in trade to different groups of countries. It is estimated that in 1991, preferential treatment was offered to 40 per cent of EU imports (see Wolf, 1995). First, owing to its special relationship with its immediate neighbours in EFTA, preferential treatment is given to imports from EFTA countries which account for over 22 per cent of imports into the EU (see section on EFTA). Second, unlike other regional groupings, the European Union consists of major colonial powers such as France and the UK which have special trade and economic relationships with their former colonies. The UK's relationships with the British Commonwealth and those of France with the African, Caribbean and Pacific (ACP) countries have led to preferential treatment in trade through such instruments as the Lomé Convention. The Lomé Convention contains a number of special agreements for privileged market access to the EU for the products of the 70 ACP countries. Goods originating from these countries can be imported into the EU free of tariffs and quantitative restrictions but they are subject to tariff quotas; those goods that are subject to market regulation within the EU are excluded. Lomé IV (signed in 1989), which expires in 1999, provides for non-reciprocal tariff concessions on bananas and other commodities. In 1992, Latin American banana producers (Guatemala, Ecuador, Honduras and Mexico) challenged the right of the EU to give preferences to the ACP countries and requested GATT to review prevailing banana regimes. The GATT panel on dispute settlement found the regimes inconsistent with GATT principles (see Raboy *et al.*, 1995). The EU banana regime which went into operation on 1 July 1993, replaced a variety of national trade restrictions by common quotas targeted mainly against Latin American producers.[1]

In addition to the ACP countries, the EU has 12 separate agreements with the Mediterranean countries which provide for immediate preferential access to the EU market for products from these countries, particularly in such products as citrus fruit, olive oil, wine and tobacco.

Together, the Mediterranean and ACP countries account for about 11 per cent of imports.

There is growing pressure for the review and possible elimination of preferential tariffs under the Lomé Convention. However, as we note below, even without such a review, trade between ACP countries and the EU has been on the decline. On the other hand, association agreements with Eastern European countries represent the most recent round of preferential trade agreements of the EU.

Trade preferences clearly hinder global trade liberalization because they discriminate against the rest of the world. Although the enlargement of the EU has a positive influence on liberalization, it is not certain that this will more than compensate for the negative effect of preferences.

EU Protectionism

The Common Agricultural Policy (CAP) is one of the most explicit forms of EU protectionism. It involves producer subsidies, limits on volume of production and price controls. CAP subsidizes exports to dispose of surpluses and thus has distortionary effects on trade with the rest of the world. For example, it has adversely affected the food exports of such countries as Argentina, Australia and New Zealand. For a long time, a strong farmers' lobby prevented any reform or relaxation of this protectionist agricultural policy. However, in the nineties internal as well as external pressures have led to some reforms. Internally, agricultural financial constraints, EU accessions and the Single Market programme have led to a reform of CAP since 1992. There have been strong external pressures as a result of the Uruguay Round Agreement, which are forcing the EU to consider gradually reducing agricultural subsidies. Internally, agricultural subsidies are increasingly being viewed as a wasteful burden on the tax payers and consumers. EU enlargement adds to this burden.

Although tariffs have generally been declining, the EU has increasingly applied various forms of non-tariff barriers (NTBs) on a selective basis, to products and countries. Import barriers are applied to products of developing countries, and in particular, to manufactured exports from the East Asian NIEs, such as colour TVs, VCRs and computers. EU protectionism applies not only to the East Asian economies but also to other developing countries such as Bangladesh, the Dominican Republic and Sri Lanka. Both tariff and non-tariff barriers against imports from these countries have been quite significant (World Bank,

1991, p. 9). Winters (1993) has noted that the coverage of NTBs imposed by the EC on manufactures has grown five-fold, rising from about 10 per cent in 1966 to over 55 per cent in 1986. This level of NTBs is higher than that of either Japan or the United States. The EU product coverage of NTBs has increased by the extension of CAP protection to other primary sectors such as coal.

The EU continues to be a frequent user of anti-dumping measures. It is reported that at the end of 1994, 156 anti-dumping measures were in force. Against the Republic of Korea alone, the EU imposed 19 anti-dumping measures during 1985–90, which is twice the number of cases during 1972–84 (see Han, 1992, p. 28). These measures have also been imposed against Japan (roller bearings), India, Indonesia and Thailand (polyester yarn), and Malaysia, Mexico and the United States (3.5 inch microdiscs) (WTO, 1995a, p. 63).

In 1992, the European Commission sanctioned unilateral restrictions by France and Italy against Korean and Taiwanese footwear and by Germany and Italy against Czech steel pipes. In addition, unilateral restrictions have been imposed by individual EU members on the import of cars from Japan and iron and steel from the United States. Such restrictions have been subsequently replaced by EU-wide restrictive policies. Winters (1994) notes that the European Commission tends to adopt the national policies of the most protectionist member as EU-wide policies.

The drive towards EU protectionism may have been reinforced by several factors. First, as noted above, the exports of developing countries (particularly the East Asian NIEs) have shifted from primary products to manufactured goods which offer stiff competition to EU products. The EU's restrictive measures on such imports are intended to counter unfair competition as a result of subsidies or dumping. Secondly, the less developed members of the EU, namely Portugal and Spain which have production structures similar to those of the Asian NIEs, may be important protagonists of regional protectionism and barriers against NIE's imports to safeguard their own industries and exports within the EU. The Asian NIEs have been showing increasing trade surpluses *vis-à-vis* the EU countries (despite import liberalization they import less than they export to these countries) which further induces protectionist tendencies on the part of the EU. Persistent and high unemployment rates (average recorded unemployment across the EU was about 11 per cent in 1993) owing to prolonged recession, seem to have reinforced these tendencies.

There is a controversy over whether the EU is any more protectionist than the other regional trading blocs or major trading countries and whether it has increased world protectionism. Inadequate evidence is partly responsible for lack of unanimity on this point. Furthermore, the question may itself be somewhat ambiguous. Does it mean that the EU is more protectionist than would be the case in the absence of integration? Or does it imply that EU-wide trade policies are more protectionist than member governments' policies taken in isolation. Another interpretation may be that the EU is more protectionist than it was in the past.

Trade Diversion?

The increasing resort to non-tariff barriers discussed above is known to have increased the potential for trade diversion from developing countries, particularly in East Asia and Latin America. This trend has been accentuated since the three middle-income countries (Greece, Portugal and Spain) joined the European Union. Two reasons account for this. First, the removal of tariff barriers between old and new members has increased internal demand. Secondly, these countries demanded protection for a larger number of 'sensitive products' against external competition (see Page, 1994). The creation of the SEM in 1993 is likely to lead to further trade diversion.

In predicting the potential economic effects of the internal market, the Commission of European Communities (1988) estimated that non-EC imports would drop by between 7.9 per cent and 10.3 per cent. These estimates were based on optimistic assumptions about EU growth rates ranging from 4.5 to 7 per cent over several years. These estimates are generally taken to amount to about 5 per cent over five years. Since in actual practice growth rates have been much lower (at least till the middle of 1996), the net trade diversion effect might be even higher (trade creation is likely to be lower as it is assumed to result from growth, more efficient allocation of resources, lowering of prices and an increase in incomes in the EC which would generate additional demand for imports from developing countries). Page (1991) disaggregated the effects of the single market on different developing-country regions and estimated that the shares of exports to the EU of the four Asian NIEs (Hong Kong, Korea, Singapore and Taiwan), and of South Asia and China would decline. Besides the Single Market, closer integration between the EU and EFTA through the creation of the European Economic Area and the EC's openness to the Central and Eastern European countries (see below) are further likely to divert trade from the four Asian NIEs and other developing countries. The Asian NIEs' and EFTA countries' exports compete in such manufactured goods as textiles and clothing, telecommunications and electrical machinery.

Izam (1993) predicts negative implications of the Single Market for developing countries, particularly in the Latin American region. Latin American exports to the EC had been declining even before the creation of the Single Market, thanks to tariff and non-tariff barriers particularly under CAP.

Trade diversion is likely to be greater for such income-elastic manufactured goods as textiles and clothing, footwear and simple electronics in which developing countries compete with the European Union. Trade diversion is likely to be less severe in the case of primary products the demand for which is income inelastic (Page, 1991). Thisen (1994) argues that in the case of Africa, trade diversion is likely to occur in manufactures, particularly chemicals; it is unlikely in African primary exports which do not compete with European production. Estimates of trade creation and trade diversion resulting from the SEM vary a great deal depending on the assumptions made about growth rates in the EU and income elasticities of demand for primary products and manufactured goods.

Foreign Direct Investment and Strategies of Multinationals

We noted in Chapter 2 that FDI flows are concentrated heavily in Europe and, to a lesser extent, in East Asia. A study by the European Commission shows some empirical evidence of positive linkages between trade and FDI in the case of the EU and similarities in their geographic distribution (cited in UNECE, 1994). The largest share of investments from outside the EU, came from MNEs from the United States. They account for larger FDI inflows into Europe than intra-EU investments. Even before the formation of the European Community, the US, which was a technological leader at that time, invested significantly in Western Europe. This may partly have been due to the high wages and shortage of dollars which compelled US manufacturers to resort to offshore production. A substantial share of this was in the UK owing to common language and a better understanding of the business practices and regulations of that country, plus its links with the larger market of the Commonwealth.

Did European integration stimulate FDI inflows from the US and lead to their reallocation? A number of studies have been undertaken to answer this question. A comparison made by Scaperlanda (1967) between US FDI in the EC and that in the non-EC countries did not suggest any positive answer. Correcting for a methodological error in the Scaperlanda study, Wallis (1968) demonstrated that US FDI into the EC during 1951–64 increased consistently thus supporting the re-allocation hypothesis. Dunning (1993) provides data which suggests that in the first 15 years of existence of the EC, US investment in the EC rose faster than it might have done in the absence of integration. Considering that other regions of the world did not attract such large growth in US FDI, it would seem safe to assume that anticipation of the likely benefits from the creation of the common market was a strong motivation. Evidence seems to point to the fact that this, rather than the need to jump import barriers aimed at non-member countries, was what drove most of US investment in the sixties. Membership of the EC has been particularly beneficial for individual countries like the UK in terms of attracting FDI. In the period immediately following its accession to the EC, the rate of investments in the UK by US multi-nationals increased substantially. Studies (for example, one by Schmitz and Bieri, 1972) have also shown that US FDI inflows into the EC grew much more rapidly than those into the EFTA countries. This was most likely owing to the larger size of the united market and growing demand in the EC relative to EFTA.

1. Magnitude of FDI Inflows and their Impact

Between 1975 and 1983, the US accounted for an estimated 43 per cent of total FDI inflows into the Community compared with 25 per cent of intra-EU inflows (UNCTC, 1990). The free movement of goods provided by an enlarged protected common market permitted product specialization based on the comparative advantage of the different countries. This may have been an important consideration in the strategies of US multinationals. The dramatic increase in EU intra-firm trade by the larger, more experienced US investors shows that they have been increasingly engaging in efficiency seeking FDI based on regional division of labour. Sales by US affiliates in the EU to other US affiliates had increased from 21.5 per cent in 1966 to about 56 per cent in 1985. There was a further increase by almost 75 per cent from 1985 to 1988 (Dunning, 1993). More recent investments by US multinationals in the EU may also be partly a response to the growing internationalization of Japanese corporations and a need to maintain their global competitive position *vis-à-vis* Japan.

We noted in Chapter 6 (see also Figure 6.3) that the US share of

FDI outflows going to the tertiary sector was invariably higher than in manufacturing throughout the 1985-94 period. This suggests that despite monopolies and regulatory regimes in banking and financial services, FDI inflows into this sector in the EU continued. This is confirmed by the data on FDI inflows by sector of such major EU members as France, Germany and the United Kingdom. In France, FDI inflows into the tertiary sector (mainly in finance, insurance and business services) ranged from 63 per cent of the total in 1985 to 74.6 per cent in 1994. In no single year was the manufacturing share higher (FDI outflows from France also show a similar picture). Similarly, the German data show a preponderance of the tertiary sector and net disinvestment in manufacturing throughout the period (see OECD, 1996). In the UK also, except in 1985 and 1994, the share of FDI inflows in services was higher than in manufacturing. This situation may not seem surprising considering that the scope for investment in financial and business-related services has expanded as a result of widespread privatization, the introduction of new information technologies in telecommunications, increased tradeability of services, and transport and trade liberalization in the Single European Market (SEM).

While the US continues to invest much more in Europe than in the Americas (see Figure 6.2, Chapter 6), US FDI in Europe declined since 1993 while it increased in NAFTA, South and East Asia and Latin America. This may be explained partly by the need to diversify investments in response to the greater globalization strategies by MNEs, and, in the case of East Asia, in order to assure market access to a region which has been registering strong growth and market potential.

Japan was a relative latecomer in terms of investment in the EU. While the EU's share of Japanese FDI has been increasing rapidly, it remains much smaller than the share for North America (see Figure 6.3, Chapter 6). There was a dramatic surge in Japanese FDI in the EU, rising from US $8329 million in 1988 to US $13305 million in 1990 (see OECD, 1996). Over 50 per cent of this in 1990 went to the UK and another 21 per cent to the Netherlands. The UK has attracted Japanese FDI more than the other EU countries partly because of a more favourable industrial relations system, weaker trade unions and an important financial centre in London.

Japanese FDI in the EU in particular is attracted by good infrastructure, cost and quality of labour, and government incentives and subsidies to invest in less-developed or depressed areas (for example, Wales and Northeast of England in the UK). Many Japanese companies invest in the EU to defend and expand their market shares which are increasingly threatened by global competition (see Thomsen, 1993). A JETRO (Japan External Trade Organization) survey in 1991 (cited in Thomsen, 1993) shows that the globalization strategy of Japanese firms involved their shifting from exports to local production in the EU. Japanese companies tend to transfer production abroad when they lose comparative advantage at home. One of the most important reasons has been the need to capture larger market shares of the significant EU market for such Japanese products as consumer electronics and automobiles in which the country has achieved significant competitive advantage. This has caused some concern to many European countries, particularly France. All the more so as this FDI growth has been accompanied by a tremendous growth in Japanese exports to the EU. The resulting large trade imbalance has led to trade frictions and the imposition of restrictive measures by the European Union on the import of some Japanese goods, particularly automobiles. In contrast to the above 'market-seeking' investments, those in the chemical sector in which Japanese companies do not enjoy any competitive advantage, seem to be more 'resource' and technology seeking. This explains why Japanese companies have been acquiring smaller European chemical companies through mergers.

In 1993, Japanese FDI in the EU started declining whereas it started rising for NAFTA, Latin America and the Caribbean, and South and East Asia (see Figure 6.3).

Does Japanese FDI in the EU substitute for exports from Japan to the EU? Micossi and Viesti (1991) do not find any conclusive evidence to this effect. Assuming a substitution rate of 15 per cent in 1988 rising gradually to 25 per cent in 1993, Sumitomo Life Research Institute (1989) estimated that Japanese investment-generated sales would replace over US$67 billion worth of Japanese exports to the EU by 1993. Whether export substitution takes place will depend on the nature of individual industries. The issue of complementarity or substitution between direct investment and exports is tricky. The above evidence on substitution is not conclusive because it does not take account of the non-manufacturing and distributional activities in which the Japanese subsidiaries abroad are also engaged. These distributional activities are known to have promoted Japanese exports (Yamawaki, 1991).

With regard to automobiles, electronic goods and transport equipment, the EC's resort to anti-dumping duties and voluntary export restraints (VERs) has probably induced FDI of the tariff-jumping variety. This is observed mainly in the UK but also in Germany and Spain. Balasubramanyam and Greenaway (1993) suggest that the preferred method of market penetration by Japanese and East Asian firms in these sectors would be through exports, but when this is blocked through protectionist barriers, they resort to FDI as a substitute. This could either be a response to protectionism or in anticipation of it. They suggest that when it is of an anticipatory nature it might even succeed in pre-empting protectionism. As production by the Japanese MNEs within Europe will displace imports, there will be no need to impose tariffs and quotas. In addition, the beneficial effects of the Japanese multinationals through employment creation and investment in the EU, particularly in many of the depressed areas which have been wooing such FDI, might defuse the protectionist lobbies within the EU. This could be viewed as an incentive to liberalization. However, as it is also a substitute for exports, it is likely to be trade diverting as opposed to trade creating, particularly if such production proves to be more expensive than imports. It could also be regarded as investment diversion. On the other hand, Japanese FDI represents part of the globalization strategy of Japanese firms, particularly those with strong managerial skills and technological superiority. This form of FDI is likely to contribute to growth, intra-industry trade, and trade creation in general.

Thus, the impact of Japanese FDI on the EU and its member countries is not clearcut. On the one hand, the presence of Japanese plants in the EU should offer healthy competition to European industry thereby improving efficiency. On the other hand, it could lead to excess capacity as in the case of the US automobile industry.

2. *Intra-EU Investment and the Single European Market*

Since the formation of the European Community, intra-Community FDI flows have been increasing. Figures 7.1 to 7.4 show FDI outflows of France, Germany, the United Kingdom and Italy respectively to other EU countries, to Central and Eastern Europe and to NAFTA. They show the growing importance of intra-EU investments till 1991 (for France and Germany and 1990 for the UK). This picture is also confirmed by FDI intensity ratios for a selected number of EU investors (see Table 7.3). With the exception of the UK, the FDI intensity ratios of all other countries in the Table are higher for the European region than for the others. However, it is interesting to note that in the cases of France and Germany, FDI flows to the EU started declining since 1992, the year with which the Single European Market is associated. In the case of France, this decline coincides with an increase in FDI outflows to NAFTA and to a much less extent, Central and Eastern Europe. In the case of Germany, FDI outflows to Central and Eastern Europe and to NAFTA (since 1993) have gained at the expense of outflows to the EU. This suggests that these two countries were keen to diversify their FDI and capture market niches in NAFTA. In contrast to this situation, Italy's FDI flows have concentrated in the EU instead of NAFTA or Central and Eastern Europe (see Figure 7.4).

The European FDI outflows to NAFTA (mainly the US) consistently declined during the eighties (with the exception of the UK) whereas Figures 7.1 to 7.4 show that intra-EU FDI rose in the late eighties perhaps in anticipation of Europe 1992. Since FDI had risen to substantial levels, European investors started diverting FDI to NAFTA (particularly, the US). A number of factors seem to have motivated this shift of FDI back to NAFTA, including the need to protect or develop competitive positions *vis-à-vis* the US and Japan, to promote scale economies and to acquire technology.

It appears that regional integration and American competition have improved the competitiveness of European firms which, by the late-seventies, started investing in the US market. Growing competition resulting from Europe 1992, the openness of markets, integration of financial markets and growth of trade have also led to a growing number of strategic alliances and mergers between multinational enterprises in the European Union.

Has the Single Market of 1992 provided economies of scale and positive income and demand effects thus attracting inflows of FDI into the EU as has been suggested by Greenaway (1993) and Dunning (1993)? Increasing new or first time MNE activity by smaller US, Japanese and Asian NIE firms as well as by EU MNEs investing in other EU countries, would seem to suggest an increase in FDI inflows into the EU since 1993. However, as we noted above, expectations do not correspond to reality. Despite active policies by EU governments to attract FDI through increased liberalization of investment and regulatory regimes, FDI inflows declined in 1993 and 1994. The share of intra-EU FDI of France, and the UK declined before and after 1992 and that of Germany remained almost unchanged. This could have been temporary owing to sluggish growth, and in Germany's case, to reunification. The increase in Italian intra-EU FDI since 1991, noted earlier, was presumably in anticipation of the Single Market (see Figure 7.4).

Current trends show a decrease in FDI in Europe and North America in favour of South and East Asia where it has increased. However, this

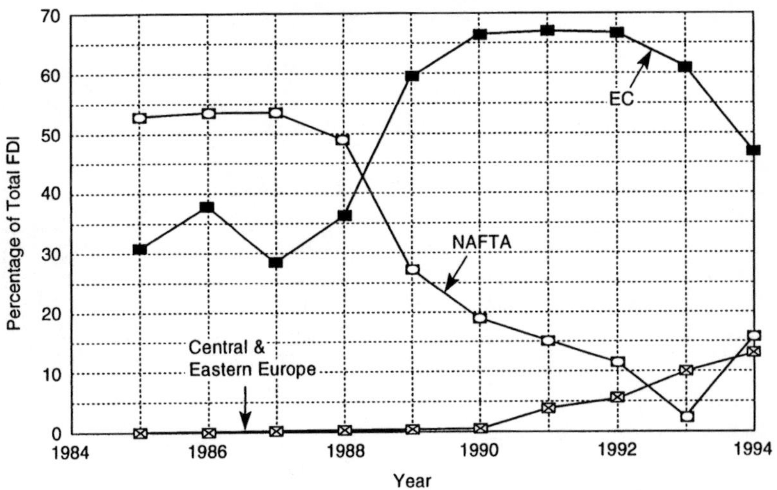

Figure 7.1 Germany: FDI Flows to EC, NAFTA and Central and Eastern Europe

Source: Based on data from OECD (1996).

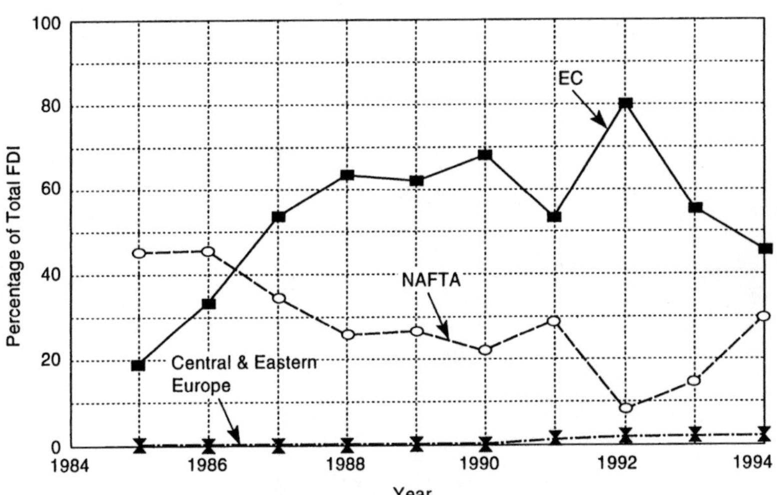

Figure 7.2 France: FDI Flows to EC, NAFTA and Central and Eastern Europe

Source: Based on data from OECD (1996).

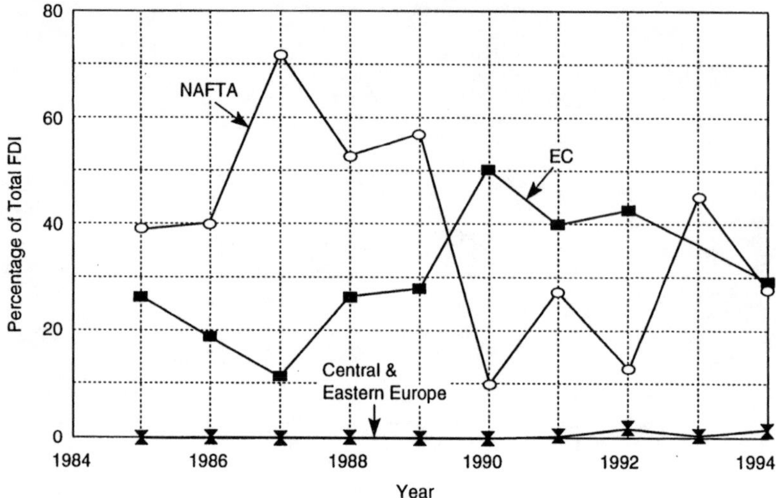

Figure 7.3 United Kingdom: FDI Flows to EC, NAFTA and Central and Eastern Europe

Source: Based on data from OECD (1996).

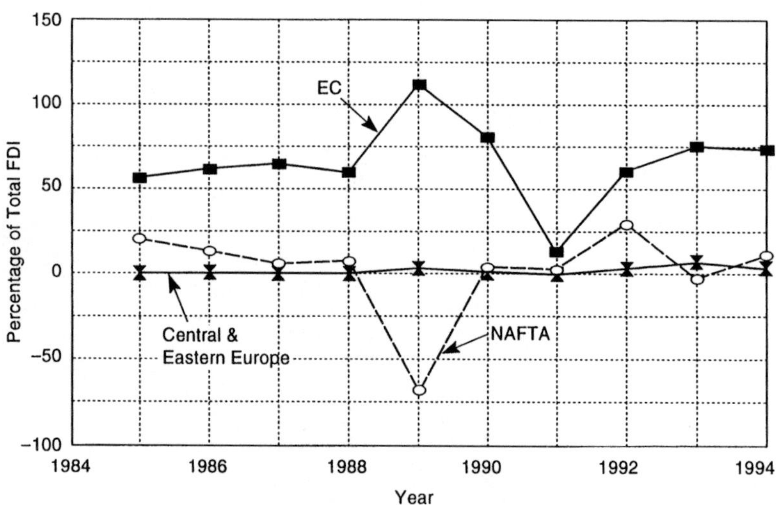

Figure 7.4 Italy: FDI Flows to EC, NAFTA and Central and Eastern Europe

Source: Based on data from OECD (1996).

Table 7.3 FDI intensity ratios of selected EU countries by host region (1990)

Country	*Host Region*				
	Europe	*North America*	*Latin America*	*East Asia*[a]	*Africa*
France	1.56	1.00	0.23	0.14	0.33
Germany	1.55	0.82	0.52	0.38	1.00
Italy	1.76	0.33	1.04	0.26	0.66
Netherlands	1.42	0.86	0.54	0.48	0.54
Sweden	1.90	0.61	0.31	0.00	0.00
United Kingdom	0.79	1.32	0.56	1.01	2.11

Source: UNCTAD (1993), p. 169.

Note: Intensity ratio: Share of host region in outward investment stock of a given country, divided by share of host region in world-wide FDI stock, excluding FDI stock in the investor country.

[a] Including Southeast Asia and the Pacific.

might once again change with the prospect of a vast single market. The European Economic Area (which includes EFTA), provides a strong motivation for more FDI from the US, the East Asian NIEs and Japan as well as intra-EU investment.

3. Investment Diversion?

Parallel to trade diversion considered above, there is also the likelihood of investment diversion. Hughes-Hallett (1994) believes that investment diversion is likely to be far more important than trade diversion, and this factor will hurt developing countries more than trade diversion. It is worth noting that accession to the EU by the southern countries of Greece, Portugal and Spain, significantly increased their attractiveness for inward FDI. However, this may have had the effect of diverting trade and investment from developing countries at similar levels of development (for example, Morocco, Algeria and Tunisia). The sharp fall in FDI into these northern African countries after 1987 suggests a possibility of investment diversion (see Figures 7.1 to 7.4).

The SEM and its protectionist tendencies (reflected in quotas, anti-dumping duties, and local content rules, etc.) are likely to encourage major investors to divert investments away from developing countries to the EU countries. However, there are circumstances under which investments may actually increase in developing countries. First, this may happen if trade creation dominates trade diversion and new investments may be needed to supply that trade. Secondly, some investments in polluting industries may be diverted to developing countries when EU environmental regulations become more strict (see Hughes-Hallett, 1994).

EUROPEAN FREE TRADE AREA (EFTA)

Countries of Europe which were not ready for far-reaching economic integration as embodied in the European Community, formed the much looser European Free Trade Association (EFTA) in November 1959 by what is known as the Stockholm Convention. Members of the Association originally consisted of Austria, Denmark, Norway, Portugal, Sweden, Switzerland and the United Kingdom. Finland became a full member of EFTA in 1985. EFTA is not a customs union with a common external trade policy. In order to prevent non-member countries exporting products to EFTA via the members with the lowest import tariffs, the group decided to establish intra-EFTA rules of origin identical to those prevailing in the EC when the UK left EFTA in 1972. Agricultural products and services are excluded from the provisions of the agreement. Unlike the EC, EFTA rejected the regional harmonization of standards and regulations.

The current and former EFTA countries are characterized by their small size, openness and extensive trade with non-European countries. Intra-EFTA trade has been limited except for trade between the Nordic countries, namely, Norway, Sweden and Finland. The small size of the market has hindered the EFTA economies from taking advantage of economies of scale and enlarged competition. This factor may have played a part in the decision by many EFTA countries to join the European Union. In EFTA countries, while manufactures are open to external competition, service industries are generally protected as they are in the European Union (Norman, 1991, p. 125).

It is generally believed that the EFTA countries engage in freer trade in manufactures than do the European Union countries. While these countries would benefit from economies of scale and competition by joining the EU, there might be some offsetting negative effects. For example, a common external tariff and trade policy for these countries would imply a possible loss of trade with the rest of the world.

EFTA countries have been unable to resist the pull-effect of the EU. The withdrawal of the UK and Denmark from EFTA in 1972 and their move to the EU triggered a series of EU free trade agreements with individual EFTA members so as to soften the blow of the loss of the huge UK market for EFTA products. This has resulted in a closer integration of EFTA countries' trade with the EU. The agreements involved largely industrial products with the exclusion of some sensitive sectors. These countries enjoy a fairly balanced trade relationship in terms of exports and imports to and from the EU. The EU accounts for between 50 and 70 per cent of EFTA international trade which is 15 to 20 per cent of their GDP (Winters, 1993).

With the current EFTA membership reduced to Iceland, Liechtenstein, Norway and Switzerland, following accession to the EU of Portugal in 1986 and Sweden, Austria and Finland in 1995, the future of EFTA has become uncertain. It is largely becoming irrelevant following the establishment of the European Economic Area (EEA) in 1992. This EFTA–EC agreement encompasses many of the features of the Single Market: the free movement of labour and capital, the harmonization of regulations affecting enterprises, consumer protection, education, the environment, research and development, social policy, competition policy, state aid, and public procurement (WTO, 1995). The main exceptions are their exclusion from the Common Agricultural Policy, the common external tariff, some elements of competition, and some, though not all, budgetary contributions. On the other hand, full membership would imply a greater degree of permanence to the arrangement and would lend greater credibility to EFTA countries in terms of attracting FDI.

A considerable amount of the independence which EFTA members were anxious to maintain by remaining out of the EU has thus been given up under the EEA. The agreement requires EFTA members to submit to much of existing and future Community legislation relating to the Single Market without any formal means of influencing its formulation. In addition EFTA countries will have to accept EU laws relating to company practices and competition policy, environment, social and consumer policy. Their major motive for agreeing to the EEA was their fear of being left out of the Single Market despite the free trade agreements they had signed with the EU. Hindley and Messerlin (1993) point out that there were some areas which these agreements had not covered such as the free movement of persons between EFTA and the EU. Furthermore, the agreements did not assure against anti-dumping actions by the EU. These authors argue that the more restrictive the trade policies of the EU become, the greater is the fear of third countries that access to this huge market will be withdrawn. They are, therefore, willing to pay a high price to assure such access even if it means sacrificing some of their independence.

The accession of EFTA countries to the European Union has implications for developing countries in that additional trade preferences will be extended to ACP and Mediterranean countries. This will promote greater economic and industrial cooperation between a large number of developed countries of Europe and the developing countries (UNCTAD, 1993).

Having examined Western European integration, we now turn to integration within Central and Eastern Europe and to the prospect for its eventual integration into the EU.

INTEGRATION IN CENTRAL AND EASTERN EUROPE?

COMECON (or CMEA) was established in 1949 with the following membership: Bulgaria, Czechoslovakia, Hungary, Poland, Romania and the USSR (Albania and East Germany joined subsequently).

During the early years, COMECON did not show any major achievements in terms of either trade or growth. Most of the transactions between members were undertaken on a bilateral basis. However, the middle of 1956 saw the start of sub-regional level planning and the establishment of joint projects and industries of crucial importance. During the seventies, several measures were adopted to implement the Comprehensive Programme of Socialist Integration. Agreements on regional specialization and location of plants and industries were made on the basis of the comparative advantage of each country in particular areas of production. More dynamic attempts were also made at joint planning through regional allocation of resources in the economic plans of each country. Supranational planning was intended to achieve economies of mass production. However, in practice, the countries did not consider the COMECON area as a single planning unit and specialization was encouraged within the existing economic structures. Inadequate coordination of new investments (despite mention of regional projects in national plans) hindered effective inter-country specialization (Dell, 1963).

COMECON members were divided on the precise ways to achieve socialist integration. While the USSR preferred central planning, Hungary and Poland opted for mixed economy measures (so-called market socialism). They advocated currency and commodity convertibility as well as decentralization of decision-making under which enterprises could purchase required inputs directly from other enterprises in other member countries. However, the Russian view prevailed.

Coordination, mainly of production rather than of investments, under COMECON suffered from several limitations. First, in the absence of rational prices and exchange rates, industrial commissions made recommendations about balancing of trade in a largely *ad hoc* and arbitrary manner. Also the purely sectoral and industrial approach failed to 'take into account intersectoral linkages resulting from changes recommended by individual permanent commissions' (Smith, 1979, p. 6).

In general, many Central and Eastern European economies, particularly Russia, continue to suffer from the pangs of transition from a socialist to a market economy. In many of these economies, including Russia, GNP per capita has actually declined due to an absolute fall in output. With the exception of Hungary, growth of per capita incomes has been negligible or negative (see Table 7.4). This has implications for the potential integration of the economies into the global trade and investment regime. Such integration requires structural adjustment measures which some of these economies are ill prepared to undertake.

Table 7.4 Basic economic indicators of Central and Eastern European economies

Country	*Per capita GNP (US$) (1994)*	*Population (millions) (mid-1994)*	*Annual GNP per capita growth rate (%) (1985–94)*	*Share of industry in GDP (%) (1994)*	*Export to GDP ratio (%) (1995)*	*Import to GDP ratio (%) (1995)*	*Share in world exports (%) (1995)*	*Share in world imports (%) (1995)*
Albania	380	3.2	–	22	–	–	–	–
Bulgaria	1,250	8.4	−2.7	35	–	–	–	–
Czech Republic	3,200	10.3	−2.1	39	59.2	63.7	0.4	0.5
Estonia	2,820	1.5	−6.1	36	90.2	85.3	0.04	0.04
Hungary	3,840	10.3	−1.2	33	29.0	35.5	0.2	0.3
Latvia	2,320	2.5	−6.0	34	29.1	39.1	0.02	0.04
Lithuania	1,350	3.7	−8.0	41	11.3	14.3	0.06	0.06
Poland	2,410	38.5	0.8	40	24.0[1]	23.0[1]	0.4	0.6
Romania	1,270	22.7	−4.5	33	23.0[2]	28.0[2]	0.13	0.17
Russia	2,650	148.3	−4.1	38	26.3	22.2	1.6	1.2
Slovak Republic	2,250	5.3	−3.0	36	62.7	59.4	0.15	0.13[1]
Slovenia	7,040	2.0	–	38	60.5[1]	55.5[1]	0.16	0.17
Ukraine	1,910	51.9	−8.0	50	25.9[2]	26.2[2]	0.2	0.2

Sources for per capita GNP, population and share of industry in GDP, World Bank, *World Development Report*, 1996; for trade data, IMF, *International Financial Statistics*, Nov. 1996.

[1] = 1994; [2] = 1993

Intra-Bloc Trade

Intra-COMECON trade expanded during the first few years. In 1948 such trade among members was 45 per cent of the total. Kaser (1967, p. 142) notes that 'between 1948 and 1954, this intra-trade rose 3.12 times in value and, if price experience was the same as in Western Europe, . . . 3.58 times in volume.' Between 1954 and 1960, intraregional trade slowed down, growing only 1.75 times in value and 1.71 times in volume.

Did COMECON (or CMEA) contribute to an increase in intraregional trade? Some authors such as Biessen (1991) and Brada (1993) believe that the volume of trade was greater than it would have been in the absence of the bloc because transaction costs of trading were reduced. Others like Robson (1987, p. 220) argue that the increase in intraregional trade was not so much due to COMECON as 'to political factors and had little to do with the Council's activities'. He attributes the failure of trade expansion to the inconvertibility of the rouble. Although an International Bank for Economic Cooperation was established in 1963 to encourage intra-bloc trade by enabling all COMECON transactions through a transferable rouble, little progress was made. This is because members of the bloc which had trade surpluses were unable to spend the transferable roubles freely on unplanned imports from other members. Rigid commodity planning hindered access of foreigners to the internal market of each country. Other barriers to intra-bloc trade included bilateral trade agreements and a slowdown of economic growth of COMECON countries particularly during the sixties.[2]

Systematic quantitative estimates to determine whether trade creation or trade diversion took place after the creation of COMECON are difficult. No doubt redirection of trade took place towards the former Soviet Union. It is, however, difficult to attribute this diversion exclusively to the creation of COMECON. The problem of identification occurs because several policy changes took place simultaneously: rapid industrialization and self-sufficiency, nationalization and central planning (Robson, 1987). Michalak (1994, p. 118) claims that 'most of the intraregional trade was the result of trade diversion after the division of Europe. This diversion was created first and foremost by political and military interference from Moscow'.

Since 1991, following the disintegration of the Soviet Union, the end of communism in Eastern Europe and the dissolution of COMECON, intra-bloc trade has declined significantly. Some estimates show that the decline has been between 15–40 per cent with the greatest decline occurring in trade between the former Soviet Union and the rest of Eastern Europe. This decline is partly explained by the reform of the Soviet foreign trade mechanism. Foreign trade decisions became decentralized to the enterprises but no foreign exchange was allocated to them to pay for imports (see Brada, 1993). The reunification of Germany, which resulted in the loss of East Germany as a major trading partner, may also have contributed to this decline.

Barriers to intra-Eastern trade persist. However, a beginning has been made towards trade liberalization among a selected number of the Central and Eastern European countries (CEECs). For example, the Central European Free Trade Area between the Czech Republic, Hungary, Poland and Slovakia came into force in March 1993. The four member countries have agreed to reduce tariffs in stages. In the first stage, tariffs on 'non-controversial' goods (which account for 30–60 per cent of the exports of individual members) will be eliminated. All tariffs and quotas on the remaining industrial goods will be eliminated by the year 2001. Finally, trade barriers on agricultural products will be phased out over a five-year period (Brada, 1993). Members have now agreed to accelerate the process of tariff reductions. As tariff levels are already low among the members, the effect of the free trade area on trade expansion may be only marginal.

The scope for expansion of the above free trade area to other CEECs, desirable though it may be, is fraught with difficulties. A major problem is the significant differences in inflation rates and misalignment of exchange rates of national currencies.

Trade Between Eastern Europe and the European Union

The CEECs are currently paying far less attention to intra-Eastern trade than trade with the European Union and Western Europe in general. Most of the CEECs have been interested in joining the European Union to ensure access to the enlarged market. Clearly, EU members have been reluctant to admit as full members such a large number of diverse countries at much lower stages of development. However, many of the more industrial countries of Eastern Europe have already obtained associate membership: the former Czechoslovakia, Hungary and Poland in 1991; Bulgaria and Romania in 1993; and Estonia, Latvia and Lithuania in 1994. The purpose of these associate membership agreements is to provide a first step towards an eventual free movement of goods, services and capital between Eastern and Western Europe. The agreements are non-reciprocal in that they involve access of goods from the CEECs free of tariffs and quantitative restrictions while the CEECs do not have to remove their own import barriers for a transition period of ten years. This is understandable since the former Soviet Union and other members of the Eastern bloc were inefficient and high-cost suppliers of goods and raw materials. The European Council held in Copenhagen in June 1993 accelerated the schedule of trade liberalization for the associated countries. With the exception of steel products and certain textiles and clothing products (so-called 'sensitive goods'), industrial imports from these countries can move freely into the EU (WTO, 1995b, p. 21). However, agriculture (in which the CEECs may have a comparative advantage) and services have been excluded from the agreements. The fear of illegal mass migrations from the CEECs, a political desire to share the wealth and security of a united Europe in order to assure political stability in Eastern Europe, and the lure of large potential markets may have been some of the motivations for the EU to offer associate membership to Eastern countries in the form of Europe Agreements.

Since 1990, the European Community's exports to Eastern Europe have increased by over 20 per cent annually (Michalak, 1994, p. 123). Exports from Eastern Europe to the EU increased even faster. Neven and Roller (1991) show that the former Federal Republic of Germany had about one-third of its trade with COMECON countries, a rather dominant position. During the eighties, a number of EU countries (namely, France, Belgium, UK, Germany and Italy) registered a fall in their exports to Eastern Europe, whereas the share of the Netherlands' exports remained more or less constant. While the EC became less important as a trading partner, countries like Austria and Finland (now members of the EU) became more important partners in East–West trade.

Market reforms and trade liberalization have enabled the Eastern European countries to redirect their trade towards western markets. It is reported that these countries 'shifted about a quarter of their trade turnover from east to west of which 80 per cent was redirected toward the EU. The EU has become the CEECs' largest trade partner, absorbing more than half of current exports from Poland, Hungary and the Czech and Slovak Republics.' (WTO, 1995b, p. 10). Germany is the single most important importer of CEEC goods. It is a natural trading partner of Central and Eastern Europe which may partly explain why it has been investing so heavily in this region since the fall of communism.

Despite the Europe Agreements, trade liberalization between the CEECs and the EU has not taken place to the extent expected. A UNECE report (1994, p. 153) notes that 'transition economies' gains in access to western markets have been partially offset by new restrictions on certain eastern exports.' Economic recession in the EU (1992–3) along with resulting fears of unemployment and heavy adjustment costs, led to import restrictions on east European goods; twenty actions in the first half of 1993 have been noted (see UNECE, 1994). The trade balance generally remains in favour of the EU which exports much more than it imports from CEEC. The economic upswing since 1994 is likely to expand trade with the CEEC. The CEEC's trade with the European Union is still limited to traditional consumer and low-technology goods.

In general, the EU is likely to benefit from open trading relations with the CEECs in the form of cheaper labour-intensive goods in which Western Europe is losing its comparative advantage. But these benefits need to be offset by the additional cost of extending the Common Agricultural Policy (CAP) at the end of the transition period specified in the Europe Agreements. Baldwin (1995) claims that the benefits from cheaper imports of goods are likely to be rather small, suggesting that the costs will outweigh the benefits.

As regards the commodity composition of East–West trade, intuitively one would expect that the comparative advantage of Eastern Europe would lie in labour-intensive and natural resource intensive commodities. However, Neven and Roller (1991) have shown that a surprisingly significant share of East–West trade consists of intra-industry trade in 'human capital-intensive industries and physical capital intensive industries'. The share of trade in labour-intensive industries is rather small. Only the Netherlands and Germany import labour-intensive goods from Eastern Europe.

A recent empirical study by Cadot, Faini and de Melo (1995) indicates that the fears among EU members of large adjustment costs of trade liberalization with the CEECs are exaggerated. On the basis of an examination of the impact on France, Germany and Italy, they show that the CEEC trade structures are not becoming competitive with those of the EU, and that their exports are not likely to cause any significant job losses in the EU countries. To the extent that total trade is intra-industry, the adjustment costs to the EU would be lower than they would be without this trade.

Foreign Direct Investment in the CEECs

With the transition from state-controlled to market economies, the role of FDI is becoming an important factor in the development and exports

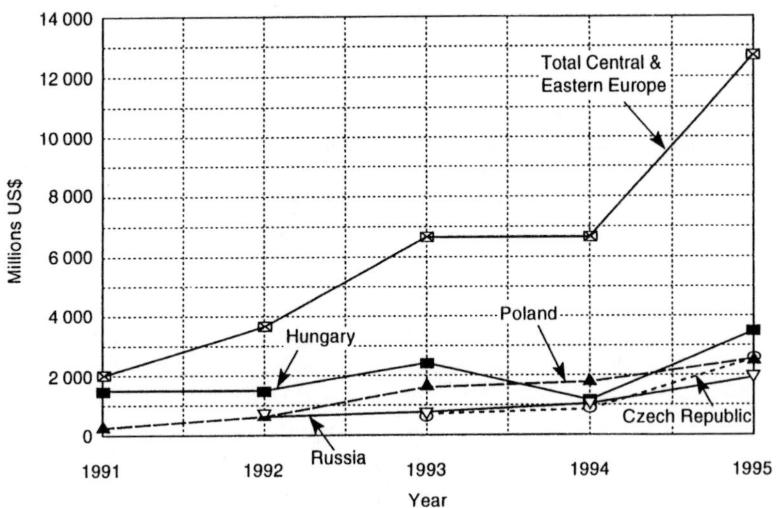

Figure 7.5 FDI Inflows into Central and Eastern Europe.

Source: Based on UNCTAD (1996), p. 64

of the CEECs. FDI is seen as one of the engines of restructuring and transformation, besides IMF loans and grants-in-aid. The bulk of FDI (nearly two-thirds of the total) is linked to privatizations under way in the region. It is estimated that there were over 55 000 foreign affiliates, and total FDI inflows into the region reached US$6.3 billion in 1994 and US$12 billion in 1995 (or 5 per cent of world FDI inflows), thus almost doubling in one year (UNCTAD, 1996, p. 64). This doubling of FDI inflows in one single year suggests that slowness and uncertainty of economic reforms and political instability did not discourage investors who must have been lured by the potentially very big market. Hungary and Poland, and to a lesser extent, the Czech Republic and Russia have been the major recipients of FDI (see Figure 7.5).

The most important EU investors in the CEECs are Austria, Finland, Germany and Italy (McMillan, 1992). Total FDI from these countries has grown since 1991 despite political uncertainty, high risks and stalling, in some cases (for example, Russia), of economic reforms. Artisian, Rojec and Svetlicic (1993, p. 13) note that the share of Western European investors 'is the highest in Slovenia, the Czech and Slovak Republics, Hungary and Poland (between 80 and 90 per cent) and somewhat lower in the CIS (60 per cent) and Romania (57 per cent). In approximately 40 per cent of the projects, 66 per cent in the case of Slovenia, the foreign parties are from the EC countries, and in about 25 per cent from EFTA'. In general, inflows of FDI have been concentrated in the more industrialized countries which accounted for 69 per cent of the region's FDI stock in 1994 (see UNCTAD, 1995a, p. 100).

It is not clear from the data whether FDI has been diverted significantly from other developing countries to Central and Eastern Europe as is often believed. FDI to the region has been below expectations. In the past few years, South and East Asia have attracted far more FDI from the EU (with the exception of Germany) than this region. For example, while the shares of FDI outflows of France and the United Kingdom to South and East Asia increased steadily since 1989, those to Central and Eastern Europe declined significantly between 1992 and 1993. In the case of Germany however, the shares of both these regions increased steadily whereas that of Africa declined between 1992 and 1993. (See OECD, 1996.)[3]

Tentative evidence suggests that FDI inflows into the CEECs are complementary to trade rather than being substitutes. In general, the presence of foreign affiliates has contributed to lowering the region's trade deficits. Foreign affiliates are tempted to locate export-oriented production in the region in view of its proximity to the EU, the availability of skills and natural resources, and relatively low wages. Generally, foreign firms tend to be more export-oriented than domestic firms. According to a UNECE (1994) survey in Hungary in 1993, foreign affiliates accounted for 52 per cent of total manufacturing exports; this share was much higher in such industries as non-metallic products (70 per cent), and machinery and equipment (60 per cent). Although Hungary has adopted a particularly export-oriented economic policy, a similar situation also obtains in other Visegrad countries (UNCTAD, 1995a). The CEECs' access to the EU market is also likely to induce capital inflows by encouraging EU firms to enter into joint ventures with Eastern European firms, and locate in Central and Eastern Europe to cater for the EU market. Also Russia and the other Commonwealth of Independent States (CIS) members offer a large potential market. However, the region continues to lack managerial and marketing expertise and organization which are abundant in the NIEs of East Asia.

Dunning (1993a) presents three possible scenarios for the future scope of inflows of FDI into the CEECs. First, he likens the CEECs' situation to that of the NIEs and suggests that substantial inflows are likely with the rapid economic development of these economies. Secondly, CEECs' economies are compared with the situation of West Germany and Japan at the end of the Second World War; massive inflows into CEECs are possible for reconstruction work as is already being done in the former East Germany. Finally, the third possibility called the 'systemic' scenario is a combination of the above 'developing-country' and 'reconstruction' models. It postulates that future inflows will be governed by the speed and extent of reorganization of the economic and legal systems. Since the initial establishment and learning costs on the part of multinationals are likely to be high, the rate of FDI inflows may be slow to begin with. In general, the existing literature suggests that a vast array of collaborative agreements, joint ventures and networking arrangements are being experimented by the multinationals during the period of transition to market economies.

Intra-CEEC Investments

At present intra-CEEC investments are not as important as FDI inflows from industrialized OECD countries. Restrictions on capital exports including outward FDI, lack of management skills, capital and know-how are some of the factors explaining this situation. (This situation is in contrast to that under COMECON where special efforts were made to increase intraregional investment flows among members). But a beginning has been made in the acquisition of productive assets in other CEECs especially by the more developed economies of the Czech Republic, Hungary and Poland. These countries have a more liberal approach to FDI outflows and inflows. Also lower wages in countries such as the Ukraine have attracted FDIs from Hungarian and Polish small and medium enterprises in the textile industry, for example (UNCTAD, 1995a, p. 107).

Some FDI in the CEECs is the result of the dissolution of the former Soviet Union and the break-up of the former Czechoslovakia. Thus, the Russian Federation has major investments in the CIS and the Baltic Republics, and the Czech Republic in Slovakia.

Limited intra-CEEC investments and low intraregional trade, noted above, are likely to limit regional integration within Central and Eastern Europe.

CONCLUDING REMARKS

The process of regional integration in Europe discussed in this Chapter, is perhaps, unique in the history of integration. No other region has pushed integration as far as the European Union. The scope and depth of integration has been achieved largely through supranational bodies, at times transcending national sovereignty. The membership and size of the European Common Market has also grown consistently since its creation. Its original membership of six has more than doubled, and a large number of CEECs are eager to join the EU. Some have already obtained associate membership in preparation for full membership. It was widely hoped that at least the more advanced group of these countries would be admitted to full membership by the year 2000. However, this target date has been pushed back to 2002 or later.

The enlargement of the EU by admission of all or a majority of the former communist countries will make it the biggest regional bloc in the world. This may have the salutary effect of diluting the protectionist tendencies of the Union. But this process of enlargement is likely to be a protracted one. Much will depend on the implementation of market reforms and democratization by these countries and the outcome of the Maastricht Treaty Review Conference. The future size of the EU budget, reforms of the CAP and of the regional aid programme, *inter alia*, will determine how soon and how many new members can be accommodated.

Intra-EU trade has expanded significantly during the past two to three decades. Some of this trade creation has been at the expense of trade with the rest of the world, particularly with developing countries and, to a lesser extent, with other industrialized countries. EU protectionism, in particular, the CAP, anti-dumping measures and VERs seem to be important factors accounting for this trade diversion – factors which have led to charges of a 'Fortress Europe'.

STATISTICAL APPENDIX

Table A 7.1 Indices of intraregional trade intensity of the EEC members

	1970	*1975*	*1980*	*1985*	*1990*	*1994*
Austria						
Belgium–Luxembourg	0.31	0.42	0.41	0.76	0.62	–
Denmark	1.47	0.16	1.14	1.12	0.99	1.04
Finland	1.44	1.40	1.14	1.23	1.02	0.95
France	0.34	0.37	0.49	0.68	0.69	0.84
Germany	2.29	2.35	3.16	3.56	3.70	4.35
Greece	1.52	1.80	1.43	1.31	0.99	–
Ireland	0.19	0.28	0.28	0.30	0.27	–
Italy	1.89	1.67	2.12	1.84	1.83	2.06
Netherlands	0.64	0.55	0.64	0.68	0.78	0.88
Portugal	1.69	1.00	0.69	0.68	0.55	0.75
Spain	0.54	0.40	0.38	0.99	0.84	0.98
Sweden	1.83	1.91	1.47	1.22	1.14	1.15
United Kingdom	0.83	0.85	0.61	0.79	0.59	0.59
Total EEC	1.23	0.94	1.40	1.56	1.54	2.02
Belgium–Luxembourg						
Austria	0.47	0.58	0.59	0.73	0.82	–
Denmark	0.68	0.10	1.15	1.10	0.93	–
Finland	0.48	0.50	0.43	0.65	0.72	–
France	2.96	2.77	2.69	3.22	2.87	–
Germany	2.30	2.33	2.12	2.15	2.06	–
Greece	0.80	1.09	0.75	1.07	1.03	–
Ireland	0.32	0.52	0.51	0.65	0.60	–
Italy	0.90	0.82	1.04	1.10	1.20	–
Netherlands	4.13	3.77	3.65	4.02	3.54	–
Portugal	0.70	0.68	0.92	0.74	0.93	–
Spain	0.57	0.57	0.53	0.63	0.90	–
Sweden	0.85	0.94	0.91	0.93	0.88	–
United Kingdom	0.49	0.94	1.38	1.88	1.30	–
Total EEC	1.76	1.41	1.84	2.04	1.83	–
Denmark						
Austria	1.18	0.76	0.76	0.69	0.65	0.79
Belgium–Luxembourg	0.33	0.36	0.51	0.60	0.59	–
Finland	2.55	2.10	2.62	2.91	3.20	4.25
France	0.37	0.42	0.74	0.77	0.85	0.98
Germany	1.23	1.26	1.94	1.87	1.89	2.47
Greece	0.67	0.76	1.02	1.51	1.33	–
Ireland	1.02	0.65	0.90	1.35	0.83	–
Italy	0.71	0.89	0.98	0.82	0.91	0.98
Netherlands	0.50	0.56	0.95	1.04	1.24	1.14
Portugal	0.88	0.62	0.71	0.60	0.82	0.84

(*Continued on page 192*)

Table A 7.1 *continued*

	1970	*1975*	*1980*	*1985*	*1990*	*1994*
Sweden	6.92	5.97	7.19	7.94	7.87	8.29
United Kingdom	2.50	2.50	2.39	2.10	1.60	1.48
Total EEC	1.38	1.31	1.57	1.57	1.50	1.87
Finland						
Austria	0.66	0.72	0.59	0.64	0.77	0.81
Belgium–Luxembourg	0.49	0.37	0.39	0.51	0.64	–
Denmark	2.73	0.28	3.48	4.19	3.71	4.23
France	0.58	0.53	0.65	0.68	0.90	0.95
Germany	1.03	0.86	1.09	1.10	1.29	1.55
Greece	1.23	0.91	1.36	0.91	1.01	–
Ireland	1.36	1.31	1.07	0.94	0.95	–
Italy	0.49	0.29	0.47	0.42	0.60	0.77
Netherlands	1.01	0.60	1.06	0.95	1.16	1.54
Portugal	0.68	1.17	0.62	0.81	1.11	0.85
Spain	0.67	0.56	0.50	0.52	0.85	1.08
Sweden	6.35	7.99	9.57	8.71	9.08	9.14
United Kingdom	2.37	2.18	1.89	1.87	1.62	1.96
Total EEC	1.36	1.00	1.32	1.32	1.39	1.77
France						
Austria	0.52	0.59	0.59	0.60	0.54	0.80
Belgium–Luxembourg	2.65	2.48	2.27	2.60	2.44	–
Denmark	0.60	0.05	0.62	0.78	0.78	1.02
Finland	0.51	0.50	0.44	0.57	0.58	0.61
Germany	1.89	1.65	1.48	1.62	1.57	1.86
Greece	1.11	1.24	1.74	1.33	1.25	–
Ireland	0.39	0.63	0.75	0.79	0.65	–
Italy	2.05	1.88	2.18	2.06	1.95	2.27
Netherlands	1.15	1.10	1.09	1.28	1.39	1.31
Portugal	1.32	1.29	1.31	1.60	1.62	2.27
Spain	1.43	1.25	1.46	1.96	2.29	3.15
Sweden	0.57	0.59	0.68	0.89	0.68	0.90
United Kingdom	0.52	0.92	1.05	1.29	1.30	1.77
Total EEC	0.52	0.92	1.05	1.29	1.30	1.77
Germany						
Austria	3.42	3.49	3.96	4.22	3.55	4.20
Belgium–Luxembourg	1.93	1.83	1.92	2.12	1.89	–
Denmark	1.41	0.15	1.73	2.10	1.76	2.09
Finland	1.24	1.06	1.06	1.35	1.25	1.36
France	1.72	1.61	1.74	1.87	1.69	2.08
Greece	1.43	1.94	1.80	1.75	1.51	–
Ireland	0.50	0.53	0.60	0.84	0.62	–
Italy	1.59	1.41	1.51	1.48	1.55	1.78

	1970	1975	1980	1985	1990	1994
Netherlands	2.12	2.08	2.15	2.29	2.04	2.07
Portugal	0.36	0.48	0.65	1.09	0.88	1.18
Spain	0.98	0.80	0.78	1.08	1.25	1.37
Sweden	1.43	1.52	1.52	1.67	1.46	1.73
United Kingdom	0.44	0.63	1.00	1.36	1.15	1.39
Total EEC	1.47	1.10	1.62	1.78	1.62	2.18
Greece						
Austria	1.23	0.92	0.46	1.11	1.00	1.27
Belgium–Luxembourg	1.01	0.51	0.50	0.62	0.58	–
Denmark	0.22	0.05	0.87	0.71	0.88	1.12
Finland	0.37	0.11	0.31	0.60	0.94	1.15
France	0.87	1.10	1.06	1.38	1.40	1.25
Germany	1.99	2.29	1.91	2.40	2.19	2.86
Ireland	0.17	0.09	0.17	0.79	0.27	0.76
Italy	1.98	1.76	1.89	2.34	3.22	3.79
Netherlands	1.35	1.29	1.41	1.17	0.93	1.20
Portugal	0.46	0.15	0.77	0.33	0.34	0.58
Spain	0.64	0.90	0.32	0.47	0.58	1.05
Sweden	0.56	0.72	0.26	0.52	1.01	0.89
United Kingdom	0.81	0.74	0.69	1.21	1.11	1.16
Total EEC	1.23	0.99	1.17	1.49	1.52	1.99
Ireland						
Austria	0.05	0.20	0.40	0.54	0.44	0.44
Belgium–Luxembourg	0.40	0.98	1.38	1.35	1.26	–
Denmark	0.10	0.03	0.74	0.95	1.10	1.13
Finland	0.09	0.34	0.56	0.81	0.68	0.86
France	0.45	0.66	1.13	1.47	1.54	1.73
Germany	0.27	0.85	1.01	1.20	1.17	1.44
Greece	0.22	0.21	0.70	0.90	0.86	–
Italy	0.29	0.58	0.61	0.77	0.83	0.92
Netherlands	0.45	1.35	1.37	1.96	1.58	1.76
Portugal	0.10	0.15	0.52	0.67	0.66	0.65
Spain	0.39	0.47	0.68	0.81	0.90	1.05
Sweden	0.20	0.48	0.71	1.16	1.22	1.52
United Kingdom	8.28	8.19	7.24	5.67	5.21	5.15
Total EEC	1.58	1.47	1.84	1.89	1.76	2.10
Italy						
Austria	1.38	1.74	2.03	1.89	1.62	1.85
Belgium–Luxembourg	0.92	0.85	0.86	0.95	0.93	–
Denmark	0.60	0.05	0.66	0.82	0.77	1.00
Finland	0.40	0.43	0.46	0.71	0.76	0.72
France	1.88	1.91	2.08	2.34	2.28	2.38
Germany	2.03	1.93	1.81	1.84	1.81	2.12
Greece	1.93	2.52	2.68	3.11	2.98	–

(*Continued on page 194*)

Table A 7.1 *continued*

	1970	*1975*	*1980*	*1985*	*1990*	*1994*
Ireland	0.34	0.47	0.45	0.43	0.45	0.51
Netherlands	0.99	0.92	0.88	0.86	0.81	0.83
Portugal	1.29	1.01	1.29	1.29	1.86	2.11
Spain	1.04	1.02	1.09	1.03	1.96	2.11
Sweden	0.58	0.50	0.59	0.69	0.75	0.73
United Kingdom	0.49	0.66	0.98	1.15	1.04	1.19
Total EEC	1.26	0.99	1.39	1.48	1.51	1.90
Netherlands						
Austria	0.69	0.72	0.73	0.80	0.80	0.84
Belgium–Luxembourg	3.46	3.47	3.91	4.55	4.06	–
Denmark	0.91	0.13	1.80	1.51	1.69	1.61
Finland	0.66	0.53	0.63	0.83	0.89	1.01
France	1.48	1.49	1.46	1.75	1.56	1.65
Germany	3.09	3.16	2.98	3.47	2.67	2.72
Greece	0.81	0.91	1.18	1.57	1.59	–
Ireland	0.55	0.71	0.70	0.89	0.95	–
Italy	1.02	1.02	1.08	1.16	1.17	1.11
Portugal	0.58	0.66	0.85	0.93	0.99	1.05
Spain	0.63	0.60	0.48	0.51	0.99	1.00
Sweden	1.01	0.93	0.98	1.07	1.10	1.17
United Kingdom	0.91	1.33	1.28	1.59	1.51	1.49
Total EEC	1.74	1.42	1.87	2.13	1.88	2.14
Portugal						
Austria	1.18	1.24	0.91	0.98	0.79	0.87
Belgium–Luxembourg	0.41	0.84	0.84	1.20	0.89	–
Denmark	1.84	0.18	1.79	2.12	2.30	2.87
Finland	2.15	1.63	1.77	2.07	2.07	1.96
France	0.70	0.99	1.50	2.21	2.25	2.75
Germany	0.62	1.10	1.40	1.64	1.66	2.15
Greece	0.48	1.52	0.57	0.51	0.87	–
Ireland	0.71	1.13	0.61	1.08	0.80	–
Italy	0.60	0.69	1.14	0.82	0.76	0.86
Netherlands	0.61	0.65	1.17	2.00	1.54	1.52
Spain	1.00	1.35	2.08	2.62	5.36	6.79
Sweden	2.24	3.11	2.61	2.44	2.56	2.07
United Kingdom	2.77	3.21	2.48	2.54	1.86	2.21
Total EEC	1.13	1.14	1.52	1.81	1.82	2.45
Spain						
Austria	0.34	0.41	0.29	0.38	0.49	0.64
Belgium–Luxembourg	0.55	0.82	0.71	0.85	0.85	–
Denmark	0.72	0.07	0.52	0.63	0.57	0.77
Finland	0.42	0.94	0.50	0.59	0.53	0.63

	1970	*1975*	*1980*	*1985*	*1990*	*1994*
France	1.58	2.02	2.35	2.66	2.99	3.72
Germany	1.15	1.14	1.05	1.12	1.32	1.61
Greece	0.56	2.20	0.99	0.74	1.29	–
Ireland	0.60	0.55	0.56	0.64	0.50	–
Italy	1.28	0.71	1.50	1.43	2.14	2.33
Netherlands	1.14	1.10	0.95	1.56	1.26	1.22
Portugal	5.41	4.51	5.60	5.45	8.07	12.43
Sweden	0.65	0.60	0.58	0.61	0.59	0.63
United Kingdom	1.19	1.13	1.17	1.46	1.22	1.54
Total EEC	1.14	0.92	1.28	1.44	1.65	2.25
Sweden						
Austria	1.23	1.18	1.08	0.98	0.96	1.07
Belgium–Luxembourg	0.79	0.73	0.87	1.30	1.06	–
Denmark	6.44	0.66	8.34	8.42	7.10	8.47
Finland	6.90	7.47	7.71	7.90	8.50	8.79
France	0.78	0.72	0.85	0.84	0.78	0.96
Germany	1.16	1.08	1.28	1.36	1.40	1.54
Greece	0.50	1.60	0.85	0.67	0.78	–
Ireland	0.68	0.93	0.93	1.05	0.90	–
Italy	0.62	0.56	0.73	0.68	0.86	0.96
Netherlands	0.97	0.90	1.17	1.25	1.40	1.57
Portugal	1.16	1.10	1.48	0.92	0.84	0.73
Spain	0.90	0.84	0.68	0.75	0.96	0.89
United Kingdom	1.67	1.62	1.65	1.68	1.50	1.91
Total EEC	1.34	1.02	1.39	1.47	1.41	1.84
United Kingdom						
Austria	0.87	0.67	0.44	0.42	0.45	0.58
Belgium–Luxembourg	0.88	1.14	1.41	1.36	1.47	–
Denmark	1.70	0.16	2.06	1.71	1.35	1.44
Finland	1.66	1.33	1.30	1.21	1.20	1.73
France	0.60	0.82	1.03	1.62	1.45	1.67
Germany	0.57	0.66	1.04	1.28	1.19	1.32
Greece	0.99	0.98	0.82	0.76	1.08	–
Ireland	8.00	9.16	9.23	8.33	8.07	–
Italy	0.55	0.56	0.74	0.87	0.96	1.16
Netherlands	0.96	1.20	1.91	2.55	1.86	1.89
Portugal	1.91	1.59	1.62	1.29	1.28	1.33
Spain	1.03	0.79	0.87	1.22	1.37	1.59
Sweden	1.77	1.77	1.88	2.39	1.54	1.99
Total EEC	0.95	0.79	1.30	1.56	1.40	1.82

Source: Our estimates based on data from IMF, *Direction of Trade Statistics Yearbook*.

8 Future of Regional Blocs

The nineties are witnessing several simultaneous trends in trade, investment and production patterns. The trend towards trade liberalization which had already begun in earnest by the mid-eighties during the protracted negotiations of the Uruguay Round, gained momentum following its successful conclusion. Uncertainties as to its outcome had provoked several regional trade agreements as possible alternatives to the multilateral trading system. While the Uruguay Round Accord was finally concluded in 1994, some lacunae in its provisions (notably, failure to reach agreements on agriculture, services and trade-related investment measures) and ambiguities and loopholes in the GATT, notably Article XXIV, have in part, led to an increasing reliance on new forms of regional arrangements. These are aimed at boosting trade- and investment-led growth and improving member countries' abilities to remain competitive.

In this global context, the new regional arrangements of the nineties, unlike earlier experiments, seem here to stay. In fact the pace of regionalization today has created a dynamic of its own whereby countries left out of any such arrangements are either forming new blocs or endeavouring to join existing ones (Preusse, 1994). As a result, many regional blocs will expand their membership and, if present trends are any indication, integration within them is likely to intensify: closer trade linkages are likely to be accompanied by increasing investment and production ties. This will inevitably increase pressures for greater regional harmonization of national policies relating to many socio-economic factors, all aimed at facilitating trade and investment, such as common environmental rules, common labour standards, customs regulations and procedures, and liberalization of trade in services. The EU stands out as having accomplished the greatest degree of integration of any regional arrangement. NAFTA countries too have established a certain degree of freedom in the movements of capital and labour and services between the members. Even APEC, although not a formal regional bloc, has begun taking initiatives towards the harmonization of trade-supporting measures.

As we noted in Chapters 3 to 7, the nature and form of regional blocs vary a great deal. The four main varieties considered in the book are: development economic cooperation (SADC), free trade areas

(NAFTA, AFTA, LAFTA, SAPTA), customs unions (MERCOSUR, SACU) and single regional markets (the European Union). Free trade areas are more prevalent than customs unions since they do not involve any loss of sovereignty of national governments. A comparison between NAFTA and the European Union clearly highlights these differences.

Deep integration, as in the European Union, involves the establishment of regional institutions and mechanisms (for example, the European monetary system and the social charter) which require some sacrifice in national autonomy and decision-making. This is not easily accepted by all member countries. The UK, for example, has opted out of the social charter (Protocol on Social Policy annexed to the Maastricht Treaty) which establishes work standards and a minimum wage and industrial relations procedures. On the other hand, NAFTA, being a free trade area, does not call for explicit harmonization of national policies or the creation of regional institutions to do so. Even in areas where members have agreed to common standards, as in labour and environment, it is left to the individual countries, rather than to any supranational body, to monitor and ensure compliance. It is unlikely that in the future this bloc will move towards wider or deeper integration of the type witnessed in the European Union. Indeed a clause in the NAFTA agreement provides that any new members will need to negotiate separately for entry into NAFTA.

TRADE AND INVESTMENT LINKAGES

Traditionally regional blocs were created to benefit from static gains from trade and improved resource allocation. However, static gains in the form of increased intraregional trade are inadequate to increase welfare within the member countries and the bloc as a whole. It is therefore necessary to aim at dynamic gains through increased FDI flows, technological advance and higher economic growth. We noted in Chapter 2 that FDI and trade can be both substitutes and complements. We have shown that in the liberalization framework prevailing in most countries today (as distinct from the earlier import-substitution model), FDI that is complementary to trade expansion is likely to contribute to growth, economic welfare and global integration of the national economies. On the other hand, FDI that is a substitute for trade can be welfare reducing and trade diverting.

Internationalization of production and business is at the heart of increased dynamism of trade expansion and investment flows noted above. But as we shall discuss below, it is not clear whether growing anti-dumping practices, VERs and stringent rules of origin requirements by most regional arrangements (but particularly, NAFTA and the EU) will limit such linkages to a regional level at the expense of globalization. There is already evidence of this trend with Japanese FDI in electronics. For example, Japanese MNEs in the EU are turning increasingly to intraregional sourcing in order to abide by rules of origin requirements rather than seeking the most efficient sourcing available on the world market (Han, 1992).

A similar tendency among the US multinationals operating in the NAFTA countries was noted in Chapter 6. However, in the case of large US multinationals with global operations covering Europe, North America and Japan, it is unclear whether a widespread shift will occur in their strategies from globalization to regionalism.

Distortions in international resource allocation have the effect of diverting trade and investment and as a result, worldwide efficiency in production. Such corporate responses to regional blocs could enhance global fragmentation. We have noted how the globalization of the production process has been a major factor in promoting economic integration. However, the regionalization of production by the more powerful multinational firms in response to regional protectionism would give an impetus to regional as opposed to global free trade. Once implanted within the region, the MNEs which have been the champions of global free trade and investments, are likely to become less vulnerable and therefore less opposed to trade barriers.

BLOCS AND BIG BROTHERS

Is a formal regional bloc a precondition for trade and investment dynamism? The experience of East Asia seems to show that it is not (while the ASEAN experience indicates that it helps). These countries were able to achieve very rapid economic growth rates and export expansion through unilateral trade and economic liberalization, despite recessionary and protectionist trends in the OECD countries. This is not to suggest that institutional regional integration of the kind the European Union has adopted, and which creates an enlarged single market, has no role to play in inducing large FDI inflows. However, it must be noted that despite intra-EU trade expansion and increase in FDI inflows, EU members' growth rates have remained very low, especially in the nineties. In most OECD countries, output and productivity growth rates have declined relative to the fifties and sixties.

The ability of different regional arrangements to achieve trade and investment dynamism depends to a large extent on their level of development, the rates of growth of the member countries, the degree of liberalization achieved, and on intra- as well as extraregional linkages.

The dynamic gains from regional blocs – enlarged size of the market and economies of scale – are more likely to occur if the bloc has at least one 'big brother' as a member. Indeed this is an emerging phenomenon in most of the blocs that we have discussed in this book. This is shown below. Each of the following six regional groupings has a big brother which ensures a reasonably large size of the market:

1. The EU: Germany;
2. NAFTA: United States;
3. MERCOSUR: Brazil;
4. SADC: South Africa;
5. ECOWAS: Nigeria; and
6. SAARC: India.

In the case of ASEAN, Singapore acts as an economic leader or a big brother in an economic sense, rather than physical. While East Asia does not have a formal regional bloc, the strong linkages among the countries of the region could not have been achieved in the absence of large inflows of FDI initially from the US and later from Japan. Even within APEC, which started off as a loose consultative forum, the main impetus to integration has come from the dominant economies of Japan and the United States.[1]

BUILDING BLOCKS OR STUMBLING BLOCKS?

Do regional blocs act as stumbling blocks or building blocks towards multilateral trade and globalization? The views on this question remain divided.

Those who support the building block notion believe that regional integration, by reducing tariff and non-tariff barriers, even though at a regional or sub-regional level, is bound to facilitate the process of trade liberalization. Furthermore, the enlarged size of the regional markets and greater economies of scale within blocs are likely to contribute to greater competitiveness of the partners. This should eventually pave the way for progressive opening up of their markets to foreign goods from outside the region. The resulting increase in competition will enhance the ability of firms to secure access to markets in third countries. This process will thus progressively encourage globalization of trade, production and investment.

Furthermore, if the world were grouped into three major trading blocs (US, a possible Japan-dominated East Asia and the European Union), it would be easier to negotiate global reduction in trade barriers than if all the countries entered into such negotiations individually (Summers, 1991). The ability of Europe to speak with one voice is often cited as having helped the multilateral process. Similarly, APEC's cohesive approach to the Uruguay Round negotiations is credited with having contributed to their successful conclusion.

Some authors (for example, Summers, 1991; Krugman, 1991) argue that most of the serious efforts at regional integration have taken place among 'natural trading partners' where, even in the absence of formal agreements trade intensities have been or would be high (for example, trade between the NIEs of East Asia, trade among the industrialized countries of Europe or between Canada and the US). In these cases, regional agreements have merely reinforced existing tendencies. From this perspective, they are unlikely to be trade diverting and, therefore, cannot be considered as stumbling blocks. Rather, by promoting these natural trading relationships, they are more likely to become building blocks in the sense that they encourage other potential trading partners to liberalize their own trading regimes in order to gain access to the regions.

Summers (1991) cites trade agreements between the US and several Latin American countries as providing incentives to these countries to reform their domestic policies and to liberalize their trade and investment rules. However, the other side of the argument is that such agreements also have the tendency to divert trade away from competitive exporters such as the Asian NIEs which might be more efficient producers (see Chapter 6). The effect of US–Latin American bilateral agreements might push the Asian NIEs into creating their own inward protectionist bloc. While it could be argued that a regionally competitive environment may provide incentives at a regional level, a globally competitive environment provides an even greater incentive for more countries to deregulate and liberalize in order to remain competitive.

Sceptics view the emergence of regional blocs as contributing towards the regional fragmentation of trade which is inimical to multilateralism. Rivalry among the three major trading blocs of the EU,

NAFTA and the East Asian region (which although not a bloc, could well be pushed into becoming one) raises the potential for trade conflicts rather than easing global trade negotiations. These powerful trading blocs have sizeable and growing markets which does not make it imperative on them to respect rules of multilateralism or facilitate their enforcement. In fact, those who benefit from trade diversion (in the US through NAFTA, for example) may be inclined to oppose an open multilateral trading system (see Krueger, 1993). Indeed, there is evidence of countries like Portugal and Spain, once targets of EU anti-dumping duties, moving for such action against third countries following their accession to the EU (see Hindley and Messerlin, 1993).

The EU, in particular, is viewed with concern. It is the most likely bloc to withdraw support for multilateralism given its growing membership and higher level of intraregional than extraregional trade. Furthermore, its multitude of different preferential agreements with other regions, for example, EFTA, ACP countries, and the CEECs, undermine the GATT MFN principle of non-discrimination and open competition.

The Asian regional bloc, it is feared, could give Japan control over the region's rapidly growing markets. Through its investments and offshore production, Japan could manage regional specialization in a manner which inhibits the free entry of firms and products from outside the region. It could thus extend its invisible barriers to these other dynamic markets making access to them by third countries as difficult as access to its own market.

US initiatives in the Western Hemisphere are another major threat to globalization. A growing concern is that the world's leading trading nation, once the strongest protagonist of free trade, is tending to move away from multilateralism and that is likely to have a domino effect. Trade and budget deficits and hardships resulting from structural adjustment forced on the US as a result of trade liberalization, have created a build-up of domestic pressures to protect certain sensitive sectors from external competition.

The US trade policy of 'aggressive unilateralism' is a case in point (Bhagwati, 1991; Oppenheim, 1992). Japan- and Cuba-bashing by the US and threats of retaliatory action is but one example of trade conflicts.[2] Threats of US-Japan and US-China trade wars are frequently heard. So far they have been barely averted. As we noted in Chapter 5, such possible trade wars will have serious consequences for FDI throughout East Asia. Some of these trade disputes may be inevitable considering the rapid expansion of trade and investment in the region (see APEC, 1995). But they represent a threat to multilateralism and globalization.

With increasing frequency American policy-makers have been invoking Section 'Super 301' of the US 1974 Trade Act which was updated in 1988. Under this Section, specific countries can be named as offenders if their trade practices (for example, violation of the intellectual property rights convention or inadequate labour legislation) are considered unacceptable by the US, regardless of whether they are acceptable to the WTO or any other treaty. The US resorted to Super 301 against Brazil, China and India in 1989 and Japan in 1990, under threat of tariff retaliation (see Bhagwati, 1991, p. 22).[3] Managed trade of this kind is clearly in violation of the WTO principles of multilateralism. It can divert trade from the rest of the world to the US to serve its national interest of reducing the budget deficit and improving national welfare.

Krueger (1993, pp. 23–4) notes 'there is little question that protectionist pressures have increased in North America and in Europe'. New events in the early nineties, namely, the Central and Eastern European countries' desire for integration into the world economy, and the long drawn out negotiations under the Uruguay Round, renewed protectionist tendencies. In the past protectionism was more than compensated by rising real incomes and declining costs of transportation and communications which led to growth of world trade outpacing world output. But is there any guarantee that this scenario will hold in the future?

Whether regional blocs are building blocks or stumbling blocks will thus clearly depend on the policy responses of the United States, the European Union and Japan to the constantly evolving trade and investment climate and to domestic constraints.

Empirical Evidence

In Chapter 2, we identified conditions under which regional blocs will be compatible with the GATT/WTO and globalization more generally. To recapitulate, these conditions are: (a) they should contribute to net trade creation rather than trade diversion or, in other words, both intraregional trade and extraregional trade (with the rest of the world) should expand, (b) they should be investment and growth inducing, resulting in an expansion of total trade, (c) they should facilitate multilateral trade negotiations. These three conditions are most likely to be met only within an 'open' regional arrangement, that is, one that does not discriminate against non-members, and, therefore, best conforms to the spirit of the GATT. It is now time to examine whether the regional blocs or groupings discussed in Chapters 3 to 7 fulfil these conditions.

Taking the case of the African region first, none of the three groupings considered are likely to act as stumbling blocks towards globalization. Neither are they likely to contribute much to the process with the exception perhaps of SADC thanks to the participation of South Africa and to a lesser extent, Zimbabwe.

As in the case of Africa, South Asia's share of world trade is quite small which makes the SAARC grouping relatively insignificant for influencing the process of globalization. Within the region, recent policies of economic liberalization, greater emphasis on trade and liberalization of foreign investment, are some of the factors conducive to globalization. It could be argued that the demonstration effects of trade liberalization in other regions of the world have contributed to these changes in South Asian countries. In addition, in order to maintain their credibility in global negotiations, these countries cannot afford not to liberalize.

In the case of ASEAN, intraregional trade has not expanded much but extraregional trade has, thus leading to overall trade creation rather than diversion. The ASEAN region has also attracted FDI inflows which have fuelled trade expansion. Thus this grouping fulfils the above conditions (a) and (b). ASEAN also fulfils condition (c) since it acts with one voice on all international issues including trade. Even with ASEAN's expansion to include Vietnam and Cambodia and perhaps Myanmar and Laos, the group will remain sufficiently cohesive to be able to negotiate easily among the members as well as with non-members.

While APEC is not a regional bloc, its large membership, including such major global traders as the United States, Canada, Japan, and, more recently the Asian NIEs, makes it a significant forum for influencing multilateral trade negotiations. It could well counteract protectionist tendencies by the two major regional arrangements of NAFTA and the EU. The East Asian economies (comprising the four Asian 'tigers' of Hong Kong, Korea, Singapore, and Taiwan; China; Japan and the ASEAN-4) in particular have threatened to form a retaliatory bloc should they suffer increasing discrimination in the form of anti-dumping actions, VERs and other non-tariff barriers raised by NAFTA and the EU. Given their increasing clout and importance as markets and as sources of FDI, for both NAFTA and EU countries, the latter cannot afford to ignore such a threat. To this extent, the possibility of a Japan-dominated East Asian bloc could deter protectionism by other blocs.

The situation regarding the remaining blocs, namely, NAFTA and the European Union is less clearcut. As we noted above and in Chapters 6 and 7, protectionist tendencies there have been growing. However, empirical evidence suggests that in the case of NAFTA the scope for trade diversion remains limited since NAFTA members are natural trading partners with current low tariff barriers. But the scope for investment diversion may be more real. Asian NIEs fear that at least part of US investments might be diverted to Mexico and other Latin American countries with which the US signs bilateral agreements. A similar situation seems to prevail in the case of Western Europe. While tariffs have declined a great deal, non-tariff barriers have increased. The possibility of trade and investment diversion in the case of the EU also exists (see Chapter 7).

To conclude, in general it would appear that 'open' regional blocs (as opposed to discriminatory, restricted membership blocs) are likely to facilitate the process of freer multilateral trade. The WTO and APEC are working towards that goal. While this is a positive trend, it may be offset, at least to some extent, by the possible negative effect on free trade of bilateral trade agreements.

Bilateral vs. Regional Agreements

There appears to have been a proliferation of bilateral trade agreements, interregional agreements and protectionist measures used by those regional blocs/countries that are experiencing sluggish growth and trade deficits. These trends are disturbing not only because they imply preferential or discriminatory practices against the non-participants. MERCOSUR has entered into an agreement with Chile and in 1996 Chile signed an agreement for closer economic and political ties with Canada and the European Union. There are also inter-bloc agreements such as the MERCOSUR trade agreement with the European Union and the Andean Pact free trade agreement with MERCOSUR signed in 1996. These forms of agreements for economic and trade cooperation are particularly numerous in the Western Hemisphere. For example, the Enterprise for the Americas Initiative launched by the United States aims at negotiating separate agreements with various Latin American countries as opposed to encompassing them into a wider NAFTA. This seems to imply that it will impose different conditions on different countries. Thus it is uncertain whether these bilateral agreements would be consistent with sub-regional and regional agreements. In fact it is possible that they run counter to the goals of the latter. This possibility has been voiced by a Latin American scholar in the following words:

> successive bilateral negotiations could also lead to frictions and practical problems. Overlapping arrangements can cause mismatches in the phasing of tariff reductions, inconsistencies between different dispute settlement mechanisms, and difficulties in the implementation of disparate rules of origin . . . the problem of convergence derives from the ambiguity, fuzziness and lack of clear definitions and commitments which seem to pervade many integration efforts in the region. (van Klaveren, 1996, p. 15)

The various agreements, whether at the regional or bilateral level, have steadily eroded specific provisions of the GATT which were intended to secure equitable gains for countries through multilateral free trade. We examine the main weaknesses in the GATT/WTO below.

Regional Blocs and the GATT/WTO

Baldwin (1993) suggests that the inability of the GATT to assure market access for developing countries into developed country markets and *vice versa* has been a major factor contributing to the growing reliance on regional integration agreements. An example of the weakness of the GATT and its successor, the WTO, is its inability to control the increasingly frequent resort to 'contingency protection' such as the misuse of anti-dumping actions, particularly by the EU, and the increasing use of 'fair trade laws' by the US. Canada's acceptance of the CUSFTA, and EFTA countries' acceptance of the EEA with the EU were motivated largely by the need to be less exposed to anti-dumping action or other forms of protectionism by the US and the EU respectively (Hindley and Messerlin, 1993). Not only do anti-dumping actions raise trade barriers and therefore cause trade diversion, they are also responsible for creating voluntary export restraints (VERs) and deflecting MNEs away from strategies which ensure optimization of their investment and production.

Article XXIV of GATT allows for the creation of regional blocs, as an exception to the MFN clause of Article I,[4] on two conditions. First, that free trade areas and customs unions should eventually lead to the elimination of duties and other regulations on commerce on *substantially all* trade between the members. In other words, no *partial* preferential trade arrangements are provided. Second, that there should be no increase in duties and other regulations affecting imports from third parties which are not members of the bloc. Bhagwati (1993) has noted certain ambiguities in Article XXIV. A major problem is with the interpretation of what constitutes 'substantially all trade'. This could have an across-the-board application or it could allow substantial sectors to be left out altogether from tariff reductions. In addition, the time frame for total elimination of tariffs is not specified. The scope for a loose interpretation of this Article has therefore enabled the creation of a variety of FTAs and preferential trade agreements that are not consistent with the spirit of the GATT. As Bhagwati notes, it raises the possibility of a gap between intentions and reality. For example, it does not preclude the risk of a regional bloc increasing non-tariff barriers (such as, administered protection) in the event of intensified competition among its partners. The rules of origin may also be subject to manipulation by protectionists.

The GATT (and now WTO) allowed for the creation of regional blocs simply for the sake of political realism: to ensure widespread signatory support of countries. It presented a compromise in favour of those countries which feared adverse consequences of multilateral trade liberalization at least in the short run. An underlying assumption was that 'regional agreements do not pose an *inherent* threat to efforts to promote continued integration on a world-wide basis' (see WTO, 1995, pp. 5–6).[5]

Reform of Article XXIV of GATT/WTO will be necessary to close loopholes which allow the divergence between the goals of regionalism and multilateralism. A beginning seems to have been made in this direction with the creation by WTO in 1996 of a watchdog committee to monitor the different regional arrangements in order to ensure their compliance with the GATT/WTO rules.

But monitoring of regional arrangements will increasingly involve more than just trade issues. As trade becomes more liberalized and borders more open, the role of protectionist instruments like tariffs will decline but at the same time there is increasing scope for trade friction through measures considered as non-border issues, namely, investment and competition policies and regulation of services. In fact, several studies have revealed the interconnections between these different issues. For example, some trade-related investment measures, such as local content or a minimum export requirement can have a distortionary effect on trade. In addition, increasing competition by governments and regions to attract foreign direct investment (FDI) can often lead to distortionary incentives. The past few years have seen a proliferation of bilateral and regional agreements to curb trade distorting incentives and disincentives. If regional trade frictions are to be avoided, such agreements need to be negotiated at the multilateral level under the auspices of the WTO. Other priority areas for multilateral negotiations in the years to come include agreements concerning subsidies, services and intellectual property rights.

Such agreements remain elusive to the WTO judging from its first ministerial meeting in Singapore in December 1996. The wide gap between the interests of developed and developing country members resulted in them agreeing to set up working groups on competition policy, foreign investment and transparency in government procurement. Their two-year studies could eventually lead to agreement in these areas.

Trade liberalization, on the other hand, got a tremendous boost at the Singapore meeting. Agreement to abolish tariffs in information technology products, among the fastest growing sectors, is a measure of the growing confidence in global free trade. The pact, signed by 28 countries led by the US, Canada, Japan and the European Union with seven others declaring their intention to join, covers nearly 300 items (including computers, software, semiconductors and telecommunications equipment). Negotiations on liberalizing members' telecoms markets were completed in mid-February 1997. The WTO is also committed to tackling the more difficult sectors of agriculture and services and to addressing the question of anti-dumping practices.

US attempts to link labour standards (including the right to form trade unions and the elimination of forced labour and 'exploitative' child labour) to trade, however, were overruled by developing countries, backed by Germany and the UK. They believe that such linkages could lead to new forms of protectionism.

There can be no conclusive answer as to whether regional blocs are building blocks or stumbling blocks to globalization. In future, whether regional agreements will actually hinder or help the process of multilateralism and globalization will depend on the way they are implemented *vis-à-vis* the WTO and how they will influence the trade and investment policies of non-members. The WTO will need to become more responsive to the changing dynamics in trade, investment and production if it is to prevent nations from acting unilaterally or within a regional framework to protect their own interests.

Notes

1 REGIONAL COOPERATION IN HISTORICAL PERSPECTIVE

1. A regional proposal to build two aluminium smelters to be owned jointly by Jamaica, Guyana and Trinidad had to be shelved (Payne, 1994).
2. Bhagwati (1992) believes that FTAs should not be recommended because they allow each partner to retain its original tariff structure. To prevent goods coming in via low-tariff partners, FTAs require rules of origin which can be restrictive. Therefore, Bhagwati would like WTO to recommend only customs unions which would levy common external tariffs at the lowest level. Corden (1993, p. 458) on the other hand, argues that the FTAs need not be protectionist; a country could liberalize unilaterally *vis-à-vis* the rest of the world and then form an FTA with neighboring countries 'with whom the degree of liberalization would be absolutely complete . . .' Indeed, recent FTAs like NAFTA are being formed in the context of global trade liberalization and may thus be more acceptable (see Krueger, 1995).

2 THE NEW REGIONALISM VS. GLOBALIZATION?

1. In writing on the failure of the early regionalism of the sixties, Bhagwati (1993, p. 28) notes: 'The problem was that, rather than use trade liberalization and hence prices to guide industry allocation, the developing countries attempting such unions sought to allocate industries by bureaucratic negotiation and to tie trade to such allocations, putting the cart before the horse and killing the forward motion'.
2. Bhagwati (1993) argues that regionalism in the past – failed because the United States was against it, being a staunch supporter of multilateralism. Now that the US has adopted regionalism, it is more likely to be durable and successful.
3. Many authors tend to use the term 'internationalization' interchangeably with 'globalization'. However, the two concepts are distinct. While the former refers to increasing geographical dispersal of economic activity, the latter implies a degree of 'functional integration' between these dispersed activities (see Dicken, 1992).
4. For details of such issues and alternative measures, see Anderson and Blackhurst (1993).
5. Note that as long as the value of country i's exports to country j, are equal to country j's imports from country i (that is, trade or nontrade barriers, and no transport costs and so on), the formula could be expressed in terms of imports. Assuming no trade bias:

$$\mathbf{M}_{ji} \,/\, \mathbf{M}_{wi} - \mathbf{M}_{jw} \,/\, \mathbf{M}_{ww} = 0$$

where:

M_{ji} = country *j*'s imports from country *i*;
M_{wi} = world imports from country *i*;
M_{jw} = country *j*'s imports from the world;
M_{ww} = total world imports (net of country *i*'s total imports).

The advantages of this formulation are: First, using only import data eases the data requirement – which in some cases could be a formidable task; second, since in the absence of trade bias or preference, the value of the index is zero. Any other number could simply be interpreted as country *j*'s degree of bias in favour of or against trading with country (or region) *i* relative to the rest of the world.

6. Robson (1993, p. 341) suggests that temporary market protection within a regional bloc may actually facilitate the process of external trade liberalization. In the context of Africa, he argues that regional 'exonomic integration may be the most practicable way to minimize the costs of African market fragmentation. . . .'
7. For example, it is estimated that investment induced by the Single European Market will account for dynamic growth effects of up to a 10 per cent increase in total output (Baldwin, 1989).

3 REGIONAL INITIATIVES IN AFRICA

1. In 1995, producers in Zimbabwe complained of South African 'dumping' and protested against its protective barriers against Zimbabwean textiles and foodstuffs (see Wright, 1996).
2. With the implementation of tariff reductions under the Uruguay Round agreement, the BLNS will be able to replace expensive South African imports by cheaper ones from the rest of the world. However, multilateral trade liberalization and tariff reductions are likely to affect the SACU common revenue pool. (See Davies, 1994.)
3. With the democratization of South Africa, the BLNS are engaged in renegotiation of the SACU Treaty to ensure more balanced and equitable arrangements for trade and economic cooperation. These negotiations were launched in November 1994 in Windhoek (Namibia). A Customs Union Task team, which consists of senior officials of all five participating countries, has been established to renegotiate institutional, technical and policy matters relating to the SACU Treaty.
4. A survey of private-sector firms undertaken by Maasdorp and Whiteside (1993) suggests fairly wide support for the idea of a common market. Malawi, which is not a member of SACU, is also inclined to join such a common market.
5. Data for 1974–82 'suggest that the exchange rate arrangements within the Common Market Area have influenced the spatial distribution of international trade in favour of intraregional trade' (AfDB, 1993, p. 234).

4 ASIA: ASEAN AND SAARC

1. Under the CEPT scheme, there are two tracks for tariff reductions: a normal and a fast track. Normal track tariff reductions will occur in two steps: for items with tariffs above 20 per cent, tariffs will be reduced to 20 per cent or less in five to eight years, and to 0–5 per cent in seven years. So in effect, tariffs on products in the CEPT listings are to be lowered to a range of 0–5 per cent within 15 years. In addition, 15 product groups have been identified for 'fast track' reductions. This means that items currently above 20 per cent will be reduced to 5 per cent or less within ten years (that is, by 2003) and those currently at 20 per cent will be reduced to 5 per cent or less within seven years (that is, by 2000).
2. Earlier attempts (Naya, 1980; Ooi, 1981; Devan, 1987) to measure the *ex ante* effects of PTA on trade by using the price-elasticity approach suffered certain limitations, notably, failure to account for the supply factors influencing production. The advantage of the Imada approach (who used the Armington, 1969, revised version of the Tyers methodology, 1980) is that it takes account of the supply effects as well as the income growth effects. But this approach, improved though it is, does not incorporate the dynamic effects of trade liberalization through economies of scale and learning-by-doing. To that extent, the benefits noted by Imada (1993) may have been underestimated.
3. For example, Toyota's Singapore office coordinates its intra-firm trade of parts and components: diesel engines produced in Thailand; transmissions in the Philippines; steering gears in Malaysia and engines in Indonesia. In 1995, such intra-firm exports accounted for about 20 per cent of the company's total exports of parts and components worldwide (UNCTAD, 1996).
4. India's dominant position is brought into sharp focus if we consider some basic economic indicators: India occupies 72 per cent of the region's total area, it has about 77 per cent of the population and about 78 per cent of its GNP. India's GDP is over three times the combined GDP of the other countries in the region.
5. Until July 1982, Pakistan did not permit private companies to trade with Indian companies. Since then there has been a gradual relaxation of the rules and by 1988, Pakistan's private sector was allowed to import from India from a list of 249 items. However, there are continued restrictions on the import of Indian finished manufactured goods. Much of the trade between the two countries is done either through their government trading corporations or illegally. It is estimated that about US$1 billion in intermediate and capital goods from India reaches Pakistan every year via Dubai, Singapore and Hong Kong.

5 APEC: A CASE OF OPEN REGIONALISM

1. Drysdale (1994) has projected that East Asia's share in world output in the year 2000 will reach 28 per cent, a level roughly comparable with that of Western Europe and North America. By the year 2010, East Asia is expected to overtake both these regions to become the world's largest group of economies.

2. For example, Japan agreed to accelerate by 50 per cent its cuts in industrial tariffs in line with the Uruguay Round and promised deregulatory measures worth an estimated US$10 billion; China proposed to cut tariffs on 4000 products by no less than 30 per cent and eliminate some import controls before the end of the year; and developing country members, such as Indonesia made commitments to progressively reduce their tariffs.
3. Hong Kong and Singapore pledged to abolish all tariffs by 2010 (ten years ahead of schedule) while Chile has expressed a similar 'willingness' in addition to abolishing most non-tariffs. Indonesia plans to cut tariffs no more than 10 per cent by 2003 while the Philippines plans to cut tariffs (except on agricultural imports) to 5 per cent by 2004. China announced it would cut import duties to an average of 23 per cent in 1996 and to 15 per cent by the year 2000 (de Jonquieres and Luce, 1996).
4. Not only does Japan have a trade surplus with the US and EU, but an even larger one with the NIEs, to the tune of US$46.5 billion in 1992 (Chia, 1994). The NIEs trade surplus has fluctuated reaching a peak of US$105 billion in 1987. The ASEAN countries recorded trade surpluses between 1984–8 but slipped back into deficits thereafter, due mainly to the poor performance of the Philippines and Thailand. China has been enjoying surpluses since the early nineties following a period of deficits.
5. The authors developed a 19-region global general equilibrium model to analyse the consequences of trade liberalization in East Asia compared with Pacific-wide trade liberalization on an MFN basis. Among their main conclusions was that Pacific-wide MFN liberalization would yield 20 per cent higher gains than an East Asian MFN liberalization, but that the US would gain more from the latter.
6. It is also in APEC's interest to provide a mediatory mechanism for resolving trade conflicts in the region. While it would not be a supranational dispute settlement authority, it could complement the WTO arbitration and sanctions process through mediation and dialogue between conflicting parties as a first resort.

6 THE AMERICAS: NAFTA AND MERCOSUR

1. For a detailed discussion on the Canadian debate on NAFTA and changing positions in a historical perspective, see Molot (1995).
2. Tremblay (1993) believes that the 1990–1 recession in both countries and the appreciation of the Canadian dollar were more influential than the FTA in shaping the trade balance.
3. The arguments regarding job loss in the context of the NAFTA debate bear resemblance to Wood's global estimation that increased exports from the East Asian dynamic economies will lead to a loss of unskilled jobs in the North (Wood, 1994). A number of quantitative studies have been undertaken using computable general equilibrium (CGE) models to quantify the effects of NAFTA on employment and wages in member countries. The following conclusions suggested by these models are worth noting. First, welfare gains in terms of real incomes as a percentage of GNP tend to be small for Mexico although they increase when account is taken of

removal of non-tariff barriers (NTBs) and an increase in foreign direct investment (FDI). Secondly, when static models allow for imperfect competition and increasing returns to scale (IRS), the gains are larger still. Thirdly, the dynamic models generally show highest welfare gains because they take account of the feedback effects of investor confidence, and increased labour productivity resulting from technology transfer. Fourthly, gains are more significant for Mexico than for either Canada or the US. Fifthly, contrary to expectations real wages and/or employment in the US rise as a result of trade liberalization and the wage gap between Mexico and the US wages narrows. A decline in the US wage is predicted on the assumption of lack of labour scarcity. However, if trade between Mexico and the United States acts as a substitute for Mexican immigration, wages of US unskilled labour may not decline.

4. Panagariya (1996) argues that the US is likely to benefit from NAFTA much more than Mexico because of the improved US access to the Mexican market. He claims that NAFTA will worsen Mexico's terms of trade. Mexico may also suffer from higher labour and environmental standards through loss of competitiveness (at least in some sectors) if competing developing countries do not raise these standards.
5. Unlike the US trade relationship with East Asia where US imports from that region have not resulted in US export increases there, thereby leading to trade deficits with all the countries there.
6. The Harmonized Tariff Schedule (HTS) is far more important than Generalized System of Preferences (GSP). While 45 per cent of Mexican exports to the US in 1989 were covered under HTS, GSP covered only 9 per cent (see Kim and Weston, 1993).
7. FDI is generally linked to the Mexican economic cycles. For example, it rose rapidly during the oil boom period (1979 to 1981). In 1982 and 1983, the debt crisis led to a decline in FDI but it subsequently picked up (Ortiz, 1994). In the late eighties, FDI inflows into Mexico depicted peculiar characteristics. Their countercyclical behaviour is explained by debt-equity swaps to reduce Mexico's debt burden. In 1986–88, when GDP either fell or grew very slowly, FDI inflows 'surpassed even the levels attained during the oil boom of 1978–81, when GDP grew about 8 percent on average'. (Calderón, Mortimore and Peres, 1995, p. 246).
8. The NAFTA agreement is credited with playing a role in halting capital flight and saving Mexico from disaster (*The Economist*, December 10, 1994). The US Government feared that the Mexican crisis would unleash a flood of Mexican imports and immigrants and halt the process of economic reform and democratization in that country. To counter this, the Clinton Administration led an international rescue operation involving Canada, the US and IMF and commercial banks to extend a multi-billion dollar loan to Mexico.
9. This point may be illustrated by the experience of the Japanese automobile companies (Honda, Suzuki/GM and Toyota) in Canada. In the eighties in order to attract Japanese investment, Canada granted special import duty reductions for imports of parts and components. Following the CUSFTA and NAFTA, these advantages have now been phased out (Edgington and Fruin, 1994).

10. We are grateful to Michael Mortimore of UNECLAC, Santiago for drawing our attention to this point.
11. The US-Mexico maquiladora programme is an example of what is known as 'production sharing' under the Harmonized Tariff Schedule (HTS) 9802. The processing and assembly of imported components is undertaken mainly (but not exclusively) in Mexico along the US border for re-export mainly to the US. The inputs are imported into Mexico duty-free while the goods re-exported to the US are charged duty only on the non-US value added and not on the US-made components. Most of the firms engaged in the *maquiladora* programme are subsidiaries of US multinationals which enjoy cheap labour (made even cheaper after severe devaluations) and investment incentives. But other countries such as Korea, Malaysia and Singapore have also been involved. The HTS noted above benefits mainly automobiles and spare parts, textiles and clothing, electronic components and furniture, industries which are prominent under the *maquiladora*. (For a detailed account of this programme, see Hufbauer and Schott, 1992, Chapter 5.)
12. However, it is important to note that Yeats' analysis relates mainly to exports. There is no evidence to suggest that the rise in intraregional imports has been at the expense of imports from outside the region. Overall, imports – intraregional and from outside the MERCOSUR region – have risen by as much as 180 per cent between 1990 and 1995 compared with a 50 per cent increase in total exports during this period (*The Financial Times*, 4 February 1997).
13. Foreign capital inflows (particularly portfolio investment) into Brazil have increased in the past two years so much so that in mid-1995, the Central Bank had to impose taxes on foreign borrowing and foreign portfolio investment (see Ffrench-Davis and Agosin, 1995, p. 6). In the aftermath of the Mexican crisis in December 1994, the Brazilian government may have been particularly cautious and forewarned.
14. This point is due to Diana Tussie of FLACSO, Buenos Aires.
15. According to the Chile-MERCOSUR agreement signed in 1996, during 1996 tariffs on most goods will be reduced by 30 per cent. From 2000 onwards, they will gradually fall to zero over a four-year period. Trade in food and agricultural products (this sector is heavily protected by Chile) will be subject to special treatment (see Reid, 1996).
16. This section is based on personal discussions in March 1996 with senior negotiators for the member countries of MERCOSUR and of Chile's negotiators on NAFTA and MERCOSUR.
17. The US perception of hemisphere integration is an extension of the NAFTA model which Brazil sees as going beyond the multilateral accord. Indeed, the US had opposed MERCOSUR, presumably because it would undermine her economic and political influence in the Americas. In some ways, this has turned out to be so. MERCOSUR's performance in the first few years has demonstrated significant economic and political cooperation among the partners, so much so that it has attracted the European Union to sign an agreement with MERCOSUR in early 1996. Thus, the US is beginning to lose its influence in the Southern Cone to Western Europe.

7 REGIONALISM IN EUROPE

1. In 1995, the EU(15) quota amounted to 2.5 million tonnes which is likely to be raised by 353 000 tonnes as a result of the accession of Austria, Finland and Sweden (WTO, 1995a, p. 91). The so-called 'banana' war against the import of bananas from Latin America is a clear example of resentment against an EU trade discrimination policy which is inconsistent with GATT (Uruguay Round) principles. In May 1996, the Latin American countries and the United States again complained to the WTO about discrimination by the European Union against their banana exports.
2. Some members of COMECON, for example Romania, started trading with the West thus diverting intraregional trade to the rest of the world. It is reported that Romania's trade with Western industrialized countries increased from 16 per cent in 1958 to 45 per cent in 1969 (Robson, 1987).
3. This contradicts McMillan's (1992) view that the unification of Germany may have diverted FDI to Eastern Germany and away from the CEECs.

8 FUTURE OF REGIONAL BLOCS

1. Of course there are negative aspects of the 'big brother' hypothesis, as we noted in the case of SAARC and NAFTA. In the case of SAARC, smaller members have resented the dominance of India. Similarly, in NAFTA the US domination, and in MERCOSUR, the domination of Brazil, is of some concern to smaller partners.
2. In March 1996, the US President signed the Helms–Burton bill which imposes US sanctions against non-American firms that do business in Cuba. The objective of the sanctions is to protect the business of non-American companies with the US. Canada and Mexico, which replaced American firms in Cuba, have complained that the bill violates the NAFTA agreement.
3. Brazil subsequently modified its regulations regarding intellectual property protection and was placed in the special 301 'watch list' along with Argentina.
4. Article 1 of the GATT requires signatory governments to 'extend unconditionally to all other countracting parties (members) any advantage, favour, privilege or immunity affecting customs duties, charges, rules and procedures that they give to products originating in or destined for any other country' (WTO, 1995, p. 5). This MFN rule is intended to ensure that both exporters and importers reap the economic benefits of international trade. It is also designed to strengthen the position of smaller trading nations *vis-à-vis* the larger ones.
5. An OECD study by Lloyd (1992) notes that in practice only four regional groupings comply with the GATT/WTO Article XXIV. A more recent study by a WTO official notes: 'Of the 80 working parties that have examined the conformity of agreements, only one has ever found an agreement to be fully in conformity' (see Sampson, 1996, p. 90).

Bibliography

AfDB (African Development Bank) (1993) *Regional Integration in Southern Africa*, Vol. 1, Oxford, Oxprint Ltd., African Development Bank.

Aggarwal, M.R. and P.R. Pandey (1992) 'Prospects of Trade Expansion in the SAARC Region', *Developing Economies* (March).

Aggarwal, Vinod K. (1993) 'Building International Institutions in Asia-Pacific', *Asian Survey* (November).

Ahmad, A., S. Rao and C. Barnes (1996) 'Foreign Direct Investment and APEC Economic Integration', *Industry Canada Working Paper* no. 8, Ottawa (February).

Akrasanee, N. and D. Stifel (1992) 'The Political Economy of the ASEAN Free Trade Area', in P. Imada and Seiji Naya (eds), *AFTA: The Way Ahead*, Singapore, Institute of Southeast Asian Studies.

Akrasanee, N. and D. Stifel (1994) 'A Vision of Southeast Asia in the Year 2000: Towards a Common Economic Regime', *Contemporary Southeast Asia* (June).

Alburo, F.A., C.C. Bautista and M.S.H. Gochoco (1992) 'Pacific Direct Investment Flows into ASEAN', *ASEAN Economic Bulletin* (March).

Anderson, Kym and Richard Blackhurst (eds) (1993) *Regional Integration and the Global Trading System*, Hemel Hempstead, Harvester Wheatsheaf.

Anderson, Kym and Hege Norheim (1993) 'History, Geography and Regional Economic Integration' in Anderson and Blackhurst, ibid.

APEC (1994) *Achieving the APEC Vision: Free and Open Trade in the Asia-Pacific*, Report of an Eminent Group, Singapore (August).

APEC (1995) *Implementing the APEC Vision*, Third Report of the APEC Eminent Persons Group, Singapore (August).

Ariff, Mohammed (1992) 'Commentary on Chapter 2', in P. Imada and S. Naya (eds), *AFTA: The Way Ahead*, Singapore, ISEAS.

Ariff, Mohammed and Tan Eu Chye (1992) 'ASEAN-Pacific Trade Relations', *ASEAN Economic Review* (March).

Arndt, H.W. (1994) 'Anatomy of Regionalism', in R. Garnaut and P. Drysdale (eds), *Asia Pacific Regionalism: Readings in International Economic Relations*, Pymble, Harper Educational Publishers.

Artisian, P., M. Rojec and M. Svetlicic (eds) (1993) *Foreign Investments in Central and Eastern Europe*, London, Macmillan Press.

Asian Development Bank (ADB) (1996) *Key Indicators of Developing Asian and Pacific Countries*, Manila.

Aspe, Pedro (1991) 'Mexico's Macroeconomic Adjustment and Growth Perspectives', in *Policy Implications of Trade and Currency Zones*, a symposium sponsored by the Federal Reserve Bank of Kansas City, Jackson Hole, Wyoming, 22–24 August, Jackson Hole.

Bach, Daniel C. (1997) 'Institutional Crisis and the Search for New Models', in Réal Lavergne (ed.), *Regional Integration and Cooperation in West Africa: A Multidimensional Perspective*, Trenton, NJ, Africa World Press.

Bailey, P., A. Parisotto and G. Renshaw (eds) (1993) *Multinationals and Employment*, Geneva, ILO.

Balasubramanyam, V.N. and David Greenaway (1993) 'Regional Integration Agreements and Foreign Direct Investment', in Kym Anderson and Richard Blackhurst (eds), *Regional Integration and the Global Trading System*, op.cit.

Balasubramanyam, V.N., M. Salisu and D. Sapsford (1996) 'Foreign Direct Investment and Growth in EP and IS Countries', *Economic Journal* (January).

Baldwin, R.E. (1989) 'The Growth Effects of 1992', *Economic Policy* (October).

Baldwin, R.E. (1993) 'Adapting the GATT to a More Regionalized World: A Political Economy Perspective', in Anderson and Blackhurst, *Regional Integration and the Global Trading System*, op.cit.

Baldwin, R.E. (1994) *Towards an Integrated Europe,* London, Centre for Economic Policy Research.

Baldwin, R.E. (1995) 'The Eastern Enlargement of the European Union', *European Economic Review* (April).

Bannister, Geoffrey and Patrick Low (1992) 'Textiles and Apparel in NAFTA', *World Bank PRE Working Paper*, no. 994, Washington DC (October).

Barad, Robert (1990) 'Unrecorded Transborder Trade and its Implications for Regional Economic Integration', in World Bank, *The Long-Term Perspective Study of Sub-Saharan Africa*, vol. 4, Background Papers, Washington DC.

Baumann, Renato (1993) 'Integration and Trade Diversion', *CEPAL Review*, no. 51 (December).

Behar, J. (1995) 'Measuring the Effects of Economic Integration for the Southern Cone Countries: Industry Simulations of Trade Liberalization', *Developing Economies* (March).

Bergsten, C.F. and M. Noland (eds) (1993) *Pacific Dynamism and the International Economic System*, Washington DC, Institute for International Economics.

Bernal, R.L. (1994) 'From NAFTA to Hemisphere Free Trade', *Columbia Journal of World Business* (Fall).

Bhagwati, J. (1978) 'Anatomy of Consequences of Exchange Control Regimes, in NBER', *Studies in International Economic Relations*, vol. 1, no. 10, New York.

Bhagwati, J. (1991) *The World Trading System at Risk*, Hemel-Hempstead, Harvester Wheatsheaf.

Bhagwati, J. (1992) 'Threats to the World Trading System', *World Economy* (July).

Bhagwati, J. (1993) 'Regionalism and Multilateralism: An Overview', in Jaime de Melo and Arvin Panagariya (eds), *New Dimensions in Regional Integration*, Cambridge, Cambridge University Press.

Bhalla, A.S. (1964) 'Asian Economic Cooperation with special reference to the Association of Southeast Asia (ASA)', Oxford, Institute of Economics and Statistics (unpublished manuscript).

Bhalla, A.S. (1995) *Uneven Development in the Third World: A Study of China and India*, London, Macmillan, second revised and enlarged edition.

Bhuyan, A.S. (1988) 'Regional Cooperation and Trade Expansion in Southeast Asia, in Asian Development Bank (ADB)', *Towards Regional Cooperation in Southeast Asia*, Manila.

Biessen, G. (1991) 'Is the Impact of Central Planning on the Levels of Foreign Trade Really Negative?', *Journal of Comparative Economics* (March).

Blumenfeld, Jesmond (1991) *Economic Interdependence in Southern Africa: From Conflict to Cooperation?*, Chapter 12 on 'The Economic Role of SADCC'. Cape Town, Oxford University Press.

Bouzas, Roberto (1995) *MERCOSUR and Preferential Trade Liberalization in South America: Record, Issues and Prospects; Facultad de Ciencias Sociales Latinoamericana (FLACSO)*, Buenos Aires (April).

Brada, Josef C. (1993) 'Regional Integration in Eastern Europe: Prospects for Integration within the Region and with the European Community', in J. de Melo and A. Panagariya, (eds), *New Dimensions in Regional Integration*, Cambridge, Cambridge University Press.

Breuer, Luis (1995) 'A Small Country Perspective of MERCOSUR: The Case of Paraguay', paper presented at an International Conference on NAFTA, Latin American Trade Agreements and Western Hemisphere Integration, Santiago, *Corporacion de Investigaciones Economicas Para Latino America* (CIEPLAN) (12–13 January).

Brown, D.K., A.V. Deardorff and R.M. Stern (1992) 'A North American Free Trade Agreement: Analytical Issues and a Computational Assessment', *World Economy*, (January).

Bundu, Abass (1997) 'ECOWAS and the Future of Regional Integration in West Africa', in Réal Lavergne (ed.), *Regional Integration and Cooperation in West Africa: A Multidimensional Perspective*, Africa World Press.

Cadot, O., R. Faini and J. de Melo (1995) 'Early Trade Patterns Under the Europe Agreements: France, Germany and Italy', *European Economic Review* (April).

Calderón, Alvaro, Michael Mortimore and Wilson Peres (1995) *Mexico's Incorporation into the New Industrial Order: Foreign Investment as a Source of International Competitiveness*, Economic Commission for Latin America and the Caribbean, Division of Production, Productivity and Management, Santiago.

Cassim, Rashad (1995) 'Rethinking Economic Integration in Southern Africa', *Trade Monitor*, (September).

Chia, Siow Yue (1992) 'Commentary on Chapter 4' (Policy Issues and the Formation of the ASEAN Free Trade Area) in P. Imada and S. Naya (eds), *AFTA: The Way Ahead*, Singapore, Institute of Southeast Asian Studies (ISEAS).

Chia, Siow Yue (1994) 'Trade and Foreign Direct Investment in East Asia', in Wendy Dobson and Frank Flatters (eds), *Pacific Trade and Investment: Options for the 90s*, Proceedings of a Conference, Toronto (6–8 June), Toronto.

Chia, Siow Yue and Tsao Yuan Lee (1994) 'Economic Zones in Southeast Asia', in R. Garnaut and P. Drysdale (eds), *Asia Pacific Regionalism: Readings in International Economic Relations*, Pymble, Harper Educational Publishers.

Chudnovsky, Daniel (1992) *The Future of Hemispheric Integration: the MERCOSUR and the Enterprise of the Americas Initiative*, Centro de investigaciones para la transformacion (Cenit), Buenos Aires (July).

Chudnovsky, Daniel (1994) 'Reviving South–South Cooperation: Argentina, Brazil, and the MERCOSUR', in L.K. Mytelka (ed.), *South–South Cooperation in Global Perspective,* Paris, OECD Development Centre, Documents Series.

Chudnovsky, D., A. Lopez and F. Porta (1995) 'Mas alla del flujo de caja. El boom de la inversion extranjera directa en la Argentina', *Desarrollo Economico* (April–June).

Cline, R.W. (1994) *International Economic Policy in the 1990s*, Cambridge, Mass., MIT Press.

Commission of the European Communities (1988) 'The Economics of 1992: An Assessment of the Potential Economic Effects of Completing the Internal Market of the European Community', *European Economy*, no. 35 (March).

Cooper, Richard N. (1974) 'Worldwide vs. Regional Integration: Is there an Optimal Size of the Integrated Area?', *Yale Economic Growth Center Discussion Paper* no. 220 (November).

Corden, W. Max (1993) Round Table Discussion, in J. de Melo and A. Panagariya (eds), *New Dimensions in Regional Integration*, Cambridge, Cambridge University Press.

Davies, Robert (1993) 'The Case for Economic Integration in Southern Africa', in P.H. Baker, A. Boraine, and W. Krafchik (eds), *South Africa and the World Economy in the 1990s*, Cape Town, David Philip.

Davies, Robert (1994) 'The Southern African Customs Union (SACU): Background and Possible Issues for Negotiation Facing a Democratic South African Government', in M. Sisulu, M. Nkosi, B. Setai and R.H. Thomas (eds), *Reconstituting and Democratising the Southern African Customs Union*, Braamfontein, South Africa.

Davies, Robert (1995) 'New Sources for Growth and Hope: Prospects for Southern Africa', paper prepared for North–South Roundtable Discussion on 'Moving Africa into the 21st Century: An Agenda for Renewal', Johannesburg (16–18 October).

de Jonquieres, Guy and Edward Luce (1996) 'APEC Opts for Slow and Steady Jog', *Financial Times* (25 November).

Dell, Sidney (1963) *Trade Blocs and Common Markets*, London, Constable.

de Melo, Jaime and Arvind Panagariya (eds) (1993) *New Dimensions in Regional Integration*, Cambridge, Cambridge University Press.

de Melo, Jaime, Arvind Panagariya and Dani Rodrik, (1993a) 'The New Regionalism: A Country Perspective', in de Melo and Panagariya, ibid.

DeRosa, Dean A. (1995) *Regional Trading Arrangements Among Developing Countries: The ASEAN Example*, Washington DC, International Food Policy Research Institute (IFPRI).

Devan, J. (1987) 'The ASEAN Preferential Trading Arrangements: Some Problems, Ex Ante Results, and a Multilateral Approach to Future Intra-ASEAN Trade Development', *ASEAN Economic Bulletin*, vol. 4, no. 2.

Dicken, P. (1992) *Global Shift – The Internationalization of Economic Activity*, Second Edition, New York, Guilford Press.

Dobson, Wendy (1994) 'What is NAFTA's Significance for APEC?', *Journal of Asian Economics*, vol. 5, no. 4.

Doz, Yves (1987) 'International Industries: Fragmentation Versus Globalization', in Bruce R. Guile and Harvey Brooks (eds), *Technology and Global Industry – Companies and Nations in the World Economy*, Washington DC, National Academy Press.

Drysdale, P.D. (1967) 'Japan, Australia and New Zealand: The Prospects for Western Pacific Integration', *Economic Record* (September).

Drysdale, Peter (1994) *The Future of the Asia Pacific Economy and Japan's*

Economic Diplomacy, paper presented to Emerging Asian Economies and the Role of Japan, 30th Anniversary International Symposium, Institute of Economic Research, Chuo University (25–6 June).

Drysdale, Peter and Andrew Elek (1995) *Towards APEC's Liberalization Goals of 2010 and 2020*, Institute of Developing Economies (IDE) International Symposium on APEC: Cooperation from Diversity, Tokyo (20–21 September).

Drysdale, P.D. and Ross Garnaut (1982) 'Trade Intensities and the Analysis of Bilateral Trade Flows in Many-Country World: A Survey', *Hitotsubashi Journal of Economics*, vol. 22, no. 2.

Drysdale, Peter and Ross Garnaut (1989) 'A Pacific Free Trade Area?', in Jeffrey J. Schott (ed.), *More Free Trade?*, Washington DC, Institute for International Economics.

Drysdale, Peter and Ross Garnaut (1993) *East Asia in the International System: APEC and the Challenge of Discriminatory Trade*, paper presented to the Helen Hughes *Festschrift*, Australian National University, Canberra (19–20 August).

Drysdale, Peter and Ross Garnaut (1993a) 'NAFTA and the Asia-Pacific Region: Strategic Responses', in Sidney Weintraub *et al.* (eds), *The Challenge of NAFTA: North America, Australia, New Zealand, and the World Trade Regime*, University of Texas, Austin.

Drysdale, Peter and Ross Garnaut (1994) 'Principles of Pacific Economic Integration', in R. Garnaut and P. Drysdale (eds), *Asia Pacific Regionalism*, Pymble, Harper Educational Publishers.

Dunning, J.H. (1993) 'Transatlantic Foreign Direct Investment and the European Economic Community', in J.H. Dunning, *The Globalization of Business: The Challenge of the 1990s*, London, Routledge.

Dunning, J.H. (1993a) 'The Prospects for Foreign Direct Investment in Central and Eastern Europe', in Dunning, ibid.

The Economist (1994) 'A Dream of Free Trade', London (19 November).

The Economist (1994) 'Happy Ever NAFTA?', (10 December).

The Economist (1996) 'Pakistan's Least Favoured Nation' (27 January).

The Economist (1996) 'South America: Getting Together' (29 June).

Eden, L. (1994) 'Multinationals as Agents of Change: Setting a New Canadian Policy on Foreign Direct Investment', *Industry Canada Discussion Paper* no. 1 (November).

Edgington, D.W. and W.M. Fruin (1994) 'NAFTA and Japanese Investment', in A.M. Rugman (ed.), *Foreign Investment and NAFTA*, Columbia, South Carolina, University of South Carolina Press.

Elek, Andrew (1992) 'Pacific Economic Cooperation: Policy Choices for the 1990s', *Asian-Pacific Economic Literature*, vol. 6, no. 1.

EUROSTAT (Statistical Office of the European Communities), *Eurostatistics*, Luxembourg.

Ezenwe, U. (1990) 'Evaluating the Performance of West African Integration Movements', in World Bank, *The Long-Term Perspective Study of Sub-Saharan Africa*, vol. 4, Background Papers, Washington DC.

Ffrench-Davis, Ricardo and Manuel R. Agosin (1995) 'Managing Capital Inflows in Latin America', University of Chile, *Department of Economics Working Paper* no. 137, Santiago (November).

Filippo, Armando di (1995) 'Transnationalization and Integration of Production in Latin America', *CEPAL Review*, no. 57 (December).

Fischer, Stanley (1993) 'Prospects for Regional Integration in the Middle East', in de Melo and Panagariya, *New Dimensions in Regional Integration*, op.cit.

Flatters, Frank and Richard Harris (1994) 'Trade and Investment: Patterns and Policy Issues in the Asia-Pacific Rim', in Wendy Dobson and Frank Flatters (eds), *Pacific Trade and Investment: Options for the 90s*, Proceedings of a Conference (6–8 June).

Foroutan, Faezeh and Lant Pritchett (1993) 'Intra-sub-Saharan Trade: Is it too Little?', *Journal of African Economies* (May).

Frimpong-Ansah, J.H. (1990) 'The Prospects of Monetary Union in ECOWAS', in World Bank, *The Long-Term Perspective Study of Sub-Saharan Africa*, vol. 4, Background Papers, Washington DC.

Garnaut, Ross (1994) 'Open Regionalism: Its Analytic Basis and Relevance to the International System', *Journal of Asian Economics*, vol. 5, no. 2.

Garnaut, Ross and Peter Drysdale (1994) *Asia Pacific Regionalism – Readings in International Economic Relations*, Pymble, Harper Educational Publishers.

Gestrin, M. and L. Waverman (1994) 'Extension of NAFTA to Latin America', in A.M. Rugman (ed.), *Foreign Investment and NAFTA*, Columbia, South Carolina University Press.

Gibb, R. and W. Michalak (eds) (1994) *Continental Trading Blocs: The Growth of Regionalism in the World Economy*, Chichester, John Wiley & Sons.

Graham, E.M. (1994) 'NAFTA Foreign Direct Investment and the US', in A.M. Rugman (ed.), *Foreign Investment and NAFTA*, Columbia, University of South Carolina Press.

Greenaway, D. (1993) 'Trade and Foreign Direct Investment', in EC Commission, *European Economy – The European Community as a World Trade Partner*, Luxembourg.

Grinspun, Ricardo and Maxwell A. Cameron (eds) (1993) *The Political Economy of North American Free Trade*, London, Macmillan Press.

Han, Sung-Taik (1992) *The European Economic Integration: The Impact on Asian Newly Industrialising Economies*, Paris, OECD Development Centre (June).

Hanlon, J. (1989) *SADCC in the 1990s: Development on the Frontline*, London, Economic Intelligence Unit (September).

Harmsen, Richard and Michael Leidy (1994) 'Regional Trading Arrangements', in IMF: *International Trade Policies: The Uruguay Round and Beyond*, vol. II, Background Papers, Washington DC.

Harris, R.G. (1993) 'Globalization, Trade and Income', *Canadian Journal of Economics* (November).

Hazlewood, Arthur (1979) 'The End of the East African Community: The Lessons of Regional Integration', *Journal of Common Market Studies*, vol. 18, no. 1.

Hill, Hal (1994) 'Australia's Asia Pacific Connections', in Wendy Dobson and Frank Flatters, *Pacific Trade and Investment: Options for the 90s*, Proceedings of a Conference, Toronto.

Hindley, B. and P.A. Messerlin (1993) 'Guarantees of Market Access', in Anderson and Blackhurst, *Regional Integration and the Global Trading System*, op.cit.

Hodder, Rupert (1994) 'The West Pacific Rim', in R. Gibb and W. Michalak (eds), *Continental Trading Blocs: The Growth of Regionalism in the World Economy*, Chichester, John Wiley & Sons.

Hufbauer, G. (1990) 'An Overview', in G. Hufbauer (ed.), *Europe 1992: An American Perspective*, Washington DC, Brookings Institution.

Hufbauer, G. and J. Schott (1992) *North American Free Trade: Issues and Recommendations*, Washington DC, Institute for International Economics.

Hufbauer, G. and J. Schott (1993) *NAFTA, An Assessment*, Washington DC, Institute for International Economics.

Hufbauer, G. and J. Schott (assisted by Diana Clark) (1994) *Western Hemisphere Economic Integration*, Washington DC, Institute for International Economics (July).

Hughes-Hallett, A.J. (1994) 'The Impact of EC-92 on Trade in Developing Countries', *World Bank Research Observer* (January).

Hurrell, Andrew (1994) 'Regionalism in the Americas', in A.F. Lowenthal and G.F. Treverton (eds), *Latin America in a New World*, Boulder, Westview Press.

Imada, P. (1993) 'Production and Trade Effects of an ASEAN Free Trade Area', *Developing Economies* (March).

Imada, P. and S. Naya (eds) (1992) *AFTA: The Way Ahead*, Singapore, Institute of Southeast Asian Studies (ISEAS).

Industrial Development Corporation (1995/2) 'Trade Integration and Economic Development in Southern Africa', *Manufacturing (Trading Conditions)*, Sandton, South Africa (October).

IMF, *Direction of Trade Statistics Yearbook*, Washington DC.

IMF, *International Financial Statistics Yearbook*, Washington DC.

Izam, Miguel (1993) 'European Integration and Latin American Trade', *CEPAL Review*, no. 51 (December).

Johnson, Omotunde E.G. (1995) 'Regional Integration in Sub-Saharan Africa', *Journal of European Integration* (Winter/Spring).

Joshua, F.T. (1989) 'Experience of African Regional Economic Integration', *UNCTAD Review*, vol. 1, no. 2.

Kaser, Michael (1967) *COMECON-Integration Problems of the Planned Economies*, London, Oxford University Press.

Khan, A.R. (1994) *Overcoming Unemployment*, Geneva, ILO.

Kim, Han Soo and Ann Weston (1993) 'A North American Free Trade Agreement and East Asian Developing Countries', *ASEAN Economic Bulletin* (March).

Kitson, M. and J. Michie (1995) 'Trade and Growth: A Historical Perspective', in J. Michie and J.G. Smith (eds), *Managing the Global Economy*, Oxford, Oxford University Press.

Klaveren, A. van (1996) *Chile: The Search for Open Regionalism*, Santiago, Institute for International Studies, University of Chile, (mimeo).

Kojima, K. (1975) 'International Trade and Foreign Investment: Substitutes or Complements', *Hitotsubashi Journal of Economics* (June).

Kosacoff, B. and G. Bezchinsky (1994) 'New Strategies of Transnational Corporations in Argentina', *CEPAL Review*, no. 52 (April).

Krueger, A.O. (1993) 'The Effects of Regional Trading Blocs on World Trade', in Sidney Weintraub *et al.* (eds), *The Challenge of NAFTA: North America, Australia, New Zealand and the World Trade Regime*, Austin, University of Texas.

Krueger, A.O. (1995) 'NAFTA: Strengthening or Weakening the International Trading System?', in J. Bhagwati and A.O. Krueger, *The Dangerous Drift to Preferential Trade Agreements*, Washington DC, The American Enterprise Institute (AEI).

Krugman, Paul (1991) 'The Move Toward Free Trade Zones', in *Policy Implications of Trade and Currency Zones*, a symposium sponsored by the Federal Reserve Bank of Kansas City, Jackson Hole, Wyoming (August).

Kumar, Sree (1992) 'Policy Issues and the Formation of the ASEAN Free Trade Area', in P. Imada and S. Naya (eds), *AFTA: The Way Ahead*, Singapore, ISEAS.

Kumar, Sree (1994) 'Johor-Singapore-Riau Growth Triangle: A Model of Subregional Cooperation', in M. Thant, M. Tang and H. Kakazu (eds), *Growth Triangles in Asia – A New Approach to Regional Economic Cooperation*, published for the Asian Development Bank, Oxford University Press, Hong Kong.

Labàn, Raul and Patricio Meller (1995) 'Trade Strategy Alternatives for a Small Country: The Chilean Case', paper presented at an International Conference on NAFTA, Latin American Trade Agreements and Western Hemisphere Integration, Santiago, 12–13 January.

Lal, Deepak (1993) 'Trade Blocs and Multilateral Free Trade', *Journal of Common Market Studies* (September).

Lawrence, Robert (1991) 'Emerging Regional Arrangements: Building Blocks or Stumbling Blocks?', in *Policy Implications of Trade and Currency Zones*, a Symposium sponsored by the Federal Reserve Bank of Kansas City, Jackson Hole, Wyoming, 22–4 August, Jackson Hole.

Lipsey, R.G. (1995) 'The Case for the FTA and NAFTA', *Canadian Business Economics* (January–March).

Lipsey, R.G., D. Schwanen and R.J. Wonnacott (1994) *The NAFTA, What's In, What's Out, What's Next*, Toronto, Policy Study 21, C.D. Howe Institute.

Lipsey, R.G. and Patricio Meller (1997) *Western Hemisphere Trade Integration*, London, Macmillan.

Lloyd, P. (1992) 'Regionalism and World Trade', *OECD Economic Studies* no. 18, Paris (Spring).

Lundahl, M. and L. Petersson (1991) *The Dependent Economy – Lesotho and the Southern African Customs Union*, Boulder, Westview Press.

Maasdorp, G. and A. Whiteside (1993) *Rethinking Economic Cooperation in Southern Africa: Trade and Investment*, Konrad Adenauer Stiftung, occasional paper.

Martin, Will, P.A. Petri and K. Yanagishima (1994) 'Charting the Pacific: An Empirical Assessment of Integration Initiatives', *International Trade Journal* (Winter).

Mayer, Marina and Harry Zarenda (1994) 'The Southern African Customs Union: A Review of Costs and Benefits', *Development Bank of Southern Africa Working Paper* no. 19, Halfway House, South Africa (March).

McCarthy, Colin (1992) 'The Southern African Customs Union in a Changing Economic and Political Environment', *Journal of World Trade* (August).

McCarthy, Colin (1994) 'Regional Integration of Developing Countries at Different Levels of Economic Development: Problems and Prospects',

Transnational Law and Contemporary Problems (Spring).

McCarthy, Colin (1994a) 'Revenue Distribution and Economic Development in the Southern African Customs Union', *South African Journal of Economics*, vol. 62, no. 3.

McCarthy, Colin (1995) 'Regional Integration in Africa: Part of the Solution or Part of the Problem?', in Stephen Ellis (ed.), *Africa Now*, London, James Curry Publishers.

McCarthy, Colin (1995a) *Integrating Unequals: Post-Apartheid South Africa and Her Neighbours*, paper prepared for the Second Pan-European Conference on International Relations, Paris (13–16 September).

McConnell, James and A. MacPherson (1994) 'The North American Free Trade Area: An Overview of Issues and Prospects', in Gibb and Michalak, *Continental Trade Blocs: The Growth of Regionalism in the World Economy*, Chichester, John Wiley & Sons.

McMillan, C.H. (1992) 'Foreign Direct Investment Flows to the Soviet Union and Eastern Europe: Nature, Magnitude and International Implications', *Journal of Development Planning*, no. 23.

Meade, J. (1955) *The Theory of Customs Union*, Amsterdam, North Holland Publishing Co.

Michalak, Wieslaw (1994) 'Regional Integration in Eastern Europe', in Gibb and Michalak, *Continental Trade Blocs*, op.cit.

Micossi, Stefano and Gianfranco Viesti (1991) 'Japanese Direct Manufacturing Investment in Europe', in L. Alan Winters and Anthony J. Venables, *European Integration: Trade and Industry*, Cambridge, Cambridge University Press.

Molot, M.A. (1995) *The North American Free Trade Agreement: Policy or Investment Led?*, paper prepared for the Conference on 'NAFTA, Latin American Trade Agreements and Western Hemisphere Integration', Santiago, Chile (12–13 January).

Morrison, Allan J. and Kendall Roth (1992) 'The Regional Solution: An Alternative to Globalization', *Transnational Corporations* (August).

Mortimore, M. (1995) *Insights into the Processes of Industrial Restructuring and International Competition in Latin America*, Santiago, ECLAC (mimeo).

Mundell, R.A. (1957) 'International Trade and Factor Mobility', *American Economic Review* (June).

Naidu, G. (1994) 'Johor-Singapore-Riau Growth Triangle: Progress and Prospects', in M. Thant, M. Tang and H. Kakazu (eds), *Growth Triangles in Asia: A New Approach to Regional Economic Cooperation*, published for the Asian Development Bank, Oxford University Press, Hong Kong.

Naya, S. (1980) *ASEAN Trade and Development Cooperation: Preferential Trading Arrangements and Trade Liberalisation*, Geneva, UNCTAD.

Naya, S. and P. Imada (1992) 'The Long and Winding Road Ahead for AFTA,' in P. Imada and S. Naya (eds), *AFTA: The Way Ahead*, op.cit.

Ndulu, Benno J. (1994) 'Foreign Resource Flows and Financing of Development in Sub-Saharan Africa', in UNCTAD, *International Monetary and Financial Issues for the 1990s, vol. IV*, Research Papers for the Group of Twenty-Four, Geneva.

Neven, D.J. and L.H. Roller (1991) 'The Structure and Determinants of East-West Trade: A Preliminary Analysis of the Manufacturing Sector', in L.

Alan Winters and Anthony J. Venables (eds), *European Integration: Trade and Industry*, Cambridge, Cambridge University Press.

Nogues, Julio and Rosalinda Quintanilla (1993) 'Latin America's Integration and the Multilateral Trading System', in de Melo and Panagariya, *New Dimensions in Regional Integration*, op.cit.

Norman, Victor D. (1991) '1992 and EFTA', in L. Alan Winters and Anthony J. Venables (eds), *European Integration: Trade and Industry*, Cambridge, Cambridge University Press.

OECD, *National Accounts*, several years.

OECD (1996) *International Direct Investment Statistics Yearbook*, Paris.

Okamoto, Yumiko (1995) *Liberalization and Economic Growth*, IDE International Symposium on APEC: Cooperation from Diversity, Tokyo (20–21 September).

Okigbo, P. (1967) *Africa and the Common Market*, London, Longmans.

Oman, C. (1994) *Globalization and Regionalization: The Challenge for Developing Countries*, Paris, OECD Development Centre.

Ooi, G.T. (1981), 'The ASEAN Preferential Trading Arrangement (PTA): An Analysis of Potential Effects and Intra-ASEAN Trade', *Research and Discussion Papers* no. 26, Singapore, Institute of Southeast Asian Studies.

Oppenheim, P. (1992) *Trade Wars – Japan versus the West*, London, Weidenfeld & Nicolson.

Ortiz, Edgar (1994) 'NAFTA and Foreign Direct Investment in Mexico', in A.M. Rugman (ed.), *Foreign Investment and NAFTA*, Columbia, South Carolina University Press.

Ozawa, T. (1992) 'Foreign Direct Investment and Economic Development', *Transnational Corporations* (February).

Page, Sheila (1991) 'Europe 1992: Views of Developing Countries', *Economic Journal* (November).

Page, Sheila (1994) *How Developing Countries Trade*, London, Routledge.

Panagariya, Arvind (1994) 'East Asia and the New Regionalism in World Trade', *World Economy* (November).

Panagariya, Arvind (1996) 'The Free Trade Area of the Americas: Good for Latin America?', *World Economy* (September).

Panchamukhi, V.R. (1995) 'Economic Cooperation in South Asia: The Crisis of Perceptions', in S. Ghosh and S. Mukherjee (eds), *Emerging South Asian Order: Hopes and Concerns*, Calcutta, Media South Asia.

Panchamukhi, V.R. (1995a) 'SAARC Strategy for Sustained Growth', *Financial Express* (10 April).

Pangestu, M., H. Soesastro and M. Ahmad (1992) 'A New Look at Intra-ASEAN Economic Cooperation', *ASEAN Economic Bulletin* (March).

Payne, Anthony (1994) 'The Politics of Regional Cooperation in the Caribbean: The Case of CARICOM', in Andrew Axline (ed.), *The Political Economy of Regional Cooperation – Comparative Case Studies*, London, Pinter Publishers.

Petri, Peter A. (1994) 'The Regional Clustering of Foreign Direct Investment and Trade', *Transnational Corporations* (December).

Petri, Peter A. (1994a) 'Is the United States Bowing Out of Asia?', in R. Garnaut and P. Drysdale (eds), *Asia Pacific Regionalism: Readings in International Economic Relations*, Pymble, Harper Educational Publishers.

Petri, Peter A. (1995) 'The Interdependence of Trade and Investment in the Pacific', in Edward K.Y. Chen and Peter Drsydale (eds), *Corporate Links and Foreign Direct Investment in Asia and the Pacific*, Pymble, Harper Educational, Australia.

Porter, Michael E. (ed.) (1986) *Competition in Global Industries*, Boston, Harvard Business School Press.

Preusse, Heinz G. (1994) 'Regional Integration in the Nineties: Stimulation or Threat to the Multilateral Trading System?', *Journal of World Trade Law* (August).

Pupphavesa, W., N. Poapongsakorn and M. Grewe (1994) 'Thailand's Trade Strategy Under AFTA', in Wendy Dobson and Frank Flatters (eds), *Pacific Trade and Investment: Options for the 90s*, Toronto.

Purvis, Douglas D. (1972) 'Technology, Trade and Factor Mobility', *Economic Journal* (September).

Raboy, D.G., T.L. Simpson and B. Xu (1995) 'A Transition Proposal for Lomé Convention Trade Preferences: The Case of EU Banana Regime', *World Economy* (July).

Ramstetter, E.D. (1994) *Characteristics of Foreign Multinationals in Selected Asian Economies and their Role in Host Economy Exports*, paper prepared for the Joint Conference on Promoting South-South Cooperation in the Asia-Pacific Region, Colombo (16–18 February).

Reid, Michael (1996) 'MERCOSUR Survey', *The Economist*, (12 October).

Robson, P. (1967) 'Economic Integration in Equatorial Africa', in A. Hazlewood (ed.), *African Integration and Disintegration: Case Studies in Economic and Political Union*, London, Oxford University Press.

Robson, P. (1987) 'Integration among Centrally Planned Economies', in Peter Robson, *The Economics of International Integration*, London, Unwin Hyman, Third Edition.

Robson, P. (1993) 'The New Regionalism and Developing Countries', *Journal of Common Market Studies* (September).

Ros, Jaime (1992) 'Free Trade Area or Common Capital Market? Notes on Mexico-US Economic Integration and Current NAFTA Negotiations', *Journal of Interamerican Studies and World Affairs* (Summer).

Rosenthal, G. (1993), 'Regional Integration in the 1990s', *CEPAL Review*, no. 50 (August).

Rugman, A.M. and G. Gestrin (1994) 'NAFTA and Foreign Direct Investment', *Transnational Corporations* (February).

Safadi, Raed and Alexander Yeats (1994) 'NAFTA: Its Effect on South Asia', *Journal of Asian Economics*, vol. 5, no. 2.

Safarian, A.E. (1992) *Direct Investment Issues for the 1990s: An Overview*, Centre for International Studies (CIS), University of Toronto.

Sampson, G.P. (1996) 'Compatibility of Regional and Multilateral Trading Agreements: Reforming the WTO Process', *American Economic Review*, Papers and Proceedings (May).

Sapir, A. (1992) 'Regional Integration in Europe', *Economic Journal* (November).

Scaperlanda, A. (1967) 'The EEC and US Foreign Investment: Some Empirical Evidence', *Economic Journal*, vol. 77.

Schmitz, A. and J. Bieri (1972) 'EEC Tariffs and US Direct Investment', *European Economic Review*, vol. 3.

Schott, Jeffrey J. (1991) 'Trading Blocs and the World Trading System', *World Economy* (March).

Schwanen, D. (1994) *Trade, Jobs and Investments in the 'New Economy': What Have We Learned from the 1988–1993 Period*, paper presented at a C.D. Howe Institute Seminar (22 November).

Seebach, D. (1993) 'Globalization: The Impact on the Trade and Investment Dynamic', Ottawa, *Department of Foreign Affairs and International Trade*, Policy Staff Paper, no. 93/07 (June).

Shiells, Clinton (1995) 'Regional Trading Arrangements', in *International Trade Policies: The Uruguay Round and Beyond*, World Economic and Financial Surveys, Washington DC, IMF.

Siv, Sichan (1995) 'Aiding with Trade', *Cooperation South*, New York, UNDP (October).

Smith, Alan H. (1979) 'Plan Coordination and Joint Planning in CMEA', *Journal of Common Market Studies* (September).

Smith, Murray (1993) 'The North American Free Trade Agreement: Global Impacts', in Anderson and Blackhurst, *Regional Integration and the Global Trading System*, op.cit.

Srinivasan, T.N., J. Whalley and I. Wooton (1993) 'Measuring the Effects of Regionalism on Trade and Welfare', in Anderson and Blackhurst (eds), *Regional Integration and the Global Trading System.*

Sumitomo Life Research Institute (1989) *Development of Overseas Direct Investment of Japan and its Impact on Trade Balance*, Tokyo (November).

Summers, L. (1991) 'Regionalism and the World Trading System', in *Policy Implications of Trade and Currency Zones*, a symposium sponsored by the Federal Reserve Bank of Kansas City, Jackson Hole, Wyoming, 22–4 August, Jackson Hole.

Thisen, J.K. (1994) 'The European Single Market and its Possible Effects on African External Trade', Geneva, *UNCTAD Discussion Papers*, no. 78 (January).

Thomas, Rosalind (1995) 'South and Southern Africa: Restructuring Economic Cooperation Initiatives to Encourage Growth and Diversity', *Courier* no. 154 (November–December).

Thomsen, Stephen (1993) 'Japanese Direct Investment in the EC: The Product Cycle Revisited', *World Economy* (May).

Tremblay, R. (1993) 'Macro-Based International Competitiveness with Free Trade', in A.R. Riggs and Tom Velk (eds), *Beyond NAFTA: An Economic, Political and Sociological Perspective*, Vancouver, The Fraser Institute.

UNCTAD, *Direction of Trade Statistics Yearbook.*

UNCTAD, *Handbook of International Trade and Development Statistics.*

UNCTAD (1993) *World Investment Report 1994 – Transnational Corporations and Integrated International Production*, New York.

UNCTAD (1994) *World Investment Report 1994: Transnational Corporations, Employment and Workplace*, Geneva.

UNCTAD (1995) *Foreign Investment in Africa*, Geneva.

UNCTAD (1995a) *World Investment Report 1995 – Transnational Corporations and Competitiveness*, Geneva.

UNCTAD (1996) *World Investment Report – Investment, Trade and International Policy Arrangements*, Geneva.

UNCTC (1990) *Regional Economic Integration and Transnational Corporations in the 1990s: Europe 1992, North America and Developing Countries*, New York, UN.

UNCTC (1991) *World Investment Report 1991: The Triad in Foreign Direct Investment*, New York, UN.

UNCTC (1992) *World Investment Report 1992: Transnational Corporations as Engines of Growth*, New York.

UNECE (1994) *Economic Survey of Europe in 1993–1994*, Geneva, UN.

UNECLAC (1994) *Open Regionalism in Latin America and the Caribbean* – Economic Integration as a Contribution to Changing Production Patterns with Social Equity, Santiago.

UNECLAC (1995) *La inversion extranjera en América Latina y el Caribe*, Informe 1995, Santiago.

Unger, Kurt (1994) 'Foreign Direct Investment in Mexico', in L. Eden (ed.) *Multinationals in North America*, Industry Canada's Research Series, vol. III, Calgary, University of Calgary Press.

Urata, S. (1993) 'Globalization and Regionalization in the Asia-Pacific Region', *Business and the Contemporary World* (Autumn).

Urata, S. (1993a) 'Changing Patterns of Direct Investment and the Implications for Trade and Development', in C.F. Bergston and M. Noland (eds), *Pacific Dynamism and the International Economic System*, Washington DC, Institute for International Economics.

Veiga, Pedro da Motta (1995) *Brazil's Strategy for Trade Liberalisation and Economic Integration in the Western Hemisphere*, paper prepared for the Inter-American Dialogue's Hemispheric Integration Conference, Washington DC (27–8 October).

Wadhva, Charan D. (1994) 'Regional Economic Cooperation: SAARC, ASEAN and other Countries of Asia-Pacific Region', in Bhargava *et al.*, *South Asia: Towards Dynamism and Cooperation*, Bombay, Popular Prakash Private Ltd.

Wallis, K.F. (1968) 'The EEC and the United States Foreign Investment: Some Empirical Evidence Reexamined', *Economic Journal* vol. 78.

Walters, Jon (1989) 'Renegotiating Dependency: The Case of the Southern African Customs Union', *Journal of Common Market Studies*, vol. 28, no. 1.

Watanabe, Toshio (1991) 'Prospects for Asia in the 1990s', *Technology and Development*, no. 4.

Waverman, Leonard (1994) 'Post-NAFTA: Can the USA, Canada and Mexico Deepen Their Economic Relationships?', *Centre for International Studies (CIS)* Working Paper no. 1994–8, University of Toronto, Toronto.

Weintraub, Sidney (1992) 'US-Mexico Free Trade: Implications for the United States', *Journal of Interamerican Studies and World Affairs* (Summer).

Wells, Louis T. Jr. (1993) 'Conflict or Indifference: US Multinationals in a World of Regional Trading Blocs', *Development and International Cooperation* (December).

Weston, Ann (1994) *The NAFTA Papers – Implications for Canada, Mexico and Developing Countries*, Ottawa, North–South Institute.

Winters, L. Alan (1993) 'The European Community: A Case of Successful Integration?', in de Melo and Panagariya, *New Dimensions in Regional Integration*.

Winters, L. Alan (1994) 'The EC and Protectionism: The Political Economy', *European Economic Review* (April).

Wise, Mark (1994) 'The European Community', in R. Gibb and W. Michalak (eds), *The Growth of Regionalism in the World Economy*, Chichester, John Wiley & Sons.

Wolf, Martin (1995) 'Cooperation or Conflict? The European Union in a Liberal Global Economy', *International Affairs*, vol. 71, no. 2.

Wong, John (1985) 'ASEAN's Experience in Regional Economic Cooperation', *Asian Development Review*, vol. 1, no. 3.

Wonnacott, R.J. (1993) 'The NAFTA: Fortress North America?', *C.D. Howe Institute Commentary* no. 54 (November).

Wood, Adrian (1994) *North–South Trade, Employment and Inequality – Changing Fortunes in a Skill Driven World*, Oxford, Clarendon Press.

World Bank (1991) *Global Economic Prospects and Developing Countries*, Washington DC.

World Bank, *Trends in Developing Economies*, several years.

World Bank, *World Development Reports*, several years.

World Bank (1994) *East Asia's Trade and Investment: Regional and Global Gains from Liberalisation*, Washington DC (July).

World Bank (1994a) 'Coping with Changes in the External Environment', *Caribbean Division Report No. 12821* (June).

WTO (World Trade Organization) (1995) *Regionalism and the World Trading System*, Geneva (April).

WTO (1995a) *Trade Policy Review: European Union* – Report by the Secretariat, Geneva, WT/TPR/S/3 (30 June).

WTO (1995b) *Trade Policy Review: European Union*, Report by the European Communities, Geneva, WT/TPR/G/3 (30 June).

Wright, S. (1996) 'Regional Cooperation and Growth in Southern Africa', *International Executive* (May–June).

Yam, T.K., T.M. Heng and L. Low (1992) 'ASEAN and Pacific Economic Cooperation', *ASEAN Economic Bulletin* (March).

Yamawaki, Hideki (1991) 'Exports and Foreign Distributional Activities: Evidence on Japanese Firms in the United States', *Review of Economics and Statistics* (May).

Yamazawa, I. (1992) 'On Pacific Economic Integration', *Economic Journal* (November).

Yamazawa, I. (1994) 'Asia Pacific Economic Community: New Paradigm and Challenges', *Journal of Asian Economics*, vol. 5, no. 3.

Yamazawa, I. (1996) 'APEC's New Development and its Implications for Nonmember Developing Countries', *Developing Economies* (June).

Yeats, Alexander (1996) 'Does MERCOSUR's Trade Performance Justify Concerns About the Effects of Regional Trade Arrangements? Yes!', Washington DC, World Bank (mimeo.), cited in the *Financial Times*, 4 February 1997 – the paper was not made available to the authors.

Young, Soogil (1993) 'East Asia as a Regional Force for Globalism', in Anderson and Blackhurst, *Regional Integration and the Global Trading System*, op.cit.

Young, Soogil (1993a) 'Globalism and Regionalism: Complements or Competitors?', in Bergsten and Noland, *Pacific Dynamism and the International Economic System*, op.cit.

Zhan, Xiaoning James (1993) 'North American Economic Integration and its Implications for the Exports of China and Hong Kong', *UNCTAD Discussion Papers* no. 72 (October).

Author/Name Index

African Development Bank (AfDB) 48, 49, 52, 53, 57, 59, 209
Aggarwal, M.R. 89
Aggarwal, V.K. 119, 120
Agosin, M.R. 138, 213
Ahmad, A. 113
Akrasanee, N. 80, 83
Alburo, F.A. 82
Anderson, K. 24, 26, 29, 33, 208
APEC 98, 202
Ariff, M. 73, 77
Arndt, H.W. 101
Artisian, P. 187–8
Aspe, P. 127

Bach, D.C. 65
Bailey, P. 24
Balasubramanyam, V.N. 23, 172–3
Baldwin, R.E. 159, 186, 205, 209
Bannister, G. 132
Barad, R. 49
Barnes, C. 113
Baumann, R. 7, 148
Bautista, C.C. 82
Behar, J. 147
Bernal, R.L. 131
Bezchinsky, G. 152
Bhagwati, J. 23, 24, 156, 201, 202, 205, 206, 208
Bhalla, A.S. 5, 96
Bhuyan, A.S. 92
Bieri, J. 170
Biessen, G. 183
Blackhurst, R. 24, 29, 208
Blumenfeld, J. 48
Bouzas, R. 143, 151
Brada, J.C. 183, 184
Breuer, L. 142
Brown, D.K. 130
Bundu, A. 64
Bush, G. 19, 154

Cadot, O. 186
Calderón, A. 212
Cameron, M.A. 123
Cassim, R. 60
Chia, S.Y. 74, 77, 85, 107, 108, 111, 211
Chudnovsky, D. 142, 151, 152, 153
Chye, T.E. 73
Cline, R.W. 159, 161
Cooper, R.N. 21
Corden, W.M. 208

Davies, R. 59, 61, 62, 209
De Jonquieres, G. 211
De Melo, J. 1, 24, 186
Deardorff, A.V. 130
Dell, S. 10, 181
DeRosa, D.A. 79
Devan, J. 210
Dicken, P. 208
Dobson, W. 139
Doz, Y. 23
Drysdale, P. 21, 32, 114, 118, 119, 126, 156, 210
Dunning, J.H. 170, 174, 188–9

Eden, L. 124, 140–1
Edgington, D.W. 135, 212
Elek, A. 98, 105, 118
Ezenwe, U. 63

Faini, R. 186
Ffrench-Davis, R. 138, 213
Filippo, A. di 147
Fischer, S. 9
Flatters, F. 109, 110
Foroutan, F. 44, 65
Frimpong-Ansah, J.H. 64
Fruin, W.M. 135, 212

Garnaut, R. 21, 32, 114, 118, 119, 126, 156
GATT, 165, 214
Gestrin, G. 127

Gestrin, M. 123
Gochoco, M.S.H. 82
Graham, E.M. 138
Greenaway, D. 23, 172–3, 174
Grewe, M. 78
Grinspun, R. 123

Han, S.-T. 25, 167, 198
Hanlon, J. 54
Harmsen, R. 9
Harris, R. 23, 109, 110
Hazlewood, A. 4
Heng, T.M. 72
Hill, H. 73, 109
Hindley, B. 180, 201, 205
Hodder, R. 117
Hufbauer, G. 123, 125, 126, 128, 131, 154, 213
Hughes-Hallett, A.J. 178
Hurrell, A. 143

Imada, P. 75, 76, 210
IMF 31, 32, 89, 90, 99, 106, 128, 129, 145, 146, 160, 182, 195
Industrial Development Corporation 62
Izam, M. 169

Japan External Trade Organization (JETRO) 172
Johnson, O.E.G. 61, 66
Joshua, F.T. 40, 41–2

Kaser, M. 183
Khan, A.R. 26
Kim, H.S. 130, 138–9, 212
Kitson, M. 25
Klaveren, A. van 205
Kojima, K. 23
Kosacoff, B. 152
Krueger, A.O. 201, 202, 208
Krugman, P. 25, 200
Kumar, S. 79–80, 85

Labàn, R. 152
Lal, D. 25
Lawrence, R. 24, 25
Lee, T.Y. 85
Leidy, M. 9
Lipsey, R.G. 123, 124, 126
Lloyd, P. 165, 214
Lopez, A. 151, 152
Low, L. 72
Low, P. 132
Luce, E. 211
Lundahl, M. 59, 61

Maasdorp, G. 61, 209
MacPherson, A. 125, 129, 154
Mahathir bin Mohamad 25, 69
Martin, W. 114
Mayer, M. 59
McCarthy, C. 11, 48, 52, 58, 61, 64
McConnell, J. 125, 129, 154
McMillan, C.H. 187, 214
Meade, J. 1
Meller, P. 123, 152
Messerlin, P.A. 180, 201, 205
Michalak, W. 183, 185
Michie, J. 25
Micossi, S. 172
Molot, M.A. 22, 140, 211
Morrison, A.J. 36–7
Mortimore, M. 140, 212
Mundell, R.A. 23

Naidu, G. 85
Naya, S. 75, 76, 210
Ndulu, B.J. 66
Neven, D.J. 185, 186
Nogues, J. 7, 9
Norheim, H. 26, 29, 33
Norman, V.D. 179

OECD 22, 26, 83, 111, 133, 134, 135, 136, 137, 138, 150, 171, 175, 176, 188
Okamoto, Y. 82, 110
Okigbo, P. 3, 4
Oman, C. 18, 20, 22, 23, 36
Ooi, G.T. 210
Oppenheim, P. 25, 201
Ortiz, E. 137, 212

Page, S. 168, 169
Panagariya, A. 1, 24, 80, 145, 156, 212
Panchamukhi, V.R. 91, 94
Pandey, P.R. 89
Pangestu, M. 86
Payne, A. 8, 208

Peres, W. 212
Petersson, L. 59, 61
Petri, P.A. 33, 84, 108, 111
Poapongsakorn, N. 78
Porta, F. 151, 152
Porter, M.E. 23
Preusse, H.G. 196
Pritchett, L. 44, 65
Pupphavesa, W. 78
Purvis, D.D. 23

Quintanilla, R. 7, 9

Raboy, D.G. 165
Ramstetter, E.D. 112
Rao, S. 113
Reid, M. 213
Robson, P. 4, 18, 183, 209, 214
Rodrik, D. 24
Rojec, M. 187–8
Roller, L.H. 185, 186
Ros, J. 127
Rosenthal, G. 155
Roth, K. 36–7
Rugman, A.M. 127

Safadi, R. 132
Safarian, A.E. 127
Salisu, M. 23
Sampson, G.P. 214
Sapir, A. 164, 165
Sapsford, D. 23
Scaperlanda, A. 169–70
Schmitz, A. 170
Schott, J. 24, 123, 125, 126, 128, 131, 154, 213
Schwanen, D. 123, 124, 126
Seebach, D. 124
Shiells, C. 130
Siv, S. 96
Smith, A.H. 181
Smith, M. 130
Srinivasan, T.N. 33
Stern, R.M. 130
Stifel, D. 80, 83
Sumitomo Life Research Institute 172
Summers, L. 24, 200
Svetlicic, M. 187–8

Thatcher, M.H. 55
Thisen, J.K. 169
Thomas, R. 58
Thomsen, S. 172
Tremblay, R. 211
Tussie, D. 213

UNCTAD 21, 27, 28, 34, 35, 43, 56, 62, 63, 67, 82, 95, 110–11, 139, 152–3, 177, 180, 187, 188–9, 210
UNCTC 21, 140, 170
UNECE 169, 185–6, 188
UNECLAC 150, 152
Unger, K. 128
Urata, S. 82, 84, 86, 112

Veiga, P. da M. 154
Viesti, G. 172

Wadhva, C.D. 95
Wallis, K.F. 170
Walters, J. 59
Watanabe, T. 108
Waverman, L. 123, 127
Weintraub, S. 125
Wells, L.T. 36
Weston, A. 127, 130, 138–9, 212
Whalley, J. 33
Whiteside, A. 61, 209
Winters, L.A. 167, 179
Wise, M. 161, 162
Wolf, M. 165
Wong, J. 71
Wonnacott, R.J. 123, 126, 138
Wood, A. 211
Wooton, I. 33
World Bank 26, 33, 70, 99, 131, 132, 160, 166–7, 182
Wright, S. 209
WTO 161, 167, 180, 185, 213, 214

Yam, T.K. 72
Yamawaki, H. 172
Yamazawa, I. 98, 112, 120
Yeats, A. 132, 149
Young, S. 26, 116, 130

Zarenda, H. 59
Zhan, X.J. 131

Subject Index

Africa 3–4, 27, 28, 30, 31, 32, 33, 34, 35, 40–68, 169, 203
COMESA 53–4
economic indicators 44, 45–6
ECOWAS 11, 14, 63–7, 68, 199
intraregional trade 43–4, 48–53, 60–2, 65–6
PTA 47, 49, 53–4, 62, 210
regional groupings and their membership 40–3
SACU 11, 15, 58–63, 64, 65, 67, 197, 209
SADC and SADCC 2, 11, 15, 40, 42, 43, 44–57, 196, 199, 203
trade diversion 168–9
trade intensity indices 31, 32
African, Caribbean and Pacific (ACP) countries 163, 164, 165, 166, 180, 201
African Economic Community 53, 68
AFTA *see* ASEAN Free Trade Area
agricultural subsidies 166; *see also* Common Agricultural Policy
Americas 121–57
MERCOSUR 141–53; *see also* MERCOSUR
NAFTA 121–41; *see also* North American Free Trade Agreement
Western Hemisphere integration 154–6
see also Latin America; United States
Andean Pact 2, 7, 8–9, 13, 204
Angola 48, 55
anti-dumping measures 17, 103, 105, 123, 124, 132, 167, 172, 190, 198, 201, 203, 205, 207
APEC *see* Asia Pacific Economic Cooperation
Arab Common Market 9
Arab Maghreb Union 9
Argentina 141–2, 146, 147, 148, 149, 150, 151, 152, 153, 155
automobile industry 143, 151, 153
FDI 149, 150, 151, 152, 153
intensity indices 146
intraregional trade 145–6
tariff and non-tariff barriers 143, 144
ASEAN *see* Association of Southeast Asian Nations
ASEAN Free Trade Area (AFTA) 15, 69, 75–81, 84, 87
prospects for 79–81
ASEAN Industrial Complementation 71–2
ASEAN Industrial Joint Ventures (AIJVs) 72
ASEAN Industrial Projects (AIPs) 71–2
Asia 4–6, 24, 25, 26, 27, 28, 30, 32, 33, 34, 35, 36, 69–97, 198, 199, 210
AFTA 75–81; *see also* ASEAN Free Trade Area
APEC 98–120
ASEAN 71–87; see also Association of Southeast Asian Nations
economic indicators 69, 70
FDI 33, 81–5, 86, 95–6, 171–8
multinationals 85–7
possible East Asian bloc 24–5, 200–1, 203
SAARC 87–97, 203; *see also* South Asian Association for Regional Cooperation; intra-SAARC trade
trade intensity indices 30, 32
Asia Pacific Economic Cooperation Forum (APEC) 11, 15, 18, 19, 20, 24–5, 28, 35, 36, 37, 38, 69, 98–120, 156, 196, 200, 203

Bogor Summit 103
challenges and prospects 116–19
economic indicators 98–9
multinationals 111–13
open regionalism 20–1, 101–6
Osaka Summit 103–4, 211
Pacific Free Trade Area 113–16
regionalization/globalization of investments 109–13
role in multilateralism 203, 204
Seattle Summit 102–103
structural adjustment 111–12
trade patterns 106–9
Uruguay Round 38, 119–20, 200
Asia Pacific investment code 102, 103, 120
Asian NIEs 53, 117, 200–1
exports 108, 110, 112, 167
FDI inward 109, 110, 111
FDI outward 81–2, 110, 111
trade 78, 106–8, 109, 166–7, 211
trade diversion 168–9
Association of Southeast Asia (ASA) 2, 5, 6, 13
Association of Southeast Asian Nations (ASEAN) 2, 5, 12, 15, 29, 69–87, 95–7, 106–12, 114, 115, 117, 119, 203
AFTA 75–81
Australia 75, 100, 101, 103, 108–9, 119, 166
Brand-to-Brand Complementation Scheme 83, 210
economic indicators 69, 70
FDI 81–5, 86, 109, 110
intra-ASEAN investment 84–5
intra-ASEAN trade 72–5, 106–7
Japan and 12, 81–2, 109
multinationals 85–7
NAFTA effects of 75, 86
possible cooperation with SAARC 71, 96
PTA 71–2, 78
Singapore's role 72–3, 199
Asunción Treaty 141, 143, 144, 145
Australia 75, 108–9
Australia–New Zealand CER Agreement 80, 119

automobiles sector
ASEAN 83, 109, 110, 210
MERCOSUR 143, 144, 147, 153
NAFTA 131, 140, 141

Baltic Free Trade Agreement 10
bananas 165, 213–14
Bangladesh 90, 91–3, 166
Benelux customs union 9
'big brothers' 198–9, 214
bilateral agreements 8, 19–20, 48, 60, 94, 119, 155, 204–5
vs regional agreements 204–5
South Africa 60
US 19–20, 119, 200, 204
BLNS (Botswana, Lesotho, Namibia and Swaziland) 58–62 *passim*, 209
Botswana 58–63 *passim*, 209
Brazil 141–55 *passim*, 199, 202, 213, 214
FDI 149–52
intraregional trade intensities 145, 146
MNE strategies in 152
Protocol 21, 153
trade 145–8, 153
Western hemisphere integration 154–5

Canada 121–40 *passim* 36, 75, 98, 99, 106, 155, 156, 203, 205, 207
intraregional trade intensity 128–9
Canada–US Free Trade Agreement (CUSFTA) 123–4, 140
Caribbean 7–8, 28, 35, 130–1
Caribbean Common Market (CARICOM) 2, 7, 8
Caribbean Free Trade Association (CARIFTA) 7
Caribbean Investment Corporation 8
CEAO (West African Economic Union) 4, 67
Central African Customs Union 4
Central American Common Market (CACM) 2, 7, 12

Central and Eastern European countries (CEECs) 180–90, 201, 202
  Europe Agreements 166, 184–5
  FDI 173–4, 175–6, 186–9
  intra-bloc trade 183–4
  intra-CEEC investments 189
  trade with EU 184–6
Central European Free Trade Area 10, 15, 184
CFA franc 4, 65, 66, 67
Chile 98, 99, 142, 152, 155, 156, 204, 211, 213
  MERCOSUR 152, 204, 213
China 5, 6, 26, 75, 78, 82, 84, 86, 88, 91, 95, 96, 117, 119, 168, 202, 203
  FDI 109–11
  Hong Kong and 106–7
  NAFTA and 131, 133
  PAFTA and 114–15
  SAARC and 91, 95–6
  US and 104, 114, 116–17, 202
Closer Economic Relations (CER) Agreement 80, 119
CMEA *see* Common Market of the Centrally Planned Economies
Cohesion Fund 159
Colonia Protocol 152
commodity price shocks 1–2
Common Agricultural Policy (CAP) 158, 159, 165, 166, 167, 169, 180, 186, 190
Common Effective Preferential Tariff (CEPT) 76–8, 79, 210
common external tariff (CET) 3, 4, 8, 10, 14, 38, 60, 63, 66, 78, 143–4, 156, 157, 163, 179, 180
Common Franc Zone *see* CFA Franc
Common Market of the Centrally Planned Economies (COMECON) 9–10, 15, 180–3, 214
  intra-bloc trade 183
Common Market of Eastern and Southern Africa (COMESA) 53–4, 55, 56
common market 3, 5, 7, 8, 9, 14–15, 16, 61, 64, 113, 143, 209; *see also* European Common Market
Common Monetary Area (CMA) 61, 62
Commonwealth of Independent States (CIS) 188
comparative advantage 83, 85, 92, 100, 181, 186
  loss of: 83, 71, 186
competition 11–12, 18, 59, 62, 76, 92, 179
competition policy 180, 207
competitiveness 18, 71, 78,.81, 83–4, 100, 174, 199
  lack of 53, 58
Comprehensive Programme of Socialist Integration 181
contingency protection 205
convergence criteria 161
convertible currencies 61
Cuba 201, 214
customs unions 3, 4, 7, 12, 14–15, 16, 24, 38, 42, 47, 143, 158, 197, 205, 208, 209
  see also SACU; MERCOSUR
Czech Republic 15, 167, 187, 189

Denmark 159, 179, 191–2
developing countries
  changing trade patterns 26, 27
  share of FDI 33–5
development indicators *see* economic development indicators
discriminatory integration 21

East African Community 2, 3–4, 13, 40
East African Development Bank 3–4
East Asian Economic Caucus (EAEC) 69, 117, 133
East Asian Economic Group 25, 69
East Asian NIEs *see* Asian NIE
Eastern Europe *see* Central and Eastern European countries
economic indicators, basic
  Africa 44, 45–6
  Americas 121, 122
  APEC countries 98–99

Asia 69, 70
CEECs 181, 182
EU 159, 160
economic integration 2, 3, 4, 7, 9, 10, 11, 12, 14, 20, 21, 43, 158, 163, 198
economic and monetary union (EMU) 161, 162
economic unions 14–15
economies of scale 1, 3, 11, 13, 18, 23, 36, 43, 141, 146, 147, 174, 179, 199, 210
ECOWAS 12, 14, 40, 43, 44, 45, 47, 51, 56, 61, 63–7, 68, 199
economic indicators 46
FDI 56, 66–7
intra-ECOWAS trade 51, 65–6
Single Monetary Zone 65
EFTA *see* European Free Trade Association
employment 85, 112, 123, 125, 211–12
Enterprise for the Americas Initiative (EAI) 8, 19, 154, 204
Europe 158–90
associate agreements 166, 184–5, 190
EFTA 178–80
EU 158–78; *see also* European Union
integration in CEECs 180–9
European Coal and Steel Community (ECSC) 9, 158
European Common Market (ECM) 9, 10, 161, 190
European Community (EC) 9–10, 26, 28, 107, 149, 158, 163–4, 169, 170, 173, 176, 178, 179, 180, 191–5
see also European Union
European Economic Area (EEA) 168, 178, 179–80, 205
European Free Trade Association (EFTA) 9, 10, 26, 165, 168–9, 178–80
European Union (EU) 2, 15, 19, 38, 68, 105, 109, 133, 134, 135, 141, 158–78, 190, 196
deep integration 158, 159, 197
economic indicators 159, 160
FDI 133–5, 169–78; intra-EU investment 173–8; investment diversion 178; magnitude and impact of inflows 170–3
intraregional trade 163–5
Kennedy Round 38
MERCOSUR and 149, 150, 156, 204
multinational enterprises 169, 170, 171, 172, 173, 174, 198
preferential trade 165–6
prospects for regional blocs 200, 200–1, 203–4
protectionism 2, 101, 107, 166–8, 172–3, 204, 205; *see also* protectionism
SACU and 60, 62–3
trade diversion 168–9
trade patterns 163
trade with Latin America 156
Treaty of Rome 158
see also Single European Market Programme; Maastricht Treaty
Exchange Rate Mechanism (ERM) 161
export promotion 23

Finland 159, 179, 185, 192
fixed exchange rates 66, 161
'flying geese' development pattern 83, 100–1
foreign direct investment (FDI) 19–20, 23
Africa: ECOWAS 66–7; SACU 62–3; SADC 54–7
APEC 102, 109–13
Asia 33, 174, 177; ASEAN 81–5, 86, 87, 109, 110; SAARC 95–6
CEECs 173–4, 175–6, 186–9
EU 169–78
export substitution 23, 172, 173, 188, 197
GATT/WTO 206, 207
dynamic gains from 147, 197
intraregional *see* intraregional investment
investment diversion 39, 75, 84, 86, 121, 123, 138–9, 157, 173, 174, 178, 188

FDI *cont.*
investment incentives 84, 110, 149, 206
investment and trade linkages 14, 67, 71, 107, 112, 139, 140, 169, 197–8
liberalization of 22, 24, 38, 54, 82, 84, 86, 88, 95, 103, 110, 123, 124–5, 133, 138, 174, 203
market seeking 137, 171, 172
MERCOSUR 144, 149–53
NAFTA 127, 133–41
promoting globalization 201, 202–4
regionalization' of 17, 33–6
resources seeking 55, 66, 109, 135, 172
substitute for trade/exports 23, 140, 172, 173, 18, 197
'tariff jumping' 83, 111, 139, 170, 172–3; *see also* substitute for trade/exports
trends in flows 33–6
'fortress' Europe 19, 24, 121, 190
France 4, 65–7, 165, 171, 192
FDI outflows 173–4, 175, 188
francophone countries 4, 65
free trade areas (FTAs) 5, 7, 10–11, 14–15, 18, 20, 24, 38, 61, 83, 87, 143, 154–6, 183–4, 196, 197, 206, 208
see also under AFTA; EFTA; LAFTA; NAFTA; PAFTA; SAFTA; Central European Free Trade Area
trade and investment linkages 197–8; *see also* investment; trade linkages

General Agreement on Tariffs and Trade (GATT) 76, 101, 196, 202, 205–7, 214
APEC, and 105
Article XXIV 196, 205–6, 214
MFN rule 76, 104, 119, 120, 130, 132, 201, 205, 210, 214
regional blocs and 205–7
see also Uruguay Round; World Trade Organization
Generalized System of Preferences (GSP) 81, 110, 130, 212, 214
Germany 53, 171, 173, 174, 177, 184, 188, 192–3, 199, 207, 214
and CEECs 185, 188
FDI outflows 173–4, 175, 188
globalization 1, 18, 23–6, 38–9, 97, 98, 201, 207, 208
concept and meaning 22–4
regional blocs as building blocks to 37–9, 119, 199–207, 208
or regionalism 24–37; FDI 33–6; of production 36–7, 78, 135, 197–8; of trade 16, 26–33; regional blocks as stumbling blocks to 17, 199, 200–3
government procurement: transparency in 207
Greece 159, 168, 178, 193
gross domestic product (GDP): FDI/GDP ratio 33–5, 55–6, 82–3
gross fixed capital formation 55–6, 82–3
growth triangles 84–5, 119
Gulf Cooperation Council (GCC) 2, 9

Harmonized Tariff Schedule (HTS) 130, 212, 213
Hong Kong 25, 91, 98, 99, 106–7, 109, 111, 112, 119, 131, 168, 211
Hub and spoke arrangements 20
Hungary 181, 182, 184, 185, 187, 188, 189

illegal trade 49, 123, 210
import substitution 1, 7, 8, 11, 12, 18, 19, 23, 47, 52, 69, 72, 76, 81, 82, 87, 92, 116, 140, 197
India 5, 6, 55, 75, 87, 92, 95, 110, 117, 199, 202, 210
dominance in SAARC 88, 199, 214
FDI 95–6, 109
trade 73, 89–93, 94, 96, 131
Indonesia 73, 74, 76, 84–5, 167, 211

information technology (IT) 22, 23, 37, 104, 135, 171, 207
institutional integration 11, 13, 21–2, 198
intellectual property rights 104, 117, 120, 126, 202, 207
International Bank for Economic Cooperation 183
intra-firm trade 112–3, 140, 152, 170, 173
Integrated Programme of Action (IPA) 88
intraregional investment 33–6
  APEC 109–11
  ASEAN 84–5
  CEECs 189
  EU 173–8
  MERCOSUR 151–2
  NAFTA 133, 137
  SACU 62–3
  SADC 57
intraregional trade 18, 23, 26–9, 30, 31
  Africa 3, 43, 43–4; ECOWAS 51, 65–6; SACU 60–1; SADCC 48–53, 62
  APEC 106–9
  Asia: ASEAN 72–5, 107–8; SAARC 88–93
  CEECs 183–4
  EU 163–5
  MERCOSUR 145–8, 149
  NAFTA 128–9, 130
  complementarity 2, 14, 32, 72, 79, 84, 100, 131, 142, 147; lack of: 6, 13, 89
investment *see* foreign direct investment
investment code 102, 103, 120
Italy 158, 160, 161, 162, 173–4, 176, 177, 194–5

Japan 19, 24, 75, 96, 107, 117, 199, 203, 207, 211
  APEC 98, 100–1, 104, 117; FDI 109–10, 111, 112; trade 107–8, 211
  economic indicators 99
  Economic Planning Agency of Japan 108
  EU protectionism 167
  FDI: APEC 109–11, 111, 112–13; ASEAN 81–2; EU 171–3; NAFTA 135–7, 139, 212
  trade 107–8, 112
  trade conflict with US 101, 108, 114, 116, 120, 201, 202
Johor 84–5

Kennedy Round 38
Korea, Republic of 98, 99, 103, 104, 106, 107, 111, 112, 130, 167, 168

labour standards 127, 161, 196, 197, 202, 207, 212
Latin America 2, 8, 12, 19, 142, 169
  bilateral agreements with US 200
  EU banana regime 165, 213–14
  historical perspective 7–9
  WHFTA 154, 155–6
  see also MERCOSUR
Latin American Free Trade Association (LAFTA) 2, 7
Latin American Integration Association (LAIA) 7, 142
Lesotho 58–61 *passim*, 209
Lesotho Highlands Water Project 61
liberalization 13, 38, 69, 78, 196, 198
  APEC 101, 102, 118, 120
  ASEAN 76, 77, 82, 84, 86, 92, 112
  CEECs 184, 185
  COMECON 10
  ECOWAS 63, 64, 66
  EU 161, 167, 171, 173
  MERCOSUR 20, 142, 144, 146
  NAFTA 132, 133, 138, 140
  SAARC 69, 71, 88, 92, 132, 203
  SADC 43, 54
  trade liberalization 5, 12, 13, 17, 18, 20, 64, 196, 201; and open

liberalization: trade *cont.*
regionalism 21; and globalization 25, 38, 166
Lomé Convention 60, 62, 165, 166

Maastricht Treaty 10, 159, 161, 162, 190
EMU 161, 162
Review Conference 190
social charter 162, 197
Malaysia 5, 6, 71, 79, 103, 104, 117
FDI 75, 82–3, 84–5
intraregional trade intensity indices 6, 73, 74
trade 72, 73, 79, 80, 86, 112
maquiladora programme 128, 137, 139, 213
market integration 11, 21–2, 95
Mediterranean countries 165–6, 180
MERCOSUR 1, 11, 15, 28, 32, 35, 141–53, 155, 156–7, 197, 199, 213
bilateral agreements 20, 156, 204, 213
economic indicators 121, 122
FDI 35, 135, 149–53; intraregional FDI 151–2; magnitude of inflows 149–51; MNEs' strategies 152–3
intraregional trade 28, 145–8, 149
trade diversion 148–9
Treaty of Asuncion 143–5
Western hemisphere integration 155–6
mergers and acquisitions 23–4, 172, 174
Mexico 20, 121–41 *passim* 154, 167, 212, 213
APEC, and 98, 99, 106
employment and wages impact of NAFTA 125, 211–12
FDI inflows 133–8, 140, 151, 212
intraregional trade intensity indices 128–9
maquiladora programme 128, 137, 139, 213
Middle East 9, 31
monetary union 4, 10, 61, 62, 64, 65, 161; *see also* economic and monetary union
Most-Favoured-Nation (MFN) rule 205, 214
see also GATT
Mozambique 48, 62
Multi-Fibre Arrangement (MFA) 81, 94, 101, 110
Multilateral Investment Guarantee Agency 54
multilateralism 1, 16, 17, 19, 25, 68, 113, 121, 154, 200, 201, 202–4, 207
multinational enterprises (MNEs) 36–9, 170, 197–8
APEC 109, 110, 111–13
ASEAN 85–6, 210
ECOWAS and trading multinationals 67
EU investment 169–73
regionalization of production 25, 36–7, 198
SADC 55, 57
strategies: and globalization 22–4, 198, 25; MERCOSUR 149, 152–3, 157; NAFTA 135, 139–41, 157, 213
see also foreign direct investment

Namibia 55, 58–63 *passim*, 209
natural trading partners 185, 200, 204
Nepal 89, 90, 91–2
Netherlands 158, 160, 171, 185, 194–5
new regionalism 17–22
see also regionalization
NIEs *see* Asian NIEs
Nigeria 4, 65, 199
non-tariff barriers (NTBs) 8, 101, 199, 203, 204, 206
ASEAN 72, 75, 76, 79, 80
EU 159, 165–7, 169
MERCOSUR 143, 157
NAFTA 31, 32, 157
SAARC 92, 93, 96
SACU 59
SADC 52, 53

North America 26–8, 30, 32
North American Free Trade Agreement (NAFTA) 2, 8, 11, 15, 19, 25, 121–41, 196
  APEC, and 107, 119, 156
  ASEAN, and 75, 86, 133
  as building block 156
  comparison with EU 197
  comparison with MERCOSUR 156–7
  EU investment in 173–4, 175–6
  FDI 127, 133–41; investment diversion 138–9; strategies 139–41
  impact on employment and wages 125, 211–12
  intra-NAFTA trade 128–9
  and multilateralism 24, 200–1, 203–4; GATT 105; Uruguay Round 38
  North–South integration 19
  objectives and content 126–8
  protectionism 24, 25, 117, 203–4; *see also main listing under* protectionism
  trade diversion 130–3
  US domination 199
  Western hemisphere integration, and 154–6

OECD countries 22, 26, 198–9
  see regionalism

Pacific Basin Economic Council (PBEC) 100, 101
Pacific Economic Cooperation Conference (PECC) 100, 101, 102
Pacific Free Trade Area (PAFTA) 100, 102, 105, 113–16
Pacific Trade and Development Conference (PAFTAD) 100, 101
Pakistan 5, 82, 87, 88, 89, 90, 91, 92, 93, 97, 210
Paraguay 141, 142, 143, 144, 145–6, 148, 152
Philippines 5, 6, 71, 73, 74, 79, 80, 82, 83, 96, 98, 99, 104, 106, 112, 114, 211
Poland 15, 180, 181, 182, 184, 187, 189
policy harmonization 8, 10, 11, 14, 21–2, 64, 79–80, 103–4, 105, 158, 161–2, 196–7
Portugal 159, 160, 161, 162, 167, 168, 178, 179, 194–5, 201
preferential trade 55, 71, 93, 113, 131, 165–6, 180, 205
Preferential Trade Area (PTA) Treaty for Eastern and Southern Africa 2, 53–4, 62–3
  Charter on Multinational Industrial Enterprise 57
Preferential Trading Arrangement (PTA) *see* Association of Southeast Asian Nations
'prisoner's delight game' 118–19
privatization 57, 66, 138, 151, 187
protectionism 7, 20, 26, 101, 102, 114, 117, 149, 156, 198, 201–2, 203, 206, 207
  ASEAN 72, 78, 80, 109
  EU 2, 17, 75, 101, 107, 162, 166–8, 172–3, 190, 204–5
  GATT and 205
  NAFTA 2, 17, 24–5, 117, 203–4
  in OECD countries 81, 198
  SACU 59, 60
  SAARC 87
  US 201–2, 205
Protocol 21 143, 153

quantitative restrictions 3, 10, 59, 75, 76, 79, 162

reciprocity 115–16, 119–20
regional blocs *see also under individual regional groupings*
  'big brothers' in 198–9
  building blocks for multilateralism and globalization 17, 37–9, 119, 199–207, 208
  future of 196–207
  loose groupings 14–15
  reasons for bloc formation 1–2
  stumbling blocks 17, 199, 200–3
regional integration 2, 25, 40, 142, 149
  growth inducing 38, 39, 202–4

regionalism
  bilateral vs regional agreements 204–5
  GATT/WTO, and 205–7
  globalization, or 24–26
  historical perspective 3–16, 17–8; Africa 3–4; Asia 4–6; industrialized countries 9–11; Latin America and the Caribbean 7–9; lessons from past experience 11–14; Middle East 9
  new regionalism 18–20
  open regionalism 20–22, 37, 39, 101–6, 202–4
regionalization
  FDI 33–6
  production, of 36–7, 197–8
  world trade 26–33
rules of origin 103, 198, 205, 206
  Africa 55
  AFTA 78
  MERCOSUR 149
  NAFTA 126, 130–1, 138–9, 156–7
Russia 181, 182, 187, 188, 189

SAARC *see* South Asian Association for Regional Cooperation
SACU *see* South African Customs Union
SADC *see* Southern African Development Community
SADCC *see* Southern African Development Coordination Conference
'sensitive products' 72, 77–8, 168, 179, 201
services 26, 43, 55–6, 120, 171, 207
SIJORI growth triangle 84–5
Singapore 5, 70, 86, 199, 207, 211
  APEC 98, 99, 106
  FDI 82–3, 84, 84–5, 109, 111
  intraregional trade intensity indices 74
  NTBs 79
  role in ASEAN 71–3, 79, 199, *see also* Asian NIEs
share in world trade 106
Single European Act 1986 10
Single European Market Programme 10, 24, 25, 97, 116, 159, 161–2, 166, 168, 171, 173, 179–80
  and EFTA 180
  and intra-EU investment 173–8
  investment diversion 178
  trade diversion 116, 168
South Africa 32, 41, 45, 65, 67, 199, 209
  SACU 58–63 *passim*
  SADC 47–50, 52–3, 55, 56–7, 199, 203
South African Customs Union (SACU) 11, 12, 45, 56, 58–63, 64–67 209
  FDI 62–3
  intra-SACU trade 60–1
  trade with SADC 62
South American Free Trade Area (SAFTA) 154–5
South Asian Association for Regional Cooperation (SAARC) 5–6, 14, 69, 71, 87–97, 203
  economic indicators 69, 70
  FDI 95–6
  India's dominance 88, 199, 210, 214
  Integrated Programme of Action 88
  intra-SAARC trade 88–93
  NAFTA impact of 131–2
  SAPTA 69, 93–5
  shares in world trade 73
South Asian Preferential Trade Agreement 69, 93–5
Southern African Development Community (SADC) 44–57, 199, 203
  Cross-Border Investment Facility 57
  FDI 54–7
  intraregional trade 48–53, 62
  and PTA 53–4

Southern African Development Coordination Conference (SADCC) *see* Southern African Development Community
Soviet Union 181, 183–4, 185
  see also Russia
Spain 159, 160, 161, 178, 193, 194–5
Sri Lanka 87, 90, 91–2, 166
Stockholm Convention 178
structural adjustment 13, 54, 55, 93, 119, 181
Structural Fund 159
subsidiarity principle 162
subsidies 166, 207
Swaziland 58–63 *passim*, 209
Sweden 158, 159, 160, 177, 178, 179, 191–5

Taiwan 81, 98, 106, 107, 111, 167, 168
  see also Asian NIEs
Tanzania 3–4
tariff reductions
  AFTA 76–8, 210
  APEC 103–4, 211
  ECOWAS 63
  MERCOSUR 147
  PAFTA 116
  SAPTA 93–4
textile sector 75, 93, 94, 109, 110, 112, 114, 130–1, 132
Thailand 5, 6, 71, 72, 73, 74, 74–5, 77, 78, 79, 80, 82, 84–5
  and APEC 98, 99, 103, 106, 109
tiered development 83, 100–1
trade
  Asia's share in world trade 72, 73
  cooperation in APEC 101–2, 103, 104, 115–16
  EU: with CEECs 184–6; patterns 163, 164; preferential 165–6; protectionism 101, 107, 166–8, 172–3, 205
  frictions 101, 104, 137, 172, 201, 204–5, 206
  globalization 22–3
  inter-firm 23, 112, 124, 170, 173, 186
  intra-firm trade 83, 124, 140, 152, 153, 170
  intra-industry trade 124, 146–7, 184
  intraregional *see* intraregional trade
  linkages 197–8
  regionalization of world trade 26–33
  three possible trading blocs 24–5, 200
  see also bilateral agreements; multilateralism
trade creation 13, 18, 25, 33, 37, 39, 64, 102, 121, 162, 163, 169, 173, 178, 202–3
trade diversion 13, 18, 25, 37, 197, 200, 202, 204–5, 214
  ASEAN 75
  CEECs 183, 185
  ECOWAS 64
  EU 116, 162–3, 168–9, 178
  MERCOSUR 148–9, 156–7
  NAFTA 130–3, 138, 156–7
  SACU 56, 60
trade intensity indices 29–32, 107, 208–9
  ASEAN 73, 74
  EU 163, 191–5
  MERCOSUR 145–6
  NAFTA 128–9
  SAARC 89–92
trade negotiations 38
  see also General Agreement on Tariffs and Trade; Uruguay Round; World Trade Organization
trade-related investment measures (TRIMs) 120, 206
trade-related intellectual property rights (TRIPs) 120
transition economies *see* Central and Eastern European countries

UEMOA *see* West African Monetary Union
United Kingdom 158–63, 165, 179, 191–5, 207
  ERM 161

UK *cont.*
FDI: inflows 169–72; outflows 173, 174, 176, 188; and EFTA 178–9
intensity ratio 173, 177
social charter 162, 197
United States (US) 19, 24, 167, 205
aggressive unilateralism 201–2
APEC 98, 99, 100, 101, 104, 105, 106, 107, 108, 119, 199; FDI 109, 110, 111; PAFTA 113–14; trade disputes 114, 116–17, 120
ASEAN 75, 81
bilateral agreements 19–20, 119, 141, 200, 204
EU: FDI 169–70, 170–1
Helms–Burton bill 214
India 96
Mexican debt crisis 212
multinationals 170, 198; regionalization of production 36–7; strategies and NAFTA 139–41
NAFTA 121–41 *passim*, 199, 214; FDI inflows 111, 134, 135, 136–7; FDI outflows 133–5, 137; intraregional trade intensity indices 129–30
'Super 301' (of US Trade Act) 202
WHFTA *see* Western Hemisphere Free Trade Area
WTO *see* World Trade Organization
Uruguay 141, 142, 143, 144, 145–6, 147, 149, 150, 152
Uruguay Round 22, 25, 77, 117, 132, 154, 156, 166, 196
APEC 101, 102, 116, 119–20, 200
NAFTA 132–3
regional blocs and multilateralism 38

Vietnam 5, 71, 84, 111
Voluntary Export Restraints (VERS) 132, 166, 172, 190, 198, 203, 205

wages 125, 211–12
West African Clearing House (WACH) 64, 65
West African Economic Union (CEAO) 4, 67
West African Monetary Agency 64
West African Monetary Union (UEMOA) 64, 65
Western Hemisphere Free Trade Area (WHFTA) 154–6
World Bank: Multilateral Investment Guarantee Agency 54
World Trade Organization (WTO) 25, 40, 76, 91, 105, 113, 116, 120, 167, 202, 204, 214
regional blocs and 205–7
see also General Agreement on Tariffs and Trade

Zimbabwe 44, 45, 47, 48, 49, 50, 52, 54, 55, 56, 57, 62, 203, 209